The Evil Dead Companion

THE *EVIL DEAD* EXPERIENCE...

"The Evil Dead *blew me away. Totally. Blew me right through the back doors, through the lobby and into the street, figuratively speaking... It was over the top, it was like a thunderstorm in a bottle, just relentless.*"
— *Stephen King*

"*...the* ne plus ultra *of low-budget gore and shock effects...*"
— Variety

"*...a shoestring tour de force...*"
— Los Angeles Herald-Examiner

"*...an instant classic, probably the grisliest well-made movie ever...*"
— Los Angeles Times

"*A ferociously original horror film... the camera has a kind of nightmarish fluidity; it dips and slides and then zooms in so fast you want to plaster your hands over your eyes, crazily exhilarating shots that make you want to leap up cheering.*"
— Twilight Zone

"*I like it when [the audience] screams... when they jump, it's a surface reaction — a cheap thrill — but I like the fact that they jump... I like to know a secret that they don't know. They don't know it's coming, but I do.*"
— *Sam Raimi, writer/director,* the Evil Dead *trilogy*

"*At this screening, two guys got up, screamed and ran out of the theatre... out in the lobby they were laughing so hard they were hitting each other on the back... there aren't many films that can do that, that can make people go nuts.*"
— *Bruce Campbell, actor,* the Evil Dead *trilogy*

"*There was a lot of pain involved with that movie... I remember how strange it was, staying up all night and sleeping through the day. I felt like a real zombie, but I was twenty years old, and it was very exciting, and I was with friends.*"
— *Ellen Sandweiss, actress, The Evil Dead*

The Evil Dead Companion

Bill Warren

TITAN BOOKS

THE EVIL DEAD COMPANION
ISBN 1 84023 187 4

Published by
Titan Books
a division of
Titan Publishing Group Ltd
144 Southwark Street
London SE1 0UP

First edition July 2000
10 9 8 7 6 5 4 3 2

Photo credits:
Front cover photograph by Mike Ditz © Renaissance Pictures Ltd.
The Evil Dead images © 1982 Renaissance Pictures Ltd.
Evil Dead II images © 1987 Rosebud Releasing Corp.
Army of Darkness images © 1992 Universal Pictures.
All other material © Renaissance Pictures Ltd unless otherwise stated: pp30, 39, 59, 80, 81, 115 © Tom Sullivan; pp 97, 160 courtesy of Mark Dutton; pp101, 102 © Renaissance/Avco Embassy; p135 © Amsco Studios; pp135, 148, 169, 234, 238, 242, 244, 247 courtesy of *Fangoria*; pp137, 138 © Renaissance/Universal Pictures; pp158, 159 © Dark Horse Comics Inc; pp165, 166 © Tristar Pictures Inc; p168 © Paramount Pictures; p169 © Warner Bros Inc; p171 © Renaissance/MCA TV; p173 © Renaissance/Studios USA Television; p174 © Circle Films; p178 © THQ, © Heavy Iron.

I want to express my thanks to Rob Tapert, Sam Raimi, Bruce Campbell, Scotty Spiegel, Josh Becker, Phil Gillis, Ellen Sandweiss, Tony Timpone, Stephen King, Beverly Warren, Wade Brown, Sue Binder, Tamara Dow, David J. Schow, Sharon Stone, Harold Warren, Leslie Swigart, Judy McClay, Sean McLaggan, Mike Watt, Harlan Ellison, Jeanne Cavelos, Dave McDonnell, Greg Nicotero, Howard Berger, Robert Kurtzman and John Cameron. Thanks also to David Barraclough, Gillian Christie, Bob Kelly and Chris Teather at Titan.

Titan Books would like to thank Tom Sullivan and Patrick Reese at Dark Age Productions, Tony Timpone at *Fangoria*, Mark Dutton, Stephen Jones, Tim Lucas, Kim Newman, Richard Pitt and THQ for their help.

Did you enjoy this book? We love to hear from our readers. Please e-mail us with any comments at: readerfeedback@titanemail.com, or write to us at the above address.

Titan Books are available through most good bookshops or direct from our mail order service. For a free catalogue or to order telephone 01858 433169 with your credit card details, e-mail asmltd@btinternet.com or write to Titan Books Mail Order, Bowden House, 36 Northampton Road, Market Harborough, Leics, LE16 9HE. Please quote reference EDC/MO.

A CIP catalogue record for this title is available from the British Library.

Printed and bound in Great Britain by MPG Books Ltd, Victoria Square, Bodmin, Cornwall.

Thanks especially, and most particularly, to Bill Thomas and David Pollison, to whom this book is dedicated.

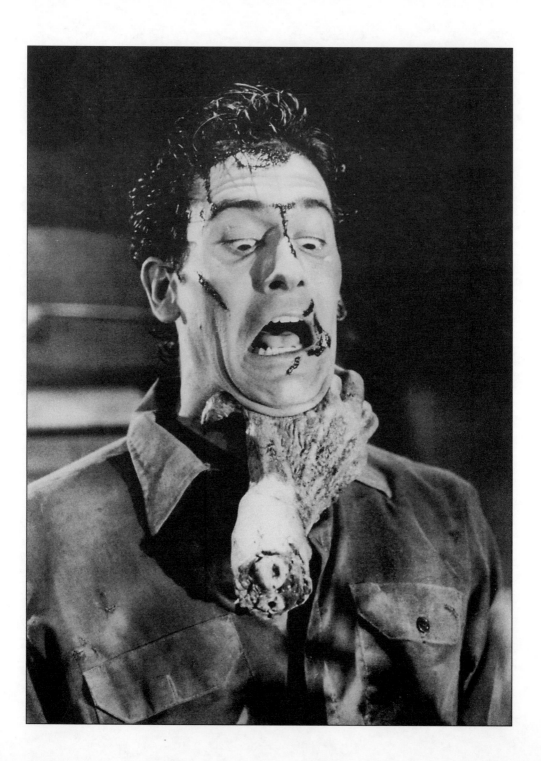

CONTENTS

INTRODUCTION

THE CURTAIN GOES UP: BLOOD IN THE AISLES

15 October 1981, the Redford Theater in Detroit, Michigan, one of the grandest old movie palaces of the Midwest. Searchlights sweep the sky, limousines pull up in front of the theatre, letting out elegantly-clad people for the première of a new movie. The balcony fills with giddy teenagers. Outside the theatre, three nervous young men in tuxedos are greeting friends, relatives and others.

It's a festive occasion, with excitement running high among everyone — it's clearly an Event. The audience is excited, anticipation mounts. From below the stage, a gigantic Wurlitzer organ rises, playing Bach's Toccata and Fugue in D flat minor.

The curtains part, the lights go down, and the projector beam from high in the theatre stabs down at the screen. It's the first public showing of *Book of the Dead* — soon to be retitled *The Evil Dead*.

On screen, a group of college-age youngsters go to a cabin in the woods where they find a tape recording left by a mysteriously-vanished Professor of antiquities. Unknown to the five, the recording rouses demons of the forest, who soon attack. One by one, the young people are possessed by dark forces and turn against their friends. The only way out is to dismember the bodies of the possessed. Finally, just one young man survives, and on leaving the cabin he, too, is attacked by an invisible demon.

The movie is awash with blood, alive with violence, graphic, gruesome and glee-ful in its mayhem, but it's also made with verve and imagination. There isn't much time devoted to characterisation, but that doesn't matter much since the low-budget movie is so impressively cinematic. The camera becomes a player in the film, adopting the Evil Force's point of view. It swooshes, it turns upside down, it shatters windows and smashes down doors, it rushes through the woods and glides over ponds.

The kids in the balcony explode with delight, clutching each other in terror, cry-ing "gross!" at the nastier stuff, and laughing with relief when the tension is broken. The elegantly-clad audience below, many of whom have actually invested money in this gorefest, have different reactions...

That night was the culmination of a dream, and the beginning of one, too.

More movie-makers than you might imagine have begun their careers with an 8mm camera in hand, ordering siblings and friends around, directing backyard epics. But what sets Sam Raimi, Bruce Campbell and Rob Tapert apart from others who started like this is that they are *still together.* Former backyard film-maker Steven Spielberg makes features, but his assistant director and stars aren't people he went to high school with, his producer wasn't a college friend — but that *is* true of Sam Raimi.

The story behind *The Evil Dead* is a very American one. Renaissance Pictures has its origins in a bunch of teenagers playing with movie cameras; there's not likely to be another movie company anywhere with such an unusual and genuinely good-hearted history, because it's the story of friendships and a business that grew out of having *fun.* It's a buddy movie, it's the American entrepreneurial spirit coming directly out of high school hallways, local theatre and indulgent parents.

There are three main players in the *Evil Dead* game: director Sam Raimi, producer Rob Tapert and actor (and producer) Bruce Campbell, but there are several others involved as well. The most influential is probably Scott Spiegel, who knew both

Below:

Sam Raimi, Rob Tapert and Bruce Campbell attend the Detroit première of Book of the Dead, *aka* The Evil Dead.

Campbell and Raimi from high school on, who co-wrote *Evil Dead II* with Sam and after whom the second male lead in *The Evil Dead* was named. Scott was the horror movie fan of the bunch, he's still close friends with both Bruce and Sam and he was a very important source of material for this book. Scotty has done well in Hollywood himself — he co-wrote Clint Eastwood's movie *The Rookie* with Boaz Yakin, for example — but he's a movie fan under it all, and is the archivist for all the old amateur movies he made with Raimi and Campbell. In fact, Scotty made more of those Super-8 wonders than any of the others.

Josh Becker, a director himself now, also turns up in these notes from time to time. He made several Super-8 movies, often starring Bruce Campbell, and worked on *The Evil Dead* as an all-around production assistant. His reminiscences also helped here. A long student film he directed solo and co-wrote with Scott Spiegel, *Stryker's War*, metamorphosed into the feature *Thou Shalt Not Kill… Except*, which starred Sam Raimi as a Charles Manson-like cult leader and murderer. Becker also directed *Lunatics: A Love Story*, which Rob Tapert and Sam helped get financed; it co-stars Ted Raimi and Bruce Campbell. He directed episodes of several Renaissance Pictures TV shows such as *Xena: Warrior Princess* and *Jack of All Trades*. In 1997, Bruce Campbell starred for Becker in *Running Time*, an unusual, and very good, movie that appears to have been shot in one take, like Hitchcock's *Rope*. John Cameron appeared in many of the Super-8 movies, worked on *The Evil Dead*, and became an assistant director in Hollywood, often working for Sam in that capacity. He was also assistant director on *Dazed and Confused* and *Men in Black*, among others. Recently, he was co-producer of *Rushmore*, and the Coen brothers' *The Big Lebowski* and *O Brother, Where Art Thou*.

We're going to be bouncing around in time here, wandering this way and that as we pick up the loose yarns that were eventually woven into the blood-and-bile-stained fabric of *The Evil Dead* and all that followed.

The original plan for this book was simply to tell the story of how each of the three *Evil Dead* movies was made, but that changed. In interviews with the three main players in the *Evil Dead* game, Raimi, Campbell and Tapert, it became obvious that their fondest memories are of the making of the first film of the trilogy. Their eyes grow bright, they become animated and they're full of colourful anecdotes. Talking about *Evil Dead II* and *Army of Darkness* isn't the same — they enjoyed working on them, but they were produced by seasoned professionals, in seasoned-professional manner. *The Evil Dead* was made by a bunch of kids who'd filmed Super-8 movies together in the suburbs of Detroit, and an enthusiastic newcomer they met in college.

Nearly half this book is devoted to the making of that one film. You'll note the approach taken to discussing that movie is different from the approach for *Evil Dead II*, and that's different from the discussion of *Army of Darkness*. This first movie was made

by amateurs, not much different from some of you reading this now. So pay attention to the sections devoted to *The Evil Dead*. That part is unusual, and instructive.

During one of the Academy Awards telecasts she hosted, Whoopi Goldberg addressed the dreamers in the television audience. To those who hoped someday to be up on that stage accepting one of those awards, she said, don't ever forget: *you can do it*. She was right.

Sam Raimi, Bruce Campbell and Rob Tapert made a movie — and made their careers. Don't let anyone tell you otherwise: *you can do it too*. And here's how...

Above:

Sam, Bruce and

Rob on the Evil

Dead II *set.*

CHAPTER 1

YOUNG BLOOD

Sam Raimi, the fourth of five children, was born 23 October 1959, in Royal Oak, Michigan. The family name, Raimi, was Americanised from the harder-to-pronounce Reingewertz a couple of generations before Sam was born. His parents, Leonard and Celia, were both in business — his mother ran a chain of Lulu's Lingerie shops and his father owned the furniture and appliance store that his father before him had begun.

Sam has an older brother, Ivan, who co-wrote *Easy Wheels* and *Army of Darkness* with him; Ivan is an emergency-room doctor who moonlights as a screenwriter. Younger brother Ted is an actor, but sister Andrea (now Andrea Rubin) isn't in show business. The eldest brother was Sander, six years older than Sam, who loved the home magic shows that his big brother staged, but Sander drowned on a tour of Israel at the age of fifteen.

Raimi lived in Detroit, but in 1968, his family moved to the suburbs. "I always liked watching TV as a kid," Raimi says, "but the first memorable movie experience I had was *Fantastic Voyage* [1966], the trip through the human body, a mind-blowing experience. I saw it with my folks when you could still go into the movie theatres in downtown Detroit dressed in a suit and tie — we all wore ties — after eating dinner. It was a big thing to go to a movie, a very serious experience. Theatres were well kept. It was a nicer experience than it seems to be now, but maybe that was just because I was younger.

"What drew me into making movies, I think, were the home movies my father used to make of us kids and show to the family. That was a powerful experience to me, to see his manipulation of space and time on film. The fact that he could capture reality with the movie camera. At that time, in the early sixties, 16mm was the format of choice for most home movie-makers [actually, it was 8mm, but let's let Sam have his memories]. I didn't know it was possible to capture reality that way and then replay it."

Sam was fascinated to see himself on screen (to this day he happily appears in cameos roles in other directors' films), but also the idea that a moment he thought had gone forever could be brought back was a wonder and a delight to him. Because of Sander, he was already interested in magic, and Sam continued his brother's tradition of staging magic acts for parties on through high school, so in a sense his dad's movie camera seemed to be an extension of this magic.

Usually, Pa Raimi's birthday movies were perfectly conventional: "He would shoot the birthday parties; for instance, shoot the kids coming in," Sam explains. "Then he'd have a shot of the cake being presented, and then I'd blow out the candles, then he'd have a shot of some presents being unwrapped, and then the kids going home after the party."

At other times, the films played differently. "Sometimes, when he got the reels back and cut them together, they'd be out of order, so I'd see the birthday cake being blown out, then I'd see a shot of my house and the first kid arriving for the party. And I thought, 'Oh my God, he's manipulating time!' Not only could he capture reality, but he could then manipulate the sequence of events, the order in which the time flow ran. I realised I had to explore this; it was unbelievable to me. It really felt like I was cheating, knowing about this magic, that it had somehow slipped through some porthole from the future. I truly believed it shouldn't be here now. That technology couldn't exist in 1965!

"The magical qualities of film, being able to capture time and replay it, in an altered reality — you can play it faster, or slower, or in an order you choose, you can reassemble time, with the added enhancement of the *sound* of the moment, years ago, being replayed. I was living in a time warp. I thought that this magic was something I had to be involved with, that I had to consume myself with. It is so fantastic, so boggling, that anything else on Earth pales in comparison with it. It was just that magic of the filmic process itself that attracted me to it." And so he tentatively began to make films of his own.

Out West, Sam's first 8mm movie, is a strange, delirious lark of a film featuring neighbourhood children of several ages goofing around in what looks like someone's basement rec room. "It was an adorable little thing," says Sam, who in *Out West* is something of an adorable little thing himself, with his playful grin and energetic attitude.

It is ostensibly a Western, primarily because a couple of the boys are wearing cowboy hats and cap pistols; otherwise, everyone is dressed in street clothes. There's a gunfight of sorts, with everyone making up at the end. Seventh-grade Sam is prominent on screen, often grinning into the camera, sometimes waving; there are a lot of bystanders, but whether they're supposed to be characters in the film, or just happened to be in the basement at the time, it's impossible to say. Everyone is having a great time, and nothing makes any sense. Sam remembers the movie as running two

Above:

Sam Raimi

making the

award-winning

Super-8 film

Picnic.

minutes, but it seems much longer, and that's not a comment on the quality — but on the other hand, no one who sees this could really claim to be able to trace in it elements of the startling movie-making imagination that Raimi displayed later. This could be the work of any bright kid playing with his parents' movie camera, although one quick trick involving a pistol and a shot of redeye (played by a glass of water) is pretty sophisticated for a seventh-grader. However, he didn't return to movie-making for several years.

We might as well deflect from our true path for a moment to mention Sam's younger brother Ted (or Theodore, or even Teddy), who's an actor; as a geeky little kid he appeared (sometimes with his cello) in many of Sam's Super-8 movies, as well as most of his brother's movies later on (as well as movies Sam co-produced, like John Woo's *Hard Target*); his best part for Sam is still *Darkman*, in which his head is run over by a truck.

Ted was forever being victimised by his older brothers. "They used to do something like Chinese torture on me," he grins. "They would ask my dad, 'Can we torture Teddy?' Dad would say, 'Yeah, yeah, go on, do whatever you want.' They would grab me, saying 'Dad told us to do this.' They would drag me upstairs, they would tie me to the bed with belts, and put a hot light on my face, and they would drip water on my head (Sam especially loved to do this), until I told the secret. To this day I don't know what that secret was."

Ivan adds to the story: "One day when my parents were very busy, [Sam and I asked,] 'Will you give us a couple of dollars if we can prove Teddy's been bad?' Dad said, 'Well, I guess.' 'We can train him to be a better human being for a couple of dollars.' So we chained him down to the bed and put hot lights on him, asked him questions he couldn't understand. Our parents didn't know what was going on. 'My, the boys are quiet, except for those occasional screams.' Then we got bored and let Ted go after a few hours."

But sometimes Ted got his own back. "There was another game I used to play with my brothers, Sam and Ivan. I had a baseball bat, like a rubber one, and all of Sam's pals, including Bruce Campbell and Scott Spiegel, would come over and I would chase them (I was around ten, and they were around sixteen); whoever I caught I got to hit, hard. That was a fun one."

Ted caught the acting bug all on his own, and worked hard at learning his craft, while still helping out in various capacities in the *Evil Dead* trilogy. "I was twelve when I did the first one," Ted says. "I barely remember it, but I was there — barely." (Later on we'll reveal where Ted Raimi spotters, soon to be a TV game show, can find him in *The Evil Dead*.)

"In *Evil Dead II,* I got my Screen Actors Guild card by being Henrietta. I was twenty, I needed the money, I was desperate. I have four different parts in *Army of Darkness*; it used to be five, but Sam cut one out, the dirty rat — I'll get him for that, put sand in my brother's shorts, that's what I'll do. I played the terrified, cowardly, worthless general. In another scene, I was another general, a brave, one-eyed general. 'Arrr! Prince Henry! Arrr!' Then I was the worthless villager: 'I don't want to die!' And then — hey, it might still be five parts — I was the brave villager: 'You can count on my steel!' And then I was the S-Mart stock boy right at the end. KNB special effects made me braces, so I was truly, truly disguised."

Ted has cameos in almost every one of big brother Sam's movies, has played bit parts in many major Hollywood films, including *Patriot Games* and *Postcards from the Edge*, supporting roles in cheaper films like *Candyman* and *Skinner*, and a leading role in Josh Becker's even lower-budgeted *Lunatics: A Love Story*. He landed a berth on television's *seaQuest DSV*, where he played, he insists, not the series' Uhura, but its Chekhov. After that show was cancelled, he began turning up regularly on

Hercules: The Legendary Journeys and *Xena: Warrior Princess* as the gawky, comic, would-be hero Joxer. These two shows generated a Ted Raimi fandom, and he even has websites devoted to him on the Internet.

"My first brush with Sam was a fleeting memory," says Bruce Campbell. "It was in the hallway of West Maple Junior High School, which Scott Spiegel also attended. Sam was dressed as Sherlock Holmes, playing with dolls in the middle of the hallway, and I just walked around him, and headed on down the hall." (For his part, Sam says he doesn't recall Bruce that day, and that he was making a video movie with a friend. He still doesn't see all that much odd about being dressed as Sherlock Holmes and playing with dolls in a high school hallway...)

Bruce Campbell, who was born 22 June 1958 (in the same hospital as Sam was the following year), first became interested in acting in 1966. "It extended from the fact that my dad wanted to be an artist," but Bruce's grandfather, who had worked for Alcoa Aluminum "for about 150 years," Bruce says, insisted that his son Charles go into a Real Job. He ended up in advertising, but "it still wasn't artistic enough for him," Bruce adds, "so he got into this community theatre group called St Dunstain's Guild of Cranbrook."

The Guild was headquartered on the grounds of the estate of the man who founded *The Detroit News*. Bruce's dad was happy in the theatre company, and socialised with other earnest if amateur thespians (he appears in *Acting and Reacting*, a Josh Becker-directed short starring Bruce). In the winter, the productions are housed in the Pavilion, but in the summer, they stage one big production in the giant amphitheatre, a recreation of a classic Greek theatre, built with pillars and 180-degree raised seats of concrete, with reflection pools going back layer after layer. It was a mystical place to Bruce Campbell, and it's still there.

One summer, Dunstain's Guild put on the musical *The Pajama Game*, staged in one of the two theatres they use. "The shows were Friday and Saturday nights, and my mom would bundle all the kids up, me and my brothers Don and Mike, and we'd sit on little cushions we brought to watch the play. And I saw my dad in *The Pajama Game,* in these really weird clothes, with make-up on. He was singing and dancing with women that weren't my mother. He looked really happy. Something in my head said, 'Okay, if he can get away with that as an adult, if he can still be a kid, that's what I want to do.'" But the opportunity didn't seem likely to come along, because to join the Guild you had to be eighteen.

However, they did use children in various productions every summer, and in 1971, when they held auditions for *The King and I*, the Rodgers and Hammerstein musical which features dozens of them, Bruce auditioned for the important part of the

King's eldest son. He didn't get it, but was cast in a lesser role as one of the King's other sons. Then, in a twist straight out of a 1930s musical, he got a phone call...

"This kid who was going to play the son got sick, and did I want the part? I said, 'Of course,' and I did play the role. I think the show came off very well." Being in the play itself was the real thrill, though. "It was a really great experience. The next year they did *South Pacific*" — another Rodgers and Hammerstein musical — "and the people in the community theatre knew who I was then, so I became a Polynesian servant boy, in dark body make-up, like I wore in *The King and I*."

By 1973, Bruce had become, at least, taller, as well as more versatile. When the community theatre staged *Fiorello*, he played three different roles: "I was Chang the houseboy again, but I was also a World War One soldier and a New York street vendor. That became the normal thing for me, but I still wasn't old enough to actually join. I don't think I joined officially until about '78.

"One summer, the play was all adults, so I enrolled in Cranbrook summer theatre school. I spent all summer doing pretty serious work on plays; it was a labour-intensive experience where we did a different play every week — you had to learn a lot of lines. We did dramas, comedies, farces. We performed indoors at the Pavilion, which was great because that was on a real stage. We borrowed some of the old sets they'd used during the regular season, and had tons of costumes. Later on, that became the warehouse for our Super-8 films."

Which brings us to those amazing films that Bruce, Sam and Scott Spiegel made for years, along with Josh Becker, John Cameron, Bill Ward, Matt Taylor, Tim Quill, various family members and girlfriends. It's unlikely that these movies will ever be shown publicly, but for the die-hard *Evil Dead* fan, they're fascinating. You really can see ideas, however primitive, turning up that later appear in not only the *Evil Dead* movies, but *Crimewave* and *Darkman* as well.

"A buddy of mine and I used to shoot films in regular 8mm," Campbell explains, "because that's the kind of camera his dad had. It used 16mm spools that, after you exposed twenty-five feet, you pulled out and turned it over to expose the other side. The lab sliced it down the middle, spliced the two ends together, and it became fifty feet of 8mm film. The camera was an old Bell & Howell; it had plastic viewfinders on top, without any reflex viewing, and you had to wind it up to make it go. But it had the capability of single-framing — it was big on special effects."

Campbell and his pal Mike Ditz, a friend since kindergarten, could not only do the kind of simple effects discovered by Georges Méliès at the turn of the twentieth century (stopping the camera and replacing an object or person with something else), they could also produce primitive stop-motion animation, or even animation of people (pixilation): 'You stand there, Bruce, and I'll shoot one frame. Now step back-wards, another frame; another step, another frame,' and on and on for dozens of frames — and when the movie is projected, Bruce looks like he's sliding around on his feet without moving his legs.

Campbell and his pal were making very short movies, "just little scenes," as he puts it. "One was called *D-Day*, where I was playing Hitler. Violence was a big thing, for some reason; lots of carnage and mayhem in my early movies. But it was just trick-ery, very primitive and simple; we used dummies a lot, because dummies were cool. You could do a hidden cut and throw a dummy in. It was a good, cool hobby."

Below:

Rob "Rip" Tapert,
Ivan Raimi and
Sam, filming a
*short (*The Happy
Valley Kid*).*

When Campbell and Scott Spiegel met in junior high school study hall, Campbell was excited to discover that Scotty had been doing films on his own — and the films made by Spiegel and *his* friends had actual sets that they had built them-selves. "I remember watching *Night in the Sanitarium* over at this guy's house," says Bruce. "They had built *sets*! I was so impressed." Furthermore, "Scott had more of a

film-making machine set up. In his neighbourhood, he had three or four friends that worked with him in making the movies pretty industriously. But then I brought a lot of costumes with me, so I was pretty handy."

Not only did Spiegel and his friends have a more elaborate film-making technique, but their films were *shown* in a slicker manner, too. "This one guy, Matt Taylor, had actually sealed off a portion of his basement to make a projection booth. And of course," Campbell says, "that was the coolest of all. You could barely hear the projector, *and* they ran these primitive speakers out to where you sat. They shot silent, but Scott would always come up with a soundtrack on a cassette recorder, and manually synch it up."

Scott's enormous enthusiasm, encyclopedic knowledge of movie trivia, willingness to do anything for a joke, and his film-making abilities wowed Campbell. They soon began doing movies together, with Three Stooges-like titles such as *Pies and Guys*, *Inspector Klutz Saves the Day, Booby Bartenders, Three Pests in a Mess* and *Half-Wits' Holiday. Three on a Couch* shows a certain Jerry Lewis influence, too, since the title is simply swiped from one of Lewis' lesser vehicles. Campbell became adept — or at least enthusiastic — at doing slapstick falls and spills in the amateur movies that he made with Spiegel. Soon, Campbell, Spiegel and Mike Ditz met John Cameron, and they all began appearing in each others' movies.

One of the earliest films Spiegel and Campbell teamed up for was 1973's *Three Smart Saps*, directed by Spiegel and his friend Bill Ward (they directed many together), and starring them, Matt Taylor, Scott Taylor, Mike Coatney and Campbell. "That was the coolest short, because Bruce showed up with his own make-up kit and wardrobe," Spiegel says. "We were so impressed by that one because Bruce put on his moustache with spirit gum, and he had a costume with suspenders. 'Wow, this guy's a real actor.' Ordinarily, we'd wear tennis shoes, jeans and a T-shirt, but we'd throw a suit coat over it, and we thought we became instant adults."

Before joining forces with Spiegel, Campbell's films did include more serious stuff, with titles like *Supa' Bad, Day of Violence*, even *Son of Hitler*. Of course, in that one, Hitler is too young to drive himself, so his mother chauffeurs him around town in a station wagon. The shorts Bruce directed often featured his brother Don and his friends Scott Tyler and Roger Bick, but as early as *Three Smart Saps*, Campbell gave himself wholeheartedly over to Spiegel's Stooge-mad agenda.

Spiegel returned the favour by appearing in the Campbell-directed *Manhunt* in 1974, with a story inspired by Richard Connell's often-imitated 'The Most Dangerous Game'. It also featured frequent Spiegel co-star Matt Taylor. But then it was back to stuff like *No Dough Boys, The Singing Nuts, I'll Never Heil Again* and similar titles. Many are direct remakes of Three Stooges shorts, even using the original films' soundtracks.

Sam Raimi had been brought into the fold by this time, but every summer —
when most of these films were made — he was shipped off to Camp Tamakwa in Ont-
ario. There are Camp Tamakwa T-shirts visible in both *The Evil Dead* and *Evil Dead II*.
At Tamakwa, Sam became friendly with Mike Binder, and in 1993 he appeared in
Binder's semi-autobiographical *Indian Summer*, a warm-hearted *Big Chill*-like comedy-
drama set at Camp Tamakwa itself. See how it all hangs together?

Before he teamed up with Campbell and Spiegel, Sam Raimi was inspired by the
Gulf Oil commercials of the time involving pixilation, and "started moving around chess
pieces on a board, one frame at a time." Almost every kid who gets their hands on a
movie camera sooner or later tries stop-motion, if they can get away with it.

Around this time, Sam met Jim Rose, whose father had a very early home video
camera that ran reel-to-reel like audio tape recorders of the time. Sam, Jim and some
other friends began experimenting: "We began getting together almost every day after
school, shooting skits on video." Unfortunately, these shorts, often war movies, are not
currently screenable.

In Rebecca Mead's interesting *New Yorker* article on Sam (23 November 1998),
he described these little video movies as a significant learning experience. They would
begin with what they thought of as aerial shots of toy soldiers, with the video camera
taking the position of a helicopter. "And then we would cut to the soldiers themselves," Raimi told Mead, "and that would be us, being participants in the fight." The
trouble was that this seemed an incoherent mess to anyone other than Sam and Jim.
"People didn't understand why we were showing toy soldiers, and then why we were
suddenly bigger than they were... At that stage, it wasn't even about making bad
movies — we were making movies that no one could understand. The movies had to
improve, just so that people could understand what we were trying to tell them."

"We did this for a long time, or until my thirteenth birthday," Sam says, "when
my father bought me a camera." Prior to that, Sam had purchased an old silent 8mm
camera with his leaf-raking money, but this birthday present was something he never
could have afforded himself. It was a Bell & Howell Filmosonic, Super-8 with sound.
"It had sound-on-sound recording," Sam says nostalgically, "meaning they had a magnetic track that runs along the Super-8 film."

Raimi and Campbell finally met in 1975 when they took a drama course together,
and discovered they were both making Super-8 movies. This was around the same
time that Sam and Scott Spiegel took a high school biology course together, taught by
Miss Slaughter, a hip young black woman who impressed both students. (They had
met in junior high, but didn't become friends until high school; Spiegel thought of
Raimi as "one of those drama people," a poseur with pretensions to acting.) Raimi

overheard Spiegel telling a joke. "Hey," Scott said, "I'm a great detective." He pointed at the heel of his shoe. "See? I ran that down." Sam recognised the joke. "You stole that from the Stooges," he told Scott. And a friendship was born, forged in the fires of Miss Slaughter's biology class.

As Spiegel says, "We all went to groovy Groves High School, and we were all making movies separately. It all kind of blended somehow that way: you make movies, *we* make movies — great! By that time, I think Bruce and I were the most advanced film-makers, but Sam was the one with the sound Super-8 camera. We just all kind of joined in and started showing the movies at groovy Groves. It was really cool. We all acted and took turns doing whatever." Most of their films were made with the same people: Raimi, Spiegel, Campbell, Cameron, Ditz and Quill, shooting in and around Birmingham, the suburb of Detroit where Wylie E. Groves High School is located.

Raimi agrees, but points out that it was: "Bruce and Scotty who had always been big fans of the Three Stooges." Specialising in Stooge-like comedies, Sam says, "was due to Scott's influence, although I liked them. But they never entered my film-making world until I met Scott." (However, enter it they did; the influence on, say, the later feature films *Crimewave* and *Army of Darkness* is obvious, but even in *The Evil Dead* the Stooges left their mark. The bleeding wall sockets and the lightbulb that fills up with blood are gory duplications of similar shots involving water in the Stooges' *A Plumbing We Will Go*.)

"It was good doing the Three Stooges rip-offs," says Spiegel, "but when Sam came into the fold, we were doing things like *The James Hoffa Story*, shot on the exact spot where he disappeared. Bruce played Jimmy Hoffa, Sam and I were the kidnappers. We put flour in Bruce's hair; he was great. Then we did a sequel, *The Hoffa Story Part II*."

Before you reel from visions of sixteen year-olds doing a starkly serious drama about the labour leader, his criminal problems and his mysterious disappearance, rest assured that *The James Hoffa Story* and its sequel are silly slapstick comedies, very much in the Three Stooges ballpark. Bruce, looking like a teenager with flour in his hair, comes out of a restaurant (the one from whose parking lot Hoffa disappeared only two weeks before) and hangs around on the sidewalk, knowing he is due to be kidnapped, and wanting to be co-operative about it all. But when the kidnappers arrive, sent by a James Bond villain-type mastermind, they grab the wrong guy, and the rest of the film is a lot of slapstick chases and pratfalls. Finally, Hoffa is indeed kidnapped and dumped headfirst into a garbage can. To say it's irreverent is to raise the possibility that it might have *been* reverent, and that was never likely. (The sequel begins on a beach, and has no discernible plot, although we learn that the clever Hoffa has tricked his kidnappers by remaining upside down in that garbage can for six months.)

Above:
Scott, Bruce and Sam filming The James R. Hoffa Story Part II.

While Sam Raimi has, obviously, become a director, and Bruce Campbell an actor (who has directed some television shows), Sam occasionally claims that this was partly a matter of chance. He told writer Ray Greene in the *L.A. Village View* (26 Feb - 4 Mar 1993), "In the days of Super-8, we'd all pitch in directing, we'd all pitch in acting and paying for the films. It was a very communal experience — everyone did everything. And it's weird, I don't think it was a conscious decision, but eventually Bruce turned out to be the better of the actors — he had the handsome jaw and the good-looking face, so we found out that girls liked watching him. So he became the actor and I ended up behind the camera... but we just kind of fell into those roles." This is an assessment that few of Sam's Super-8 friends would agree with, including Campbell who, as noted, was interested in acting even before he met Sam Raimi.

Not all of the fun that Bruce and Sam had together was on film. During a variety show staged by the Franklin Junior Players (the summer theatre group Bruce belonged to) Sam, Bruce and Doug Sills (Sam's next-door neighbour) staged the

Bonzoid Sisters. "We came up with this idea to do fake acrobatics," Sam recalls. "The three of us were bungling acrobats called the Bonzoid Sisters. We put on long underwear and shorts, and big initials on our T-shirts: BS. We began a routine as though we didn't speak English. It's hard to explain," he admits a little helplessly, "but Bruce and Doug might jump on the stage, and I would hold up a wheel, then roll it toward them, and they would jump over the wheel. The only thing was that the wheel was only three inches high. We'd take our big bows and yell 'Hey! Hey!' and launch into our next routine. It was all just a big bunch of bull, basically."

YOU MUST TASTE BLOOD TO BE A MAN

Bruce, Sam and Scotty had great fun making short films together, and gradually their scope increased. Campbell's work elsewhere helped the Super-8 movies, because as an actor at St Dunstain's, he was able to borrow costumes. "We did a film called *I'll Never Heil Again,*" Campbell explains, "and we needed military costumes. So I went over to St Dunstain's and borrowed them — for years, in fact, old suits, old military costumes, never inventoried. It was a great resource for all that stuff."

All three of them showed their films for their friends and family, and sometimes at high school as well. Together with Mike Ditz and John Cameron, Raimi, Spiegel and Campbell formed the Metropolitan Film Group at Wylie E. Groves High School, showing each other's films to surprised audiences. They even had the sheer brass to charge admission to these screenings, but they certainly weren't in it for the money. However, the idea that they *could* charge money paid off in other ways later on, with *The Happy Valley Kid.*

Scott, the resident comedian, was funny enough that after he, Raimi and Campbell appeared on a local horror movie programme, the host invited Spiegel to return on a regular basis. "Our local horror movie TV show host, The Ghoul, who was Ron Sweed, came to Detroit around 1971 or '72 and was an instant success," Scott says. Sweed "stayed a big hit pretty much all through the seventies, but his popularity began to wane around '76-'77. By that time, we ended up on the show. He saw our short *Six Months to Live* and decided to show it on the air. Not a very scary movie to show on the show, but all of a sudden, Sam and Bruce and I, mostly Bruce and I, ended up guest-starring on his show, with Bruce doing a *Close Encounters* parody dressed as a woman. It was really cool."

Spiegel went to college for a year, but economic necessity required that he get a full-time job. He worked at a market (the Walnut Lake Market in West Bloomfield, Michigan) off and on for around twelve years, despite his goofiness and tricks. "From the store," Campbell says, "Scott could get all the boxes we ever needed. He'd get boxes, pies, any kinds of food, stuff they technically couldn't sell any more, but would look good. We could break eggs, mess around with potato salad, anything we needed. Scott was king of the pies, but the boxes were very important too, because cars could go smashing through them for a spectacular look. The heyday of the boxes was probably during *James Bombed in Here Today... Gun Tomorrow*, where cars were smashing though boxes for no reason."

James Bombed is, of course, a 007 spoof crossed with the Three Stooges. Not surprisingly, Campbell plays the secret agent, and there are indeed many boxes sent flying by cars careening down alleys. But perhaps the most memorable, if that's the word, aspect of this entertaining little movie is Campbell's moustache, which appears and disappears throughout. He was eighteen by this time, and the moustache was a soon-discarded attempt to look even older, but then, Campbell was getting older. He had finished high school in 1976, determined to become an actor if he possibly could. He applied to the Cherry County Playhouse up in Travers City in northern Michigan for an unpaid job in summer stock. Comic Pat Paulsen and a business partner owned the theatre, and every summer the theatre put on six or seven plays, one of them with Paulsen, the rest with other celebrities, big and small. The summer Campbell interned there, the other performers included Sally Ann Howes, Doug McClure and Tom Smothers.

Below
Scott Spiegel,
in make-up as
Clockwork's
villain, with
Sam Raimi.

"I had to pay for my own accommodation, but it was the single biggest binding experience for me," Campbell says now. "That summer was incredibly hard work, and it gave me lots of behind-the-scenes experiences, too. It wasn't really for acting; you were there to service the productions, and they'd rotate you. For example, I was assistant stage manager for a play when Allen Ludden was up there, then I rotated to be Tom Smothers' dresser, then I would be on set-dressing for another one, where we'd have to do all the scene changes in between. It was a real non-stop nightmare that summer, but it was the coolest thing I'd ever done."

One of the great treats was working with Tom Smothers, who turned out to be very supportive. Campbell enjoyed being Smothers' dresser: "I did his laundry, took him around, picked him up, took him here and there. He was a really nice guy." Scott Spiegel went up to Travers City to visit Campbell, and he brought with him some of their Super-8 movies: "One of the defining moments of my life was showing Tom Smothers our Super-8 movies. He laughed hysterically as he watched them, which put us in shock."

But Smothers' appreciation was genuine, and later he sent Campbell and Spiegel a cheque for $500 to help finance more of their cockamamie projects. "We actually used it toward equipment or films," Campbell swears, and the film that benefited most was the Super-8 *Mystery No Mystery*, made after he returned home in the fall.

When the summer was over, Campbell went to college at Western Michigan in Kalamazoo; he had his cousin sign him up for "a bunch of theatre classes. I didn't have time to do it, so she did it for me, but when I got there, I was tormented at the remedial nature of it all. I'd gone way beyond that already. It was, 'this is upstage, this is downstage.' I'd just been building sets and showing my movies to Tommy Smothers. I couldn't possibly stay there."

Fortunately, Bruce's father, who had continued in the advertising business, was an account executive dealing with producers of commercials: "He was the type of guy who would look over the shoulders of directors on commercial shoots, saying, 'Do you think there's enough light on the product?' He got to be friends with Vern Nobles, a guy who did a lot of local commercials, who wound up being very influential to our careers."

Although Nobles only made commercials at the time, Campbell and his friends didn't judge him, because the commercials were still "big, glossy stuff. He was pretty well-known in the city of Detroit." Campbell, Raimi and Spiegel showed Nobles some of the early films. He offered elementary, but valuable, advice, recalls Bruce, "He'd say, 'You see how the car comes in here left to right? In the shot before you had it going right to left. Keep it all going left to right.' He taught us about screen direction and editing, and actually made us aware of the crudities of what we had been doing.

"He would sometimes do a commercial on Friday and wouldn't take the equipment back until Monday, so we borrowed his stuff and did a little 16mm short, a kind of prototype. Since Vern had editing equipment, we edited it, too. It was our first taste of professional equipment, where it had double action sound, you had to use a slate, you had to synch it up. It was very complex, and we had to edit it during a certain time period, because he had to get the equipment back."

Campbell dropped out of school after half a year and went to work as a production assistant for Nobles in January of 1977, and stayed for about a year: "We did forty to fifty commercials during that time. The first job I was ever on was a big national Chevy commercial that Vern directed." Campbell kept an accurate diary during this period (but not, dammit, during the shooting of *The Evil Dead*), and he still considers keeping a journal to be one of the most valuable things he ever did as an industry professional.

Working with Nobles gave Campbell a taste of "the real stuff", as Bruce explains: "Vern studied under George Stevens — he worked on *The Diary of Anne Frank* and some other Stevens' movies in that period as his gofer. Vern married a woman who didn't like Hollywood, so he came back to Detroit. He was a guy who was constantly champing at the bit to do more and better; he always had fabulous ideas and was the best salesman I've ever seen. He's out here in California now, but doesn't do much any more. His sons are all millionaires, because bold, crazy inventiveness runs in the family." Campbell worked on Nobles' one feature, *The Magic Balloon,* which showed on television in Detroit, giving him further invaluable experience.

Meanwhile, Spiegel, Raimi and Campbell continued to make their Super-8 movies. With the input of Vern Nobles, the money from Tom Smothers, and Campbell's increasing know-how regarding production, the films became slicker and more professional, but Sam's departure for Michigan State University meant they also became less frequent. And it had other decisive effects, too.

Sam's older brother Ivan was also at Michigan State, studying medicine; when Sam arrived later on, Ivan's room-mate was Robert Tapert, whose major at the time was business. Tapert, born 14 May, 1955, "came from a middle-class upbringing, ended up going to Michigan State University, studied first humanities, and then economics," he says. "I became involved in economics because, crazy as it seems, I took an Economics 101 class from a guy who supposedly was very difficult and very demanding. But out of 1300 students, I finished number one, and so he sent me a letter that said I should go into economics. Okay, that seemed easy enough, so I did.

"While I was doing that, I always took film classes; a couple showed us all the different film movements, and I enjoyed that, but I never saw how they were going to fit into my life, because I always liked the outdoors and that kind of stuff, so I was headed toward an outdoors economic bent. Ivan Raimi came to Michigan State in the spring of 1974; we became buddies and got a house off campus together for five years. I knew Sam as Ivan's impish brother. He was always a practical joker, a magician. The first twenty minutes of time I ever spent with Sam, he showed me this magic trick at their house in Franklin, Michigan. He got me, sucked me in with his magic, and then later came up to school to visit Ivan. I watched some of his earlier movies, and thought they were funny. Finally, when he came up to college, we ended up in a Shakespeare class together. It was my last year; I was in the five-year programme and almost missed having any classes with Sam. Who, incidentally, was there the same time as Magic Johnson; Magic made a lot more money."

When Sam sat behind Rob in their Shakespeare course, Rob learned another aspect of his character. "I had never met anybody who so deliberately attempted to embarrass people in front of a large crowd," Tapert laughs, "to control the situation. Just before the class started, as Professor Upshaw walked in, in those thirty seconds in which everyone is settling down, Sam would say, way too loudly, 'You know, Rob, I agree with you; for a bald-headed jerk, he's not a bad teacher...'

"In Sam's freshman year, he suggested we all make a movie together. Ivan kind of got the ball rolling so we could get student funding, to help put on other people's movies. While ours were kind of commercial at the time, there were other people at college making movies that people really wouldn't pay to go see. We ran the Society of Creative Film-making at Michigan State; Sam was president. We started putting on a Super-8 festival every spring for two years. When we left, other people kind of picked up the ball. I guess they still have it — their annual Super-8 film awards."

The movie they made was, in many ways, the most important project any of them had worked on until then. The movie was *The Happy Valley Kid*.

Sam wrote the script about a pathetic nerd who arrives at college only to be tormented by everyone he meets, abandoned by his mother and spurned by his girlfriend. His mind snaps and, dressed as a cowboy, he guns down a few people before being killed himself. It's a comedy, but there are some touches of pathos.

Ivan was originally going to play the title role, but didn't have the time, so Sam asked Rob, originally scheduled to play the room-mate, if he would play the lead. He always enjoyed acting, and jumped at the chance. Sam didn't stop tormenting Rob, though; in the credits, he's billed as 'Rip Tapert'.

They shot the movie on and off over one wintry school term, and the production was not without its highlights. "There was a massive snow storm," Tapert explains, "and they'd shut down the campus. So we hitch-hiked to Meier's Thrifty

Acres (or Meier's Shifty Fakers), which is a big discount place, and bought a ton of film. Then Sam got in line at the liquor store, bought a keg and some cases of beer, threw a party in the hall, and filmed it." Except for the exaggeration of the lead character and what he goes through at the party, it's a surprisingly realistic depiction of a drunken college party, although one suspects at times that the cameraman too had been hitting that keg pretty hard.

When *The Happy Valley Kid* was finished, they showed it on campus, charging admission. "It got a good reaction, and I had no idea what to expect. None whatsoever," Tapert admits. "The first screening we had was the most nerve-wracking thing I had ever done. I was so nervous I couldn't be inside — a classic story — so I just listened through the doors.

"We cut another five or six minutes after the first screening, and then started running it four times a week, twice on Friday and twice on Saturday, up at Michigan State, and people started to go see it. We played to half to two-thirds filled houses. I think we did thirteen or fourteen weekends, then and at the beginning of the next fall, over the life of the movie. We left the following March.

"*The Happy Valley Kid* was the first movie that Sam had ever done without Bruce and Scott being actively involved, though they're both in it. Sam was up at State, and they came up to do big scenes and post-production only. A lot of the shooting was Sam and Ivan and me, or Sam, me and someone else." But to the surprise of both Sam and Rob, they made a profit, and the idea that they could make a film for real cinemas was planted.

That summer, back in Franklin, Sam, Scott and, occasionally, Bruce got together to make an elaborate Super-8 comedy called *It's Murder.* By this time, Campbell says, they were more systematic about making the films, largely due to the influence of Vern Nobles and the lessons learned during the making of *The Happy Valley Kid*: "The '77 period began with us getting organised, trying to get people to commit to being in the films, though none of them were professionals — they were still just our friends from school — but we'd tell them we needed them for a whole day on Saturday, you can't have a dental appointment. During that summer, we did most of the shooting of *It's Murder*, but then everybody had to go back to school that fall. So Scott and I wound up running around grabbing shots on weekends and sending them to Sam so he could cut them in. I wore other guys' outfits all the time, and did a lot of Fake Shemping."

Now that's a term that anyone who has watched Sam Raimi movies will find familiar, if puzzling. At the end of the cast list of most of his feature films to date, Raimi includes a group of 'Fake Shemps'. On the features, this really means something like

visible extras or bit players, but it meant something else in the Super-8 movies.

With his brothers Moe and Jerry (Curly), Shemp Howard was one of the original Three Stooges working on stage in the late twenties and early thirties. He left the group, but rejoined to make a series of two-reelers for Columbia. When he died in 1955, it presented a real difficulty. The shorts were not shot individually, but in batches, so there were several for which Shemp had shot some of his scenes, but not all. They hired an actor who kept his head down and pretended to be Shemp in bridging scenes, dubbing in some of Shemp's lines from other films to hide the fact that this guy wasn't who he appeared to be. Stooge fans Sam, Scott and Bruce spotted these fake Shemps immediately, and when they found it necessary to have someone double for another actor (often for many others) in one of their Super-8 movies, they called the doubles 'Fake Shemps'. And a tradition, however obscure, was born. Bruce Campbell Fake Shemps a hell of a lot in *It's Murder.*

Another important element of what would become *The Evil Dead* came aboard on *It's Murder*, and that was make-up and special effects technician Tom Sullivan. He's one of the saga's more mysterious figures. He worked on the first two films (much more extensively on *The Evil Dead*), doing a memorable job, and then basically vanished from movies. 'Ash's Evil Dead Page', a website devoted to the *Evil Dead* movies, includes an interview with Tom Sullivan conducted by Cliff Holverson. "I had been making my own films, doing masks and special effects experiments by myself in Marshall, Michigan," Sullivan told Holverson. "I started with water-dripping noises, a sound effect I can do with my mouth."

"I was a little reluctant [to get involved]," Sullivan told Bob Martin in *Fangoria* (May 1983), "but we hit it off real well right from the beginning." Sullivan designed the poster (inspired by Frank Frazetta's for *After the Fox*) and made water-dripping noises for *It's Murder*, although "shooting had been almost completed when I met them... I think I showed them everything I had, including my stop-motion dinosaur epic Super-8 short called *Time Eater*, a high school project I'd done at Wheaton North, in Wheaton, Illinois." In addition to sounding like dripping water, Sullivan created the *It's Murder* poster, and later the titles for *Clockwork*. And he carried on working with Raimi, Campbell and Tapert, providing the make-ups for *Within the Woods.*

It's Murder is a broad comedy with an intricate plot and a lot of characters. Scott plays a stupid detective, and Sam is an old man in a wheelchair, who sometimes forgets about the chair. When Scott calls to him from the foot of a spiral staircase, Sam cheerily responds, "I'll be right down!" And tumbles out of the chair to the foot of the stairs. The film is uneven, with some very bright moments, but it's hard to follow and probably too long for what it is.

There was a very important aspect to *It's Murder*, one that was almost thrown

Right:

Bruce Campbell,
Scott, Julie
Quiroz, Tim
Quill and Sam in
an It's Murder
publicity shot.
Quiroz doesn't
appear in the
finished film.

away in the film itself. As Spiegel explains, "Sam and I made a movie called *Six Months to Live,* which was really funny; we liked it, it got great responses. About that time, I had stumbled upon the twenty-minute Super-8 condensation of William Castle's *Strait-Jacket,* and added it to our cache of movies. At parties, we'd sometimes show *Six Months to Live,* which got laughs, and followed it with *Strait-Jacket,* which got screams. It's really well edited."

Scott Spiegel has loved horror movies all his life, and his apartment looks like that of the ultimate fan of Forrest J Ackerman's *Famous Monsters of Filmland.* Although horror movies scared Sam enough that he usually avoided them, Spiegel began getting him interested. "Sam kind of liked horror movies like the TV movie *Don't Be Afraid of the Dark,* so I got him to watch *House on Haunted Hill;* the scare with the old lady — he screamed! He loved the shock stuff, which is still in his repertoire. And I turned him on to *The Haunting* and all of these things."

Sam goes a bit further. "At the time, horror films scared me," he admitted, "and I didn't like being scared. It was an unpleasant experience for me. But since making my first horror film, I've come to appreciate them, and to appreciate the great artistry of the classics." In Rebecca Mead's *New Yorker* interview, he added, "The movies I see are not [horror movies]. They are stories of real people, or a mix of real people and adventure, like *The Treasure of the Sierra Madre,* which I love."

Since the short version of *Strait-Jacket* had startled their captive audiences, Raimi and Spiegel decided to include a shock sequence in the otherwise comic *It's Murder.* "We had a scare in the back seat of a car that I picked up from *I Saw What You Did,* being a big William Castle fan," explains Spiegel. "It worked so well in the original film that John Carpenter also used it for *Halloween:* the killer in the back seat." The scare sequence has a preamble, but the shot itself is simple — a menacing figure suddenly rises up in the back seat of a car the driver thought he was alone in. It still works, and if you saw it, you'd jump.

Although Scott Spiegel is still somewhat fond of *It's Murder,* and it does have some funny scenes, the others were dismayed by the audience response to the film. In fact, Campbell says, "It was a bomb, a total flat-out bomb, a two thousand dollar bomb. Sam tells the story of showing up in this big auditorium that they had to rent. One guy showed up, and halfway through he said, 'Okay, that's enough, you can turn it off now,' and he left. There was Sam just wallowing in his misery after making a killing off *The Happy Valley Kid.*" Spiegel counters by pointing out that later on *It's Murder* did play to satisfied audiences at Groves High, and eventually made back all of its money.

Rob Tapert found himself being drawn further and further into Sam Raimi's filmmaking world: "Sam and I had an apartment together up at Michigan State while Sam was working on *It's Murder.* He needed help doing the sound, and I blew off a big test I had to help Sam get ready. Somewhere in that time, the idea started formulating in my mind. Well, I know a few guys who have money, maybe I could get the money together."

Around that time, John Carpenter's *Halloween* débuted to great acclaim and big box office. "Sam and I went to see it alone," Tapert remembers, "and we were about the only people in the theatre, on a Tuesday night after it first opened in Lansing. Because we were alone, I didn't have a wild visceral reaction. I had seen a lot of drive-in movies because I liked them. I thought, 'Oh, this is pretty cool, and it's not the same as Hammer horror.' I asked him, 'Sam, can you make a movie this good, maybe better than this?' He said he didn't know, because it was pretty good.

"And then he went to see it with his girlfriend on the following weekend, to a packed theatre full of young girls, and they shrieked and screamed their way through it. We were now running *It's Murder* on campus, and the only thing in all of *It's Murder* worth waiting for was the shock scene in the car." Even though *It's Murder* was a financial catastrophe, Rob says, "It basically made us think that we could go out and make a feature-length film. So sometime in October of 1978, the idea began to grow. Let's do some sort of horror film.

"I started doing research, found *Variety* for the first time, went back and got all their rental champs [top-grossing films], and started pulling a bunch of stuff together. Eventually, I came up with information that was encouraging; some of the biggest low-budget hits had been horror movies: *Night of the Living Dead, Last House on the Left, The Texas Chain Saw Massacre*. And a lot of them had first-time directors."

Campbell was willing to be a part of it. "Fine, comedy, horror, it didn't really matter to me, but horror does lend itself more to the obvious techniques of film-making than comedy does." He began researching horror movies himself, never having seen many of them.

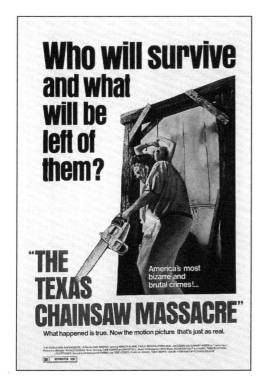

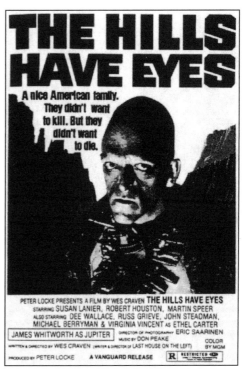

"We thought, 'Well, we can't do a slapstick because it's too odd, it's too strange. It's too risky.' A failed comedy will make less money than a failed horror movie. Even if the horror movie is bad, some kid walking down the aisles of a video store will go, 'Oh, that's got a good box,' and rent it. So we felt obligated to pick a genre that was more of a sure-fire thing at the time." Because of his love of horror movies, Scott Spiegel encouraged them, but his family obligations prevented him from becoming involved in the planning and making of the film.

They began to haunt drive-ins, paying particular attention to how audiences reacted, how they "turn their lights on during boring parts, flashing them up on the screen, honking their horns at parts they didn't like," Campbell says. "So after going to a bunch of these movies, we realised that some of the most effective ones really got relentless. We did a little chart comparing the plot, situations and budget restraints of our potential film and other successful low-budget horror movies. The early George Romero works had young cast members, and when you had no money, you get young eager people. In *The Texas Chain Saw Massacre*, it was isolated people up against an unstoppable force. *The Hills Have Eyes:* stranded people, their car breaks down in the desert, they're trapped by crazies again, and the actors were completely unknown. George Romero, Tobe Hooper, Wes Craven, all those guys started with this kind of similar formula, although I would hate to say that anybody copied from anybody, that would be unfair, but there seemed to have been good reasons why they did it that way."

With this sense of what people liked and disliked in horror movies, and an idea of an approach, "we determined, whether our movie was good or bad, to go all-out, non-stop; if we were going to make a horror film, we were terribly concerned to make a horror film with a capital H."

Horror films "juice you," as Sam Raimi says. Rob adds, "It's the roller-coaster effect. You go to a thousand films looking for the kind of movie that will really put you on that roller-coaster, and you don't know where you're going; you make the turn at the last second — or you don't make the turn, and you crash into a wall made of Styrofoam. It's the wild ride you're looking for. I know that's why I went to all of them. *The Hills Have Eyes* got me in that way. *Halloween* almost got me that way. Horror is a mass effect, and it's really at its best in theatres. It's been relegated to video, and that's not ultimately the best medium."

Tapert was enthusiastic about the idea of making a real movie that would play in real theatres, but Sam and Bruce, who had half-heartedly discussed the idea earlier, felt it was unlikely to succeed. "Poor Rob will learn it's impossible," Sam remembers thinking, "but we will humour him." So after Christmas that year, Sam returned to the apartment with Rob with an idea for a horror movie. His idea was not original; a group of young people is isolated and in danger, then killed one by one with maximum impact and suspense. He had taken ideas from *Night of the Living Dead, The Hills Have Eyes* and *The Texas Chain Saw Massacre*, added some concepts from a course in ancient history, and a few ideas left over from a short story he wrote for a writing class. Over the course of the script's creation, the original idea of basing it on the Egyptian Book of the Dead was replaced by references to Sumerian religion. Like other writers, Sam later borrowed the term 'Necronomicon' from author H.P. Lovecraft. In an interview in *Drama-Logue* (9-15 April 1987), Sam said, "My ancient history professor was giving a dissertation on Sumerian culture, and I was phasing out, as I was likely to do in those days. And she mentioned the ancient Sumerian Book of the Dead, which is actually a series of scrolls and not one bound book, as in the pictures. They were about burial rites, funerary incantations and passages explaining the trip to the netherworlds beyond death, and that suddenly pricked up my ears."

Sam's one alteration from the pattern of the films they studied was to make the central character a man rather than a woman. As Campbell says, "Sam felt that could make it even more horrifying; if you could reduce a man to scrambling and screaming and yelling and being tormented, it would be even more horrifying than a woman doing that. We figured in our own borderline chauvinistic way, that would be worse, scarier for the audience."

Sam told *The New Yorker* that through watching horror films, "I began to see that there is an art to them, and there is a craft to making suspense, and I realised how interesting the process was. I would watch the suspense build in a picture, and it would be released, and the audiences would jump and scream, and I thought, this is kind of fantastic; they are being brought to a level here, and how long can we sustain that level? And should we break it with a scare, or should we bring it down gradually, or should we end the scene on a high note? I began to understand that making a horror film was like writing a piece of music; it's like watching the work of a composer."

Tapert turned out to be the go-getter, the firebrand of the bunch. By April of 1979, he had already begun to contact potential feature distributors about handling what they intended to call *Book of the Dead*. "Rob was the first guy who said, 'Okay, let's put some numbers down on paper and see how much it would cost,'" Bruce explains. "He knew how to form a business entity; before we had either pulled the money out of our own pockets or talked to dad or borrowed this and that. If we were to get serious, we had to get money from somebody else; we didn't have enough

Below:

Sam directing

Cheryl Guttridge

in Clockwork.

money, and neither did our families. Rob contacted Phil Gillis, who was his family lawyer. Rob was a kind of rowdy kid, and this guy had bailed him out on several occasions, but had never done anything entertainment-wise. We worked out an in-kind agreement; it was determined to do a limited partnership, a very easy non-corporate entity that doesn't last forever, with individual partners responsible for paying their own taxes, a very simple structure that we used several times later."

In early 1979, as part of a film course, Raimi made *Clockwork*, a short, effective suspense piece about a woman (Cheryl Guttridge) who begins to suspect that she's not alone in her home. Outside in the snow, in the dark, a shadowy figure (Scott Spiegel) watches. *Clockwork* is taut, sophisticated and mature, easily the best thing Raimi had made up to that point. He had clearly changed from being a kid having fun with a movie camera into someone who was learning just how powerful audience-manipulating tools a camera and effective editing can be. There are a few falterings in tone, some elements that don't quite fit and the ending is bleak and nihilistic (like that of *The Evil Dead*), but it's perfectly paced, and builds smoothly to a disturbing climax. It was the first of two warm-ups for *The Evil Dead*, and the first one made after Raimi and Tapert had decided a horror film was the way to go. It shows clearly that they had the skills they would need in place.

Around the same time, Raimi and Tapert made *William Shakespeare — The Movie,* with Bruce Campbell and an actress from Michigan State. It's a few scenes from *The Taming of the Shrew*, shot outdoors in the winter. Like *Clockwork*, it was made for one of Raimi's film courses, and like *Clockwork*, it's efficiently done — but unfortunately, it's also rather boring. However, for the first time, Raimi experiments boldly with a moving camera, and even a bit of gore.

"Up until college we all pitched in, but at that time, we each started making more of our own films, directing them our own way," says Sam. "It wasn't left up to the group where to set the camera up. I had been seeing the work of other directors, and started to appreciate them critically for the first time. It was very exciting to see moving camera shots, and I decided to put in things with the camera I liked to see myself. It never occurred to me throughout high school that the camera placement was so important, or could have such a visceral effect on the audience. When I did realise that, film-making became a much more exciting medium for me."

In spring 1979, to encourage more investors to put money into Renaissance's *Book of the Dead*, they filmed *Within the Woods,* their first out-and-out horror movie, which was shot at the Tapert family farm in Marshall, in the middle of Michigan. It cost them $1,600 to film in Super-8, and it took six days. "It was really a halfway point between our Super-8 movies and a professional, low-budget, feature-length movie," says Sam. "We wrote a script from the git-go, we had professional make-up effects Tom Sullivan prepared in advance with moulds, and on-the-set make-up. And we had professional lighting, in the sense that we rented professional lights for the first time.

"And we experimented with camera speeds, taking it a little further than we had gone before, recording synch-sound at a third slower for a more monstrous effect. For instance, although we shot the movie itself at eighteen frames per second, we shot Bruce Campbell at twenty-four frames per second to give him more mass on screen, and to make him move a little differently than the other characters. And also to distort his soundtrack, to make it much slower and heavier, an inhuman pitch."

In general, they experimented with virtually all the techniques that they would use in *Book of the Dead* later that year, but in Super-8

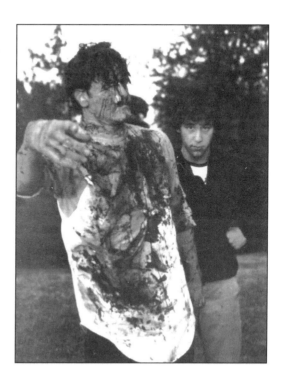

Above:
Bruce and Sam
shooting Within
the Woods.

rather than 16mm. One of the most striking aspects of the first two *Evil Dead*s is the swooping, gliding camera that flies through the woods, at times only inches above the ground. There are no camera tracks visible. Ordinarily, that kind of effect would be done with Garrett Brown's Steadicam, a large camera rig that's very heavy, very complex — and very expensive. Raimi, Campbell and Tapert didn't have the money for a Steadicam, so they invented their own variation.

In *Within the Woods,* Sam explains, "I ran with the camera hand-held for the effect of the creature advancing on the house. I could see that a wide lens helped the distortion factor. The closer you could get the object to the edge of the frame in a wide lens, it would warp as it went out of frame in a very dramatic way." For *The Evil Dead,* of course, he took it even further...

Tom Sullivan was hired to do the make-ups for the short. "That was mostly casting," Sullivan told *Fangoria.* "Building an arm, doing some make-up on Bruce — a lot of scars all over him, and popping his eye out." He also created the hand that Bruce gnaws off (an improvised action) in the course of the gory little film.

Of all the films that Raimi, Campbell, Tapert and Spiegel made until this point, *Within the Woods* is the most vivid, graphic demonstration of what they might do with this kind of material at feature length. It's swiftly-paced and involving, but still has an air of amateurism, an air that soon blew away. Scott Spiegel feels that "*Within the Woods* is far superior to *The Evil Dead* in many ways."

"It was more effective at making the audience scream than *Evil Dead* was," Sam says, "so in that way it was better. But it wasn't as professionally photographed, the sound wasn't as good, and the image quality wasn't as good, since it was Super-8. I think it did manipulate the audience better, providing more of an experience like John Carpenter did with *Halloween*." Rob Tapert agrees only in that *Within the Woods* is shorter than *The Evil Dead*. "It's eight minutes of set-up and twenty minutes of running around sticking knives in people," Rob says.

In the short film, Bruce and Ellen Sandweiss — using their own names — go on a picnic in a meadow surrounded by woods. He shows her part of a hunting arrow that he found in the area, as well as the head of a spear; and explains that he knows so much about Indians because he was a Boy Scout.

Ellen isn't very interested, but he persists: "You know this place we're stayin'? Used to be part of an old Indian burial ground. You're only cursed by the evil spirits if you violate the graves of the dead. We're just going to be eatin' hot dogs. Besides, I'll be there to protect you."

As Ellen spreads the blanket right over the camera, Bruce goes off to find wood for their fire. He starts to dig a hole, apparently to make a fire pit, and finds a wooden cross. (Were the local Indians Christians?) He digs further, coming up with various objects that are hard to identify. "Must be 200 years old," he mutters. Then he finds a knife, wrapped in cloth: "Ellen, look at this. It's an old Indian dagger. When the medicine man of a tribe died, they used to bury one of his possessions with him so he could have it in his next life."

She is disturbed by the fact that they are having a picnic on dead bodies. "All that's left now," says Bruce in joshing tones, "is Tinga, the Indian spirit of the woods who watches over and protects the medicine man's grave for all eternity." He tosses the knife aside. This is a very low angle, directly on the ground, moving in very slowly on the couple. Another cut: eerie music plays as fire erupts from the ground; we can see them in the background, apparently unaware of the fire.

Later, Ellen wakes up on the blanket; Bruce is gone. She puts on her jacket, still calling for him, gathers up their things, and leaves. Ellen trips and falls, and something odd on the ground in front of her catches her attention (though it's hard to see what it is). She looks up, and there's Bruce, hanging upside down, his face torn and shredded, one eyeball dangling.

Terrified, Ellen screams and calls out for Scotty. Weird noises come from the woods. The camera moves nervously around. She calls again. Then, in the distance, something starts rushing toward her in a fast-moving point-of-view (POV) shot through the bare branches.

Ellen screams and runs, casting frightened glances behind her as she flees. We hear something like low growls on the track accompanying a POV shot pursuing her across the pond or creek. With more screams she continues to flee toward a small house. (All she remembers about the film years later, Ellen Sandweiss says, is running through a swamp and falling up to her neck in dirty water. "It was quite thrilling and disgusting all at the same time. But I was a good runner. I still am.")

As she pounds on the door, Scott Spiegel reluctantly goes to see who it is, and opens the door just in time, apparently. They go into the house as the force withdraws.

Later, at sunset, Mary Valenti tells the terrified Ellen that she's just going to step outside and shine the light into the woods. As she steps out the door, a hideously scarred Bruce grabs Mary (to Universal horror movie music), and lifts her off the ground. He moans "Join us!" as he raises the dagger, plunging it into her throat and stabbing her with garden shears.

Above:
Within the Woods' *Monster Bruce attacking Joanne Kruse.*

Inside the house, Ellen tries to find something to use as a weapon, coming up with two large knives. A rattling doorknob scares her, and mistaking him for Bruce, she stabs Scott — but it's unclear whether this is in her imagination or for real, since we later see his body with the wooden cross sticking out of it.

Fleeing, she backs into Bruce, now in the house. He moans "You have violated the ancient ways. And so must die, to join..." He breaks off as she saws at his right hand, clutching her shoulder. Roaring, he tears at the hand himself, biting through the last tendons. He tosses the hand, with knife, onto a Monopoly board.

After a fight, she grabs the dismembered hand, still holding the knife, and stabs him. He reacts melodramatically, groaning and bleeding black fluid which also pours out of his mouth. Moaning, he collapses to the floor.

Scott Spiegel is one of the two leading actors in *Within the Woods*, but he didn't

Above and
opposite:
Bruce and
Joanne Kruse in
Within the
Woods publicity
shots.

go on to *The Evil Dead*. He isn't a partner in Renaissance Pictures, either, because, frankly, he had to earn money. "I just couldn't do it because I was supporting my family," Scott says today with some regret. However, the second male lead in *The Evil Dead* is named Scotty in honour of Spiegel, he co-wrote *Evil Dead II* with Sam, and he's a Fake Shemp in the first two movies. "I was going to be an associate producer," says Scott, "and one of the partners; I really wanted to be involved, but I couldn't quite make it."

When *Within the Woods* was finished, Rob Tapert arranged to show it at a cinema on the east side of Detroit called The Punch and Judy, in August of 1979. It was running *The Rocky Horror Picture Show* as a late show on weekends, and the cinema managers agreed to show *Within the Woods* before *Rocky Horror* on a few consecutive Saturday nights. "We patched into the sound system," Campbell recalls. "There was our crappy little Super-8 projector taking up about a quarter of the screen, with the sound system hissing and humming. But it worked, and audience members actually reacted."

Michael McWilliams of *The Detroit News* reviewed *Within the Woods* on 24 August 1979. "It will probably never be advertised alongside the glossy, big-budget horror movies of our time, but you won't easily forget a locally produced little film called *Within the Woods*. In just thirty-two minutes, it provides more chills, thrills and squeamish giggles than such recent professional duds as *Prophecy* and *The Amityville Horror* combined."

Sam and Bruce were both interviewed for the article, providing some of Raimi's earliest impish quotes. ('Impish', incidentally, is a word often used to describe Sam.) "I like it when [the audience] screams," Sam told an amused McWilliams. "When they jump, it's a surface reaction — a cheap thrill — but I like the fact that they jump... I like to know a secret that they don't know. They don't know it's coming, but I do."

McWilliams was knowledgeable enough about horror movies to spot the fruits of the drive-in research Sam, Rob and Bruce had conducted in early 1979. Sam, said

McWilliams, "has looked at *Night of the Living Dead* and knows our terror of the grave. He has looked at *Carrie* and knows the effect of a bloody arm out of the blue. He has looked at *Psycho* and knows our fear of knives and cellars. He has looked at *Taxi Driver* and knows the sometimes-psychotic rites of 'manhood'. He has looked at *The Texas Chain Saw Massacre* and knows our primal fascination with blood.

"With all this background, however, Raimi still has his failings. Above all, he's going to have to learn to limit his point-of-view shots. In the forest sequence, for example, we see things from five separate points of view." As those who know the *Evil Dead* films are aware, Raimi actually increased the number of point-of-view *shots*, but in all three films, the number of different points of view is reduced, so there are never more than three in any sequence — the evil Force, the human being in the scene and the omniscient movie director's viewpoint.

McWilliams concluded: "Raimi displays a wealth of learning in *Within the Woods*. Perhaps he will be able to make a more extended work, a feature film, in which he can clear up some of his technical deficiencies and prove that he has the personal depth to provide a context — a thematic meaning — for all his gore. Like many budding artists, Raimi is particularly skittish on this point of 'meaning.' He considers it 'silly' to take too seriously what comes to him naturally. When loosened up by a few jokes, however, Raimi can discuss underlying ideas in his work with considerable wit. For him, there are three recurrent themes: 'One, the innocent must suffer. Two, the guilty must be punished. And three, you must taste blood to be a man.'"

According to Rob Tapert, these rules originate with Sam, but "I actually don't know where they came from. The Coen brothers tried to tack another one on, that The Dead Must Walk, but we're not sure if it really stands the test of time. It does come up often, and it is certainly in the footnotes."

Sam adds, "I guess what I meant when I said that was — not to get too serious now — that it's fun to watch the innocent guy be tormented, because the audience relates to him, and if he's tormented by demons then we're afraid for him and are afraid ourselves. Also, we want to see the demons, the guilty, get their just come-uppance. The audience eventually does want to see the morality play out. I think that part of the fun of drama is that you sometimes get to see the world work out in ways it doesn't seem to want to in real life. And then, finally, 'You must taste blood to be a man' — that's the rite of passage. Bruce doesn't just taste blood, but swallows fifty gallons of it in the whole *Evil Dead* series; he had to experience violence or some kind of aggression to achieve his transition from nerd to movie hero."

Around the time *Within the Woods* was ready to be shown, Phil Gillis and Brian Manoogian completed the partnership papers for Renaissance Pictures, Ltd, and the prospectus for the sale of shares in the company, or rather, in *Book of the Dead* itself. The contract/memorandum is dated 10 August, 1979. The minimum purchase price per unit was $10,000, with a total of fifteen units planned. (The movie ended up cost- ing between $350,000 and $400,000, according to Campbell.) The prospectus care- fully explains the risk factors: it was a new partnership with no prior operating history, for example, and as usual with such documents, explains that there is no guarantee of a financial return to any investor, and that the partners (Bruce Campbell, Sam Raimi and Rob Tapert) have previously produced only three Super-8mm motion pictures. These were *It's Murder, The Happy Valley Kid* and John Cameron's *Shemp Eats the Moon*. It outlines the fiduciary responsibilities of the general partners, and their contributions and compensation. Sam's copyright in the screenplay extends to the partners. Income, state, local, capital gains taxes, compensation to the partners, depreciation, the film format and how it will be handled — everything is covered but the kind of food they'll eat on location. However, the ultimate statement is that everyone shares alike, no investor is guaranteed a return, and the partners control the content and making of the film. It's a very thorough document, forty-six pages of High Legalese; if you read it, you'd be bored.

An additional document concerning the formation of Renaissance Pictures was prepared at the same time. Included in this were a couple of charts showing how other horror films, the main inspirations for *Book of the Dead*, compared with it. They also prepared a listing of receipts for various movies released between 1968 and 1978; most of them are horror films aimed at young people, the audience Renaissance Pic- tures was aiming for with their horror movie.

Campbell doesn't claim to have understood all the details of the prospectus and contracts, but he's very respectful of Phil Gillis (who Fake Shemps in some of Raimi's features): "He wound up being pretty much the guardian angel of the whole project. He said he wanted $20,000 for his work, but he essentially folded it back into the film, and another $80,000 as well; he wound up putting about $100,000 into it. And the young guy who did the legwork on the limited partnership was Brian Manoogian; his family is related to the Masco Corporation, a Fortune 500 company, which makes Delta faucets. And he invested too, as did his brother, a friend of his and his sister. Between Phil Gillis and Manoogian, we got about two-thirds of our money."

The three partners in Renaissance Pictures convinced themselves that they could shoot *Book of the Dead* in Super-8mm and have a satisfactory blow-up to 35mm. "Michael Hinton, out in San Francisco," says Tapert, "had some sort of process that he believed in that would transfer Super-8 to 35mm. We saw something that he'd shot for Venezuela, and thought it just about got by. It looked like, say, 12mm."

"We went to a local movie theatre where we knew some of the people," Campbell recalls. They asked the management to show it: "We asked the projectionist, very cagily, 'so how does that look to you?' He said, 'It looks like a blow-up from 16mm.' And we thought, 'Yeah! Got it! It works!' But before we put all the money into that, we thought we'd better do our own test."

Raimi shot a very brief horror film in Super-8 called *Terror at Lulu's*, set in the lingerie shop owned by his mother; it was about a woman trying on lingerie late at night while being tormented by some guy. Or, Rob Tapert muses, maybe it was about mannequins coming to life and terrorising a girl who's working late doing inventory. They chose to use this as a sample because it had the financial advantage of being much shorter than *Within the Woods*. Also, there's no negative with 8mm film; what goes through the camera is physically the same film you get back, and they didn't want to lose their only print of *Within the Woods*. "Furthermore, we wanted to make sure that we shot something we intended to have blown up, so we used certain lighting ratios and other ideas that we didn't use on *Within the Woods*," Rob says.

They used the finest Super-8 camera they could get, a professional cameraman and the best lenses, and included some scenes with high contrast just to test things even more thoroughly. When the 35mm blow-up came back from Michael Hinton, they gathered in the Maple Theatre before it opened for the day, where they had persuaded the manager to allow them to show their footage.

Below:

Bruce is attacked by supernatural forces in Within the Woods.

What they saw was, to say the least, a rude shock. "It was the most horrifying experience of my entire life," Tapert recalls. Their film had grain the size of hailstones; it was unwatchable, unreleasable. "We couldn't justify the fact that it would be hailing golf balls throughout the movie, so we had to forego that technology," Raimi says ruefully. All three of the partners were crushed; there went the dreams they'd begun to believe. "We were dumbfounded," Campbell admits. "I was even more bummed-out than the other guys, because I thought, 'Okay, that's it, we can't do it.'"

But the indefatigable Tapert wasn't about to say die. "I remember sitting on the back porch of my parents' house with Bruce, and talking to him about this." Tapert suggested they simply switch over to 16mm; *Night of the Living Dead* was on 16mm, wasn't it? It took some time for him to regenerate their enthusiasm, but he managed it. In fact, Tapert now says, looking back, "It turned out to be the best thing that ever happened to us." (One of the two best things; the other was meeting Irvin Shapiro a few years later.)

The three partners bought briefcases, donned suits and played the roles of businessmen as they met with potential investors. They showed them the prospectus, and sometimes *Within the Woods* as well, and raised $85,000 of the $150,000 they were after.

They also firmed up their intentions for the film itself. "We wanted to make a picture that punished the audience for their sins against us," Sam smiles, "and we wanted to punish them with horror and gore and laughs. We were going to teach them never to come back to another one of our pictures — if there was to be such a thing. But the truth is, our goals were very limited at the time. We just wanted to make a picture that would be effective enough to play in the theatres. Certainly, we wanted to please the audience, but that was like if we ever *got* one. The goal was really to make a picture that could play in theatres. Which when we were shooting seemed like a very distant concept." Shooting, though, was now just a few months away — and they still hadn't raised the full amount they hoped for.

Their money was in a special Escrow account. In the fall, they sent a letter to the investors asking for permission to open the account short of the full amount, and to start making the movie. The investors agreed, so they began holding auditions for the three roles available. Bruce was cast as Ash, the lead. Ash's sister Cheryl, who ends up spending much of the film in make-up peering out of a trapdoor, was played by Ellen Sandweiss, who'd been in *Shemp Eats the Moon* and other Super-8 movies — and, of course, *Within the Woods*.

Ellen met Bruce and Sam in high school, where they were all involved in theatre, "both in the drama classes and the extracurricular plays," she recalls. She remembers that one of the Super-8 movies "was filmed in front of and in my house. I don't remember the name of it, I just remember I was in a long gown, and we used our living room with a grand piano."

While all of the Renaissance team, Josh Becker and Scott Spiegel all remember Ellen as a great sport, she says, "the one thing about all these guys that will stand out in my mind forever is that they always made me laugh, they always had me in hysterics over something. I remember walking down the hall with Bruce and seeing him just do a pratfall, throwing his books all over the place. I was in a play with Sam where I could never keep a straight face on stage because he would always mutter things under his breath and crack me up. I thought they were an odd lot, but they were so funny that they were a constant source of entertainment to me."

"Sam and Bruce are incredibly talented comedians, in terms of acting as well as directing, and I really hope they will get to use those talents, or put themselves in positions where they use those talents more. Although I've basically given up acting as a full-time career, if they asked me to do another movie, I would jump at it."

Teresa Seyferth, who later became a radio personality in Chicago and Los Angeles, was cast as Shelly, and Rich DeManincor (a professional diver in addition to an actor) as Scott. Both were in the Screen Actors Guild (SAG), which mandates a minimum pay scale that the Renaissance partners couldn't meet. So the two took different names: Teresa Seyferth became Teresa Tilly, then Sarah York; DeManincor became Hal Delrich since his two room-mates at the time were Hal and Del. The subterfuge didn't work, though — the two were spotted by the SAG, and fined. Bruce points out that in Detroit, SAG members are "famous for ratting on each other." DeManincor later turned up in *Crimewave* — using his own name. In *The Evil Dead*, Bruce, Ellen and Betsy Baker used their real names.

"It was very difficult to cast for a low-budget horror movie," Campbell explains,

Below:

Sam, Teresa

Seyferth and

Ellen Sandweiss

rehearsing in

the Book of the

Dead *cabin.*

"because when any girls auditioned, their boyfriends came with them because it sounded more like a porno film. I think we went through maybe ten people to get the five; it wasn't a huge paring-down process." But, difficult or not, casting was quickly completed.

Josh Becker returned to town from Hollywood; he had been the first of them to go out there. "We had no other jobs for him except as a PA [Production Assistant]," Campbell admits. "He took it begrudgingly, but we needed people who were used to working on movies. Some of our other friends who did Super-8 movies were in college by now, so we lost them. Scott had to work, so it was just Rob, Sam, Josh and I." During the making of *The Evil Dead*, Becker kept a journal, the only one of the crew to do so, and you can read the full text on his cheerfully self-promoting website, 'Becker Films: Directing from the Edge'.

"We found a local guy, Tim Philo," says Campbell, "who had photographed a couple of 16mm films for Wayne State University. We remembered seeing his films, the photography seemed good, and he was around our age. Initially, we were going to shoot in Michigan, when we thought we could get the money together like that" — Bruce snaps his fingers — "but now it was fall, so we took a scouting trip down to Tennessee."

They weren't able to start production in Michigan when they hoped; fall had gone, winter was coming on. They chose the mountains of Tennessee because they felt that, being further south than Michigan, it would be warmer; also, there were rolling, wooded hills available, and isolated cabins where they could shoot. After choosing their location, they returned to Michigan and assembled their crew. One of the crew, John Mason, had been a teacher of Bruce's at Wayne State University, which he'd briefly attended in 1978. Campbell knew Mason was eager to actually *do* something and, despite having a wife and kids, was happy to head for Tennessee with a bunch of first-time film-makers years younger than him.

"So we went down with a core; it was Rob, me, Sam, Josh, John Mason, Tim Philo. There was no such thing as a gaffer, there was no such thing as assistant cameraman or boom man, the sound guy did everything, he recorded and did it all. David Goodman, an old friend of the Raimi family, was the cook/production assistant of the crew; he'd just graduated and was gung ho to do a film; he became the guy who ran around, did transportation, and everything."

The three partners read a few books on budgeting and scheduling low-budget films, but such resources were scarce in 1979. As far as budgeting day-to-day expenses went, apart from housing and food, they decided to pay the actors $100 a week, production assistants/crew members got $40 per week (though Becker got $50 because of his greater experience). The partners allotted themselves $35 a

Above:

Rob Tapert,

Steve "Dart"

Frankel, Sam,

Tim Philo and

Josh Becker on

location in

Tennessee.

They're actually

kneeling down...

week, primarily as expenses, "but we never took it," Campbell says. "Everything just got dumped back into the movie."

Costuming was simple — people wore ordinary street clothes, but Sam Raimi was insistent that, nonetheless, the clothing not be linked to a time period. As Campbell says, "Have you ever seen old *Charlie's Angels* episodes? They're the funniest shows to watch because they always have these flared pants and big checks." So Sam dressed Bruce in blue workshirt and brown pants — unaware he was condemning him to the same costume for three movies. At least for the second two, Bruce got to wear sturdier shoes than the 'elf boots' (as he calls them) Ash wears in the first one. Ellen Sandweiss' clothes are different from the others to indicate that her character's a bit weird. The actresses wore specially made white scleral contact lenses (which turned out to be extraordinarily uncomfortable) to blank their eyes out for the scenes in which they're possessed.

It seemed obvious that they should shoot all the daytime exterior shots first, then the night exteriors, followed by the daytime interior shots, concluding with the very important night interiors. "We did those crude groupings," Campbell goes on. "The original shooting schedule was six weeks, and that's probably why we lost everybody for a while, because we went twelve weeks. We completely doubled it. We had some days where we got only two shots, and I could show you some in the film that took a whole day to get."

But that lay in the future, in the mountains, in the cabin; now it was time to begin shooting. So with their green crew, their untried cast, a script and $85,000, they headed for Tennessee.

CHAPTER 3

HOT COFFEE AND COLD BLOOD

Finally, they were on their way, with real movie equipment, real film stock, real actors and a real script, although it was only sixty-six pages long. They didn't realise that in movie industry practice, one page of a movie script is estimated to translate into one minute of running time.

Most people interested in a particular movie want to read anecdotes about the making of it, and as Rob Tapert says, with *Book of the Dead/The Evil Dead*, "the thing is one long anecdote." Everyone interviewed about the film has stories to tell — about the cold weather, the problems with the location, with the locals and with each other. Making the movie was somewhere between running the gauntlet and passing through the freezing fires of Hell, but no matter how horrible it was at the time, everyone seems to remember it as a fantastic, memorable experience. Not necessarily one they'd like to repeat, but one they are are deeply grateful and proud to have undergone.

It was November 1979 when Sam Raimi and Rob rode down to Tennessee together in a U-Haul truck. "It was kind of a bummer," Sam recalls, "because the truck was governed at 55mph — it wouldn't go any faster than that, and going up hills, it would go, like, thirty-five. It was unbelievable, a journey that lasted forever." On the way, naturally, they talked; Sam impressed Rob by outlining an especially striking scene during the trip. He knew Sam was good, but he wasn't expecting *this*.

"It was fascinating for me, I'll tell you," Tapert recalls. "It was maybe a twelve hour drive, but there was at least an hour of him explaining how he was going to do it, and I thought it was a great idea."

It's the sequence in which Ash chains Linda's body to a workbench, intending to dismember her with a chainsaw. Sam shot the scene in an unusually aggressive, spare style: there are close-ups of objects (chains, hands, lightbulbs, etc), with one sharp sound matched to each image. The cutting is very quick, with all extraneous action removed. There's nothing remotely like it in any of the Super-8 movies Raimi made, and very few scenes like it in any movie prior to *The Evil Dead*.

"I had been studying time cuts," Raimi explains, "which are jumps forward in time in movies. The most famous, and most extreme, example is the cut in *2001: A Space Odyssey*, from the bone the ape tosses to the satellite in orbit around Earth, millions of years later. I was trying to come up with a stylistic approach to the scene where Bruce feels that he must destroy this demon that resides inside the woman he loves. I really wanted to present it like a juggernaut, he's going to do it, he's going to do it — and then he can't, because he realises that he loves her.

"In the truck, I thought about this, and felt that I'd do a sequence of cuts. There would be one, two or three second takes, each developing on the previous, leading us to believe that Ash was going to destroy the woman he loves." The sequence is striking, and has the exact effect that Raimi was aiming for. We're pulled through the scene by the scruff of the neck, our certainty building with each cut that we're about to see a man hack his beloved to bloody chunks with a roaring chainsaw — only to be brought up short in sympathetic sorrow, when he weeps into his hands instead, unable to go through with it. Raimi uses similar sequences in *Evil Dead II* and *Army of Darkness*, but the effect is very different; both of those end with a satisfied Ash staring at a new mechanical appendage, and murmuring "Groovy."

Below:

Sam Raimi and

Rob Tapert pose

for the camera

whilst making

The Evil Dead.

In Josh Becker's journal, he noted that after he, Rob and Sam had watched some rushes, "Sam related film-making to being a magician. He said the only thing a magician is thinking about while performing is, 'do they know how I'm doing this trick?' If they don't, he's succeeding — period. The point also isn't to just make the film, it's to amaze yourself and everyone [else] at the same time. If you think what you're doing is neat, chances are everyone else will, too."

The optimism Tapert felt on hearing Raimi's imaginative ideas dimmed somewhat when he learned that the cabin, located for them by the Tennessee Film Commission, was not available after all. "The owners had got cold feet and pulled out," Campbell says. "So here we were with everybody sitting around, and we had to go on this desperate search. We hooked up with a local guy named Gary Holt; his famous phrase was, 'Now here's the deal I've worked out...'"

Holt was very useful to the *Book of the Dead* bunch. "He was a local hustler," Campbell goes on, "a Vietnam veteran with big rings on his fingers, and oh man, was he wired into Morristown, Tennessee. He got into early dwarf-tossing in bars around there with this black dwarf named Percy Ray, who had a Mohawk. Holt had been a

Below:

The cabin in

Tennessee.

chauffeur, too; his big boast was that he drove Elvis around a couple of times. He said, 'I ain't queer or nothin', but he had a magnetism.' Gary had produced a record in Nashville, which he played for us." In his journal, Josh Becker wrote, "It was about ten minutes long with a guy talking about the horrors of a Vietnam vet. It was too weird." Holt arranged for a press conference, resulting in some local newspaper coverage and TV interviews carried by a Knoxville station. This regional wonder was so useful that he wound up with the credit of Assistant Producer on *The Evil Dead*.

Holt found a huge, rambling old house that was perfect for the entire *Book of the Dead* company to stay in. A production meeting was held in the old house on the weekend of 10 November. "Sam spoke... and made a good show," Becker noted. "He was adroit, yet funny... He used a camp counsellor attitude [for] the whole thing, seemingly covered all the points and that was that."

After a few days, they found a cabin that they could use as the location for the movie. Of course, there were a few problems, as Rob explains: "It was completely over-grown, and cows had free run of the place; there was four inches of cow manure on all the floors. It was small, confined and had low ceilings."

And there were other potential drawbacks. Unlike the first cabin they'd chosen, the new one was, well, haunted. The Tennessee Film Commission told them the cabin dated from around the time of the Civil War. As the builder was placing the final brick on his chimney, a bolt of lightning struck him dead. "Apparently," Raimi recalls, "this cabin is in the centre of a valley that's surrounded by mountains of ore. Basically, it draws a lot of lightning to this area.

"When we got there," he goes on, "we saw that the top brick was still missing from the chimney, as though it had never been placed there. And then as we started meeting the locals, we learned more about it. After the fellow died, the place was con-sidered haunted, and no one stayed there for something like forty years. Around 1925, a family that was very poor didn't care about the haunted house story any more, and three generations of women — a mother, her daughter and the grandmother — moved in because they had no place else to go.

"The first night they were in this place, the little girl woke up to another light-ning storm and ran screaming into her mother's room, and then her grandmother's. By coincidence, both had died of natural causes the same night. So this little girl ran screaming out into the rain; searchers found her at a nearby farmhouse about half a day later, in a state of shock; she never really recovered from that. The family there raised her. And that was the whole story." Well, almost the whole story.

There was a lightning storm while they were shooting the picture. "It was very intense," Raimi remembers, "much more intense than any I'd seen before, with very loud booming lightning bolts coming a little too close for my comfort. This pick-up drives up the one-mile mud road to the cabin, and the people ask, 'Have you seen Abigail?' We ask, 'Who's that?' They explained that she was the daughter who had run off years before, the one who had found both her mother and grandmother dead in the cabin the same night. She was somewhere around sixty years old. They told us she got kind of confused during thunderstorms and would wander off into the woods, returning to the cabin, calling for her mother and grandmother. They didn't find her all the time we were there. After we left, the cabin was struck by lightning and burned to the ground." Whooooeeeee. (Bruce, of course, claims that Sam's explanation for the gutting of the house is fabricated, and that it actually burned down when some drunken revellers accidentally set fire to the place.)

Time and winter were pressing upon the plucky little band, and they went with the haunted cabin for want of anything better. However, there was all that cow flop on the floor, and a few other minor matters. Sam, Tim Philo and some of the crew went off to shoot the scenes of the car and the truck driving in the Tennessee mountains, while the rest of the *Dead* bunch began shovelling dung.

The car, incidentally, was Sam's own 1973 Delta 88 Oldsmobile, which has almost developed a fan following of its own. It appears in virtually all of Sam's movies, except for *The Quick and the Dead*. That's a Western, so it was rather hard to include the battered old vehicle.

Campbell, who seemed to be everywhere, recalls the cabin. "We worked out a deal with the owners that we would leave it no worse than we found it, which even if we destroyed the place would have been no real change. It had a power box but no power, no running water, it was just an abandoned cabin in a beautiful hollow. But it was a really cool area, very convenient. We blazed a new road because it was all overgrown, ran power in there, took out all the ceilings in the main room and tore out the middle wall."

In *Evil Dead II*, when they recreated the cabin, they built it with half the walls made of slatted wood, half with plaster, just as in the original cabin. The two rooms made into one had been done differently; the production designer for the sequel picked up on that detail probably without realising what it meant.

"We had to tear out the ceilings because we needed to light from above, and hung the lights. After we scraped all the cow manure off, we found beautiful tongue-and-groove flooring. The first week or ten days there we spent just getting the cabin ready. We brought down a guy named Steve Frankel [nicknamed 'Dart'], who could use tools; he could build anything. He built wood furniture for the cabin, he built the swing out front, he helped us trim off the front of the cabin. We had to build a trapdoor, and had to dig a cellar of sorts. We knew we could use the Tapert farmhouse in Marshall, Michigan to shoot the scenes set in the cellar, because it had a great dirt floor and rock walls all around."

Sam Raimi adds that the cows had broken down the door of the cabin, so the team replaced it. The *Book of the Dead* team also got busy "repainting the walls, getting rid of bats' nests that were in there, etc. Then we brought in furniture from a local furniture place, antique stores and the like."

Whoever had free time devoted it to digging out the hole under the trapdoor in the floor of the cabin. Eventually they completed the task, with the help of those who had been out filming the drive-by shots of the car. "We were shooting the ride up to the cabin," Raimi says, "needlessly shooting and shooting and shooting. We were stuck for, like, two weeks. I should have stopped shooting and worked on the cabin."

The first day of actual filming was Wednesday, 14 November, on the bridge. In his journal, Becker described installing the *It's Murder* beams (light plastic beams first used on *It's Murder*) under the bridge, including running a tripline allowing the car to drop the beams itself. "Things went quite well, if slow," Becker wrote. "My first job of the day was attracting the attention of some bulls that were attacking Tim and Sam as they [filmed] the long shot from a field across the street. I just sang some songs and the whole herd moved to the other end of the field."

Below:

Tim Philo filming the drive to the cabin, with Sam on the roof.

Initially, Becker's mood was positive. "Things are running well... Sam is funny and has been giving some first-rate direction. Bruce is funny and keeps Ellen particularly always laughing. Rob is dealing with the problems and not giving anyone grief, while always wanting the best for the production."

Early in the movie, as the tape recording chants the spell that awakens the demons of the forest, outside the cabin the ground cracks, smoke seeps out and red light glares. This was one of the earliest scenes shot for the movie, and done much more cheaply and quickly than you might expect. First, it was a forced-perspective shot; that is, the cracking earth in the foreground is much nearer to the camera than it appears to be. A teeter-totter arrangement cracked the earth; a buried red light became visible, and the smoke seeped out of the dirt and leaves on top of the teeterboard.

At the huge old house where they were staying, Sam prepared storyboards. (Interestingly, storyboards originated in the making of animated cartoons, to show the animators the progress of the story, with key poses illustrated, sometimes with big floating arrows indicating which direction the characters were moving, or which way the camera's point of view was intended to go. They then began to be used for live-action features, primarily for action sequences.) Aware that, like his cast and crew, he was green at this movie-making stuff, at least as far as feature films went, Raimi wanted clarity at all times. He drew stick-figure storyboards himself and mounted them on the refrigerator at their house for all to see. "They were basic illustrations," Raimi says, "starting with a head-to-toe of a figure, then the next picture would be just the two eyeballs. That would indicate a move-in from a head-to-toe shot of Bruce to an angle that featured only his eyes. However, perhaps the storyboards wouldn't indicate that the camera would start on the ground, and move up to eye level as we move in. There are changes like that which would take place from my boards to the actual execution of the shot. They were very exacting, but there was still plenty of room for interpretation when I got there."

On the other hand, Tapert says, "When we got to the set we'd never do what was on the storyboards. But I think he had already developed the style that he stuck with, visually maximising everything prior to shooting."

Sam was surprising everyone with his creativity, including long-time friend Bruce Campbell: "Sam showed more savvy during the making of *Evil Dead* than I had ever seen before. I didn't know where he was getting all this nonsense, but it was finally his chance to use every trick he had learned to that point, and he just kept laying it on. Everything became a tricky shot, and his cameraman, Tim Philo, was up to it. We all kicked around a bunch of ideas on how to shoot some stuff, and that's how we got the idea for the 'Shaky-Cam'. That's a two-by-four with a guy on either end to stabilise it, the camera in the middle; you could go over bushes and logs, it was an incredibly versatile thing." This was, of course, their new and improved replacement for the more costly Steadicam.

They had chosen Tennessee over Michigan because it was further south, and therefore likely to be warmer. It turned out to be the coldest winter Tennessee had experienced in decades (and the warmest in Michigan). "It was freezing," Campbell recalls with a shudder, "and of course the cast had to pretend it was fall. We were running around without any winter coats on. We didn't get snow, but it was freezing cold." Between takes, the shuddering actors draped themselves in blankets, but in front of the cameras, they had to smile and pretend it was a balmy autumn.

Tom Sullivan, a *Within the Woods* veteran, arrived to do the make-up. He told Cliff Holverson, of the website Ash's Evil Dead Page, "I recall Sam was very secretive about the script. I got it about three weeks before shooting began. I had time to buy supplies and do some face casts that weren't usable for what I needed them for. So the latex face castings I made from them went on the very first version of the Book of the Dead. It's Ten Commandments size, which Sam told me later was too big for Ash to grab with that necklace."

Sullivan told *Fangoria* that he was only down on the set for about three days, "mostly as a consultant, and to prepare for a few optical effects. I helped on some of the [on-set] special effects, but very minor things. For instance, the scene where Hal Delrich totally dismembers one of the possessed. That was really the most exciting thing that happened to me on *Evil Dead*. I was holding one of the dummies, and every few seconds I had an axe swinging down to within a few inches of my head, as I was being drenched in Karo syrup blood."

Below:

The Book of

the Dead.

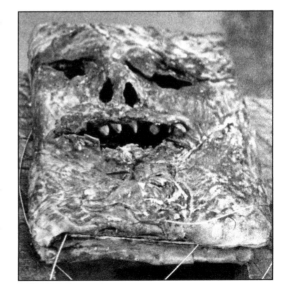

He added: "The entire job was so rushed that... the make-ups in *Evil Dead* are not what I would have done if I'd had more time. But actually I can't blame [Sam], because his direction makes my work look so darned good it's incredible."

"Once we had all the actors, the people that got possessed and stuff," Campbell recalls, "we had to get their legs moulded, or their arms, or their heads, and these casts were made directly with plaster. I remember when they took a cast of the face of Betsy Baker, who played Linda, my girlfriend in the movie. They put Vaseline on her face, then poured plaster of Paris over it, which heats up as it hardens. We gave her a piece of paper to write on if necessary. And she kept writing 'getting very light-headed' as the plaster was heating up. When it came time to pull it off, we couldn't, because her eyelashes were stuck in the plaster. We finally pulled it off, leaving her lashes stuck in the plaster and her face beet red."

Sullivan got a little too creative, in one sense, when he decided to make the sacrificial knife out of real chicken bones. Sullivan had set up shop in the laundry room of the rambling old house, and assembled the prop there. Later on, a horrible smell began wafting out of the room, and they found a bag of rotting chicken bones left over from making the knife (which turns up in the first two movies).

Campbell recalls the early production period as "some of the funniest nights. If I wasn't acting, I was a member of the crew. I just put the glasses back on, and put a coat over my bloody outfit, and moved lights around." Production at the cabin began the night of 26 November.

"I entirely understand Sam's directorial technique now," Becker wrote in his journal on 1 December. "He breaks every scene down to every possible angle and films them all, thus giving himself total latitude in the editing room. It's a viable method, but not rational for this production... Sam looks like he's on his last [legs]. Now he's really like a punch-drunk boxer. Nevertheless, he's still right on top of the action (as he says quite often) and he's getting some nice footage."

"I'd never worked so hard or so long in my life," Raimi remembers. "It got *so* cold there. After Tim Philo left and I had to operate the camera, be my own first assistant and load the cameras, etc, I also had to help blood up Bruce." They were using dyed Karo brand corn syrup for blood, and that stuff's very sticky. "My hands would be covered in syrup," Sam goes on, "and I'd realise, I gotta change the film magazine, I gotta change the lenses, so I would have to wash this blood off my hands. It was like fifteen degrees in this place, and there was no heat. The only thing we had was the coffee maker, full of coffee, not water. So I had to pour hot coffee over my hands to get the blood off them, and to warm them up enough to be able to load the 16mm cameras. It was a very hard, physically difficult experience. We should have taken days off, we should have rested, but it got to the point where we'd work eighteen hour days non-stop for, it seemed like, months."

As shooting continued, Campbell says, "the cabin was slowly being destroyed. We were using Karo syrup-based blood, tons of it, and the floor was getting horribly sticky. We'd take ashes from the fireplace to put on the floor to get rid of the stickiness, so the floor was turning from brown to this sort of grey colour."

At the cabin, they shot mostly on a night schedule to "permit filming from when it got dark at about 6.30pm to dawn," Becker noted. "However, things have gotten

pushed to the point of beginning to film last night [28 Nov] at 2.00am, then going until noon... Winter has come, the muddy driveway to the cabin has frozen, allowing access to it, and the cabin itself is now always astoundingly cold inside, even with a big fire and two space heaters. Last night, on the seventeenth take of an exterior dolly shot, the synch cable froze and we were forced to go [inside] and let it thaw."

Above:

Sam and Bruce

hard at work.

Early on in the production, jokes were possible; one night, after finishing his scenes, Campbell was so exhausted he was dopey. Rob and Sam told their confused star that he had to go shoot the wood-chopping scene right now. Then, when he swung the axe, they'd impatiently interrupt, telling him he wasn't doing it just right. Eventually they allowed him to chop the wood — which he did diligently for forty-five minutes until he became aware that Sam and Rob were falling down laughing... there was no wood-chopping scene for Ash. Still, Rob says, "We did keep that wood-chopping scene in the movie for the longest time."

Later, "We had a giant fire-cracker war on New Year's Eve," Tapert recalls. "We decided to whoop it up, and had this fire-cracker war. When you're in the back woods of Tennessee, you get, well, heh-heh-heh."

Yeah, heh-heh-heh. Out there you can run into people like Fats Derringer, someone even more colourful than Gary Holt. "Fats was a moonshine-drinking good old boy," Campbell remembers fondly. "His car, a souped-up Toronado, had bullet holes in it. I don't know how we met him, but during the shooting, it started raining and the road washed out, so we had to carry everything in the quarter mile from the highway; we shot for two nights straight, and we were crazed. But Fats Derringer makes it down the road from the highway, the only one who could make it.

"He comes bombing down this mud-slick path, drunk out of his mind, demanding to be in the movie. 'How're my friends goin' to know that I'd known a picture was here unless I been in it,' he says. Fats was a little scary, and as I said, we were a little crazy, so we said, 'Okay, Fats, let's go.' We got all the equipment back out again, and re-enacted a scene from *The Happy Valley Kid*. Don't ask me why.

"Josh played the Happy Valley Kid in the scene where he brings his story to his professor; Fats played the professor who rejected the story. First we documented Fats standing there with his girlfriend, bobbing back and forth because he was so drunk. The professor is supposed to have a long speech, rejecting the kid's script as comic book trash. But all Fats could say was 'I don't want this damn shit,' and he'd throw it back." And that's what they shot; they slated it, then ran sound, the whole nine yards.

Below: Bruce Campbell.

Campbell suspects the footage still exists, but, unsurprisingly, it didn't turn up in *The Evil Dead*.

Occasionally during shooting, when Campbell seemed a little lethargic, Rob and Sam would poke at him with sticks to arouse the actor's attention. (When Sam began production of *The Quick and the Dead*, Campbell sent him a fax asking if he was going to poke Sharon Stone and Gene Hackman with sharp sticks to get them to act.) For his part, Campbell sprained his ankle charging down a hill while goofing off with the cast and crew, but had to walk normally in the scenes shot that day. Josh Becker reveals that Bruce used a "big character builder" for some scenes in the movie. "He would take one of those plastic bottles you use to spray water on house plants, and he'd shove it up his nose and spray like a pint of water up each nostril. This would really get him into character; once he did that, he didn't care what he did."

Becker is very admiring of Campbell's willingness to do just about anything as an actor, particularly for Sam Raimi. "Sam would ask him to climb up on a roof and jump off on his neck. Bruce would take a couple of minutes to get into character, then he'd do it. In character."

Bruce also has all the attributes of a producer, too — when they did the later Super-8 movie *Thou Shalt not Kill... Except*, Josh would: "get over to Bruce's house at six o'clock in the morning when we had a 7.30am call. Bruce had already been up for two hours washing all the uniforms and pressing them. He loves to make lists and break things down, and he's liked to do that from the very beginning."

In *Fangoria* #65, Bruce Campbell told journalist Will Murray that, as a movie actor, he was pretty green while shooting *Book of the Dead*. "I didn't really know how to conduct myself 100 per cent, how big or how little to be... If the camera's really close, I had to learn to just use my eyes. If it's a long shot, then I can go crazy. I also had to learn that if we shot the opening scene and the final scene on the first day, I had to try to imagine everything in between. So it's all like a puzzle. For

Above:
Rob Tapert.

example, if we're shooting something where I'm being chased by this evil entity, I have to remember a scene I shot a week ago and compare it with what I was doing so that it will match."

Despite his work in theatre in Detroit, Campbell said, "I don't have any formal training, and I'm sure many people will say it's obvious. You get tons of theory in school. You know: 'Lie on the stage and fry like a piece of bacon.' I learned more from Sam looking through the camera and saying, 'No, cheek one inch up, nose two inches over. Now go back and land in that position.' To me, that's been as good a training as anything."

Making *Book of the Dead* provided Bruce with good experience as an actor, and it cemented a relationship. Until they began production, Rob Tapert regarded Bruce Campbell as just a friend of Sam's, but "we spent day after day for weeks together in the summer before we began production, and Bruce and I went to a lot of investor meetings together, doing this stuff.

"Bruce was living in some shabby basement apartment somewhere smoking clove cigarettes, and I remember endless times of him and me looking up *Variety*'s lists of rental champs." This period, plus the incredible efforts Bruce went to on *Book of the Dead*, firmed up their relationship as friends, and as working partners. When you go through the fires together like this, you usually emerge friends. And that happened to Tapert and Campbell.

It's a good thing they were friends. In the scene at the end, in which Ash dismembers whatever bodies are left, Tapert was one of the people who crawled under the floor of the cabin to stick his hand and leg through the floorboards to impersonate dismembered body parts. Tom Sullivan said, "The soil had been acting like a coffee filter for cow urine," and Tapert has noted that the axe blade enthusiastically swung by Bruce came through the floorboards just inches from his face.

Then there was the night the power tools disappeared. They were shooting nights and staggering back to the big old house to sleep when the sun came up. Apparently, some locals felt this meant the stuff they left behind was fair game. Sam started sleeping at the cabin to keep an eye on their equipment.

"When we came back one morning," Bruce says, "all the power tools were gone, but they didn't touch a $20,000 Arriflex camera, a $5,000 Nagra [sound recording

Below: Shooting the vine rape scene with Ellen Sandweiss.

gadget] — these had no value to these people. We had seen guys up on the hills at night, just squatting, watching us. Once, I was carrying groceries down to the cabin one morning, both arms full, and a guy with this long red beard and a hunter's outfit on, a bandoleer of shotgun shells across his chest, was coming from the direction of the cabin. What do you say? I just said, 'Good morning,' and he said 'Mornin',' and kept going. We did get a taste of the South."

Sometimes the taste was pretty colourful, like learning how to tell good moonshine from bad moonshine, a lesson that has stayed with Campbell to this day. The way you tell the difference is simple, he explains — you set the stuff on fire: "You pour a little into the lid of the Mason jar, and light it; if it's a soft blue flame, that's good. If it's an orange flame, it's been distilled in a car radiator, so you better watch out. Also, the size of the bubbles in the stuff was an indicator. If you had tiny bubbles, no troubles. We did get drunk on moonshine a couple of nights, but soon found that was a big mistake, so just before the camera rolled, we'd throw it into the fireplace. Pa-whoosh! Great blaze, and we'd start shooting." They kept the hooch in Styrofoam cups, which would slowly dissolve...

Thanksgiving was 22 November that year. "After shooting the [gnarled] hand/bridge scene until 6.30am, with two generators, a thirty-six foot crane, three fog machines and 4000 watts of light, we got up at 11.00am to go to Gary Holt's mother-in-law's house for the Thanksgiving meal," Becker wrote in his journal. It was, he noted, "probably the nicest Thanksgiving I've ever had." They watched a football game, helped a neighbouring farmer round up his cattle, and showed *Within the Woods* to Holt and his family. But work continued the next day, and over the weekend.

The cast worked hard, very hard. "We were shooting Ellen Sandweiss being chased through the woods by the force, and she's in that little night-gown, barefoot," Josh Becker recalls. "We had the camera set up on plywood for a couple hundred feet, so we could follow her with a wheelchair with the camera on it — there was no dolly on that picture. It's one of the coldest nights of the year, and we're shooting all night long. She's running and falling, and running and falling for hours. She got completely wound down, and as it was nearing dawn, she said, 'That's it, you don't get any more.' She was in tears, and just ran away. Rob and I are coiling up cables and pulling all the stuff out of there. And as we're doing this, we see blood all over the plywood; her feet had obviously been ripped to shreds by roots and stuff. And Rob says, 'I love it when actors give me that much!'"

Reminded of this, Rob's a little embarrassed. "I was kind of joking," he admits. "Taken out of context, it's kind of horrible, but at the [time], it seemed like a funny, appropriate thing." In any event, Ellen Sandweiss did give up acting, a career she had originally intended to pursue.

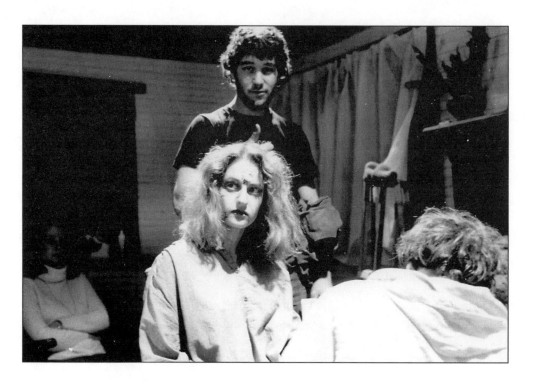

Sandweiss also recalls the making of the film: "I scraped the hell out of myself. The make-up was also horrendous — because everything was so low-budget, everything really was an ordeal. We didn't quite have the right anything, whether it was the right make-up, or enough people to help with it. Those contacts in the eyes were really something.

"There was a lot of pain involved with that movie. There was pain with make-up, pain with running through woods... In the scene where I fall back into the cellar, at one point I didn't quite make it through the hole, and slammed my head on something. I remember how strange it was, staying up all night and sleeping through the day. I felt like a real zombie, but I was twenty years old, and it was very exciting, and I was with friends."

Sandweiss had taken time off from her theatre studies at the University of Michigan to make *Book of the Dead*, but insists it wasn't the making of the film that steered her away from acting: "I went on to get a master's degree in arts administration, and went into the business end of theatre; I was manager of a symphony orchestra for a while in North Carolina. I lived in Asheville for ten years, and was involved in that career, and also got married and had children, so acting just didn't fit into my life."

Her only regret about making the movie was the scene in which she's raped by the vine: "I guess I didn't really realise what that was going to look like on the big screen; that's actually the reason I don't want my kids to see it."

While shooting continued in the cabin, Rob Tapert and others worked on the bridge, distorting it as per the script. The Tennessee road department gave them permission to do whatever they wanted to a nearby abandoned bridge, as long as they paid for the cutting and welding. The idea was to make the bridge's beams curl up like clutching fingers, and that's what they did, but the shot doesn't really work. "Normally, we could have done it much cheaper with Styrofoam beams," Bruce admits, "because we lit it so dark — we didn't have the lights to show that there was no bridge. It was actually this epic job that we did; we tore up the girders of the bridge, a hundred feet above the water. It was tremendously visually stunning, but you would never know it. It looks like it was shot in Sam's back yard."

Becker's journal described an accident that could have been serious. A winch cable was looped around one side of the bridge to bend the 'little finger' of the welded clutching hand. "Unbeknownst to anyone," Becker wrote, "the cable was also around a large tree branch that snapped when tension was applied to [it]." The branch slammed into Sam Raimi, staggering him. "Everyone thought he was okay," noted

Below:
Bruce and Sam
working on the
bridge.

Becker. "However, I... found him pale, his eyes completely bloodshot, his lips white and crusty and a small amount of blood dripping from his left nostril." He continued working the rest of the night, but passed out on the way back to their lodgings, although there didn't seem to be any lasting ill effects.

They ran into problems they didn't expect, difficulties they weren't prepared for, and shooting dragged on. They reached the end of the six weeks they'd planned for, and still they weren't done. October stretched on into November, and then December. In mid-December, a problem arose that they couldn't gallop enthusiastically over — they were running out of money and time. Josh says that something like five weeks into the picture, John Mason, in charge of the sound, had to leave, so he took over the sound recording. In fact, most of the cast and crew were getting restive, as they had lives to return to back in Michigan.

In his diary, Becker outlined what he felt were some of the reasons for the growing dissension: "Sam never shoots a master-shot of anything, therefore the cast never gets to play out a whole scene. He'll spend hours filming an insert, then not have time for three other shots. He spends very little time telling the actors what he wants; he'll do a few run-throughs, but mainly for the camera's sake, not the actors." Becker's journal alternates his excitement at working on a movie with annoyance that his suggestions were ignored, and that he was not asked to be part of Renaissance Pictures. But even he admits that he didn't participate in the arduous money raising, and in the journal itself sometimes refers to what he's written as "paranoid ravings." Still, in the thick of it he wrote: "My neck has hurt for four days, and yet, even with all this I'm still enjoying myself."

Becker still recalls the night the big change came: "I was sitting on the steps in the house, and upstairs were Sam, Bruce and Rob. They're discussing how they can take this tiny amount of money they have and somehow spread it out so they can shoot for another couple of weeks.

"Meanwhile, downstairs, it's like the camera tilts down and I can see the cast and crew. They're all going, 'So, you're driving the van? Can I ride back with you to Michigan?' 'No, no, you go in this car, and you'll go in that car.' And then you tilt back up, where Bruce, Sam and Rob are saying, 'Okay, I think we've got this worked out, we'll just offer them thirty dollars a week, and we can shoot for three more weeks.' They come downstairs, passing me on the step, and present their proposition. 'You'll get the rest from profits, because we need to shoot for three more weeks.' Everybody said, 'What? We're leaving tomorrow morning.' And they did. So, suddenly, five of us then shot for the next five weeks." Sam hastily rewrote some scenes, inventing others, to cover for the fact that, of the actors, they now had only Bruce, and Fake Shemping went on like mad (Tapert appears in drag as Ellen's character).

Bruce says, "It was such a whirlwind, non-stop, twenty-hours-a-day sort of life, it's a big jumble of who exactly said what. At one point, Josh was bitching about something, and Sam turned around and said, 'Okay, what's the first bus we can put him on?' He is right about everyone leaving, but in a way, it didn't matter to us. We'd been abandoned [by the cast and others] on *It's Murder* and every Super-8 movie we made, and that's the absolute truth."

Above:

Sam and Bruce,

after weeks

of non-stop

shooting.

Most of the cast and crew left over the two weeks beginning 23 December, leaving behind only Bruce, Sam, Rob, Josh and David Goodman, the cook and general gofer. John Cameron and Mike Ditz arrived to help out, but left after a few days. "At that point," Becker says, "I took over the lighting as well as keeping the camera clean, and Sam took over shooting. So for the remainder of the shoot, I was doing both sound recording and lighting."

Tim Philo had brought the cameras with him, borrowed from Wayne State University, and he had to take the equipment back with him when he left after the money ran out. According to Josh Becker, "Sam said, 'You can't take the Arriflex BL; I can't shoot the rest of this movie with the Arri S,' you know, the little one. But Tim said he couldn't leave it behind. Now this is Sam Raimi's logic; I love this. He goes, 'Tell you what, Tim. Leave the Arri BL, we won't use it. But what if the Arri S breaks? Then I don't have a camera; you leave the Arri BL, and we won't use it, because the Arri S isn't going to break, but I need a back-up camera.' Tim finally agrees, gets in his car and drives away. His car is not out of sight before Sam turns to me and says, 'Okay, load the BL.'" And sure enough, when the camera finally made it back to its owner, it was broken.

Sam just kept going and going. "He pretty much tested all of us on just what the limits of our stamina were," says Becker. "Every day was eighteen, twenty hours on that film. He just loved to keep going and keep going; Sam has more energy than anyone else. Once, as we were getting near the end of this thing, and he felt like he had to get everything he could down there in Tennessee before we left, which was reasonable, we shot for sixty-two hours straight."

While they were shooting, Becker explains, "we would send all the footage to DuArt, and would get the footage back twice a week, 3000 to 4000 feet of film at a time. We'd set up these giant reels of 16mm, and we'd put them on the projector, and we'd turn them on to watch them — and then everybody would fall asleep. We'd all be awakened by the flap-flap-flap of the tail of the film hitting the projector housing. We never did watch dailies down there because we fell asleep during every one of them."

"A lot got cut from the script when everyone went home," Rob Tapert admits, "but there's more tension in Bruce being driven slowly insane from being trapped in the cabin, with the girl in the cellar and the other guy dying on the couch, and him being totally unable to do anything. I bet we cut ten minutes of that story subplot. It was all character shit, of him going crazy. We shot a lot of that, but cut it out."

The defection of the cast required Rob and Josh to double occasionally for dead bodies, or Deadites banging at the door, seen from behind. As for Sam Raimi, Bruce says, "I think he pretty much had it instilled in him, okay, if you're going to be a filmmaker, then you better shine, you better do it different than everybody else. And after the others left, he started coming up with entire new sequences. The whole sequence of me alone in the cabin where everything is shot at a forty-five degree angle, he just came up with one night."

Becker claims, "anything I say about this movie will get Sam mad, but that's life. There was no ending on the script; when we got down there, nobody knew how the story ended. Rob kept asking Sam how it ended, and Sam would say, 'I don't know, but I do know I need a crane.' So Rob rented a cherry-picker crane, which sat there for weeks. Rob would say, 'I'm paying $50 or $75 a day for this thing — what's the end of the movie?' Sam kept saying he'd figure it out.

"So one day, I'm sitting there, and I'm thinking, and thinking, and I realised I knew what the end of the film should be. The camera starts on a leaf, pans to the back door of the cabin, comes down through the back door, which flies open, goes through the next door, which comes flat down, goes out through the front door, which blows out in pieces, and goes right into Bruce's mouth. I storyboarded it and showed Sam, and he said, 'I don't think so.' Oh. Okay. So the cherry-picker sits there, and the cherry-picker sits there. Finally, we shot everything we can shoot, and Rob insists that we have to shoot some kind of ending as long as we're down there. Sam says he still doesn't have an ending, but Rob says, 'Well, there's that ending Josh came up with.' Sam is very reluctant to use anyone else's ideas, since it's his movie, but Rob forced him: 'We've got to shoot *something*. That doesn't mean you have to use it.'

"So Sam operated camera on it, and I'm up in the rafters kicking that second door down. I'm the one who cut the front door to pieces so it would blow out, so the camera could go through there and hit Bruce. I basically set the whole thing up, because I thought it up, and I really wanted it to work right. It's the end of the movie; they never thought of an ending they liked better."

They also used the idle cherry-picker crane for the shot in which Ash carries Linda's body out for burial. "There's one crane up, and one crane down," according to Josh. However, Sam says that they did use the crane for more shots that didn't end up in the movie. At one point, he was up in the crane to shoot a few scenes of the bridge being altered, and he fell asleep with the camera running. After a while, people began to wonder where on earth Sam was, until someone thought to bring the crane down again.

As the shoot wore on, Becker's mood got worse, alienating him. Then Steve Frankel, "came up to me out of the blue," Becker wrote, "and said, 'Stop trying to get even, get ahead.' He didn't seem able to explain this comment very well, but related it to things I had said to him and repeated it a few times. It's stuck with me. I am trying to get even a lot of the time, to do and outdo what Sam has done, to prove myself."

Becker felt he had burned his bridges, that his hopes of ever working with Sam and the others again were dashed. Then, one morning after a late night, he and Sam talked: "Sam decided to let me in on how to make it in the directorial world: 'Make a ten-minute gem.' This is to show everyone that I can direct. He said that he and Rob and Bruce would gladly help me." And they meant it; Becker's griping may have annoyed the Renaissance partners, but he did his work, and when most of the cast and crew fled, he stuck it out and came up with some good ideas. Loyalty and perseverance matter a lot to some people.

Sam went on to play the Charles Manson-styled villain in Becker's first feature, *Thou Shalt Not Kill... Except* in 1985 (which he had conceived on location for *The Evil Dead*), while Bruce worked on the movie in a variety of capacities, along with many *Evil Dead* veterans. Becker's next feature, *Lunatics: A Love Story*, was actually made by

Renaissance Pictures, and starred Ted Raimi. More recently, his inventive and entertaining 1997 movie *Running Time* starred Bruce Campbell. Becker has directed a *Hercules* TV movie for Renaissance, several episodes of *Xena: Warrior Princess*, and some for *Jack of All Trades* as well. As he wrote at the end of his *Evil Dead* journal, "I began this shoot bitter, unhappy and a [production assistant]. I end it a fairly happy, exhausted lighting and sound man. This may have been the most difficult and the most rewarding experience of my life."

While the *Book of the Dead* crew were nearing the end of production in Tennessee, they were evicted from the place where they had been staying, because the owner was moving in a lot of brass beds and turning it into a house of ill repute, so legend has it. With nowhere else to go, they stayed in the cabin where they were shooting. "That was horrible," sighs Tapert. "One night, either I drank a cup of coffee, or I was wired and couldn't go to sleep. Everyone else did, and slept for eight hours. I couldn't fall asleep to save my life, I just couldn't. I got up and wandered around.

"When they got up, we had to put a ceiling back in this place — being the math

Below:

Sam behind

the camera.

one, I had figured it all out on paper. We need this many sheets of plywood, and this is how they all go in, and here's what we have to do. They were clearing everything out, while I fell asleep standing up in a mud puddle and just toppled over. Somebody found me and they put me on the couch, where I fell asleep again, and they couldn't wake me up. They kept asking, 'How many sheets of plywood?' 'Ah, yeah, plywood,' I'd think, and tell them something. They got the plywood, but then couldn't get me to stay awake long enough to tell them how it all fit in. But eventually it got figured out.

"Then we did a couple of really crazy things. I was wide awake and refreshed from two hours of sleep, so we went out back and lit the biggest bonfire you've ever seen in your life. We were catching the woods on fire." Bruce remembers the fire, too: "It was really stupid. It was twenty feet around. We had to make dive bombing runs past it to throw stuff on it, because it was so hot we couldn't get close. We were so lame."

Finally, they buried a time capsule in the area they'd dug out beneath the trapdoor. It contained "messages, notes, little trinkets from the film, stuff like that," Bruce explains. And lastly, says Rob, "Bruce and I took a shotgun and a hundred shells and blew up every single prop in the house. We went crazy."

But crazy or not, by the end of January 1980, they finished shooting in Tennessee.

KEEPING THE BLOOD FLOWING

They returned to Detroit, tired, battered, but with something between seventy and ninety per cent of the film in the can. Campbell says that they'd gotten all the establishing shots and most of the action, though "until we started to cut it together, we didn't know how much we were missing." Which meant getting more money, a "slow and agonising process," according to the actor. "We had well over $100,000 in bank loans at a time when the prime rate was around twenty per cent. We had to get investors to put up twice the amount of blue chip stock, but they did give us another round of money; Phil Gillis and the Manoogians, primarily. There were some new investors, because now that so much of the movie was shot, the risk was less. Principal photography, quote unquote, was completed. Har de har har. That $85,000 was supposed to get us a whole lot farther than it finally did. The final cost no one really knows, but it's probably between $350,000 and $400,000, when all is said and done. But in that spring of 1980 we did collect more money, and got some of the real actors back."

Becker says, "We did something like a week in Gladwin, Michigan, up at Bruce's family cabin, and we did a week in Marshall, Michigan, in the basement of Rob Tapert's family's farmhouse. Then there would be four days at Sam's house, then five more days at Sam's house a month later, then three more days there. Everyone was happy to show up for a week or so at a time." And as Campbell says, "We were never going back to Tennessee, for God's sake. We just needed a wooded area." Plus a location for the effects.

Tom Sullivan had been in Tennessee for three days to apply the make-ups and operate the stand-in dummies, but most of the special effects remained to be shot when everyone came back to Detroit. Raimi unrealistically expected that they could shoot the meltdown scene in a couple of hours on location at the cabin. "It was going to be pretty much suggested," Sullivan told *Fangoria*. "Some bile flowing out of a collar, some deflated clothing. That didn't entirely sit right with me." The location effects shooting involved the shot of the pencil stabbing into an ankle, a hand chewed off by one of the Evil Dead, and the scene in which another falls into the fireplace and catches fire.

The meltdown sequence, as seen in the movie, is spectacularly loathsome. The two remaining Deadites creak, crumble and slimily ooze into twitching piles of goop, with bugs, snakes, tumbling green worms and collapsing eyeballs as filigrees and decorations. Sullivan and Bart Pierce were in charge of almost all of this.

Bart Pierce, recommended by Tim Philo, was a psychology student before going into films and had worked for five years in a film lab, so he "gave us advice on how to photograph the film for the blow-up," says Campbell. "He told us to expose it a third of a stop brighter than we normally would have, and use only prime lenses, no zoom lenses — although we did use one later on anyway. The blow-up came out pretty well. Tom did the armatures and moulding and the stop-motion, while Bart Pierce did all the camera and technical supervision." Like Sullivan, Pierce had ambitions of being a movie-maker himself.

Although Sullivan and Pierce got along well, at first there was a disagreement over whether the meltdown sequence should be done in live action or by stop-motion animation, which Sullivan favoured. He was a long-time fan of the stop-motion movies of Ray Harryhausen, and was inspired by the collapse and decay of a Morlock near the end of George Pal's *The Time Machine*. "I felt that if we put stop-motion in the film, even if it wasn't the greatest," Sullivan told *Fangoria*, "it would put it into a certain genre and get people curious about it. Bart felt very strongly in favour of mechanical and fluid effects. Finally, it was almost like a Reese's Peanut Butter Cup commercial. Hey! Peanut butter and chocolate together! We figured that if we mixed the techniques, they might help to disguise each other." Combining make-up effects and stop-motion is very tricky, however, and therefore rarely done.

When they decided to use both techniques, "We went back to Sam, who showed

Left:
Tom Sullivan
and Bart Pierce
with Cheryl's
meltdown
dummy.

us a cut of the rest of *The Evil Dead,* and told us what he wanted — an ending which would be more violent than all the rest of the film, the *tour de force* of the movie. The most important thing we had to do," said Pierce, "was see that the ending matched the rest of the film [in movie-making style]. It had to have fast, rapid motion, never a still moment in the frame, and we had to shoot it in 16mm, though we could have done it in 35mm much faster. We did the mattes in the camera, using a 16mm Mitchell with a matte box using hand-cut mattes. Because we were using half-frame animation [two superimposed exposures per frame, for more fluid movement] matted with live action, just about every shot went through the camera anywhere from three to seven times."

"In the first week of August 1980," Sullivan told the unofficial website 'Ash's Evil Dead Page', "I had to leave my wife Penny again, living away an average of six days a week, enjoying a cot in the basement at Bart Pierce's home. Bart and I were in synch and having a blast developing the meltdown. Sam and Rob were away in New York in post[-production], so Bart and I started our planning in Detroit. We expanded the sequence from the eight original drawings to about thirty storyboards that I drew. We had control over the action and camera movement, lighting and the solutions to the special effects. That's why it works; we were left alone and allowed to go nuts. Later, Sam added some inspired close-ups of Bruce, and *voila!* Genius."

Because of the multiple passes (by individual shots through the camera), minor errors meant footage had to be scrapped and refilmed. One shot of Scott's head, where bile is beginning to bubble up, hair is falling out and so on, included both live action and animation elements, and had to be shot five times. By the end of their work, Sullivan and Pierce were turning out a shot every other day or so. In all, shooting the optical and mechanical effects took Pierce, Sullivan and their various assistants three and a half months.

Meanwhile, Raimi, Tapert and the others were shooting the pick-up and additional shots for the rest of the film (the opening scenes of the camera gliding over the swamp, for example). Also, the attack on Sandweiss by the vines was expanded. "We shot a major portion of that in Sam's back yard," Josh Becker explains. "In Sam's garage, we shot the scene in the cellar where Bruce is walking along and Rich goes 'Boo!' at him. The scene where the spider-webbing of the veins happens on the girl's leg was shot in Bart's basement. That was Cheryl Guttridge's leg; she was in some of the Super-8 movies, and in *Thou Shalt Not Kill... Except* for me. Her leg had to be clamped down for about five hours to do the animation on it; when she was released, she threw up."

Finally, Scott Spiegel was able to be involved: "I had a chance to work on it a lot in Bart Pierce's basement, where most of the effects were done. They shot the whole meltdown scene in Bart's garage. Teddy Raimi stands in for Ellen Sandweiss when the monster hands pop out of her stomach and back. I supplied all the meat parts from the supermarket, and boy did those start to stink after a few hours in the hot lights. I also supplied some of my girlfriends to have their heads chopped off and double for other actresses in the picture. My own girlfriend of the time doubled for Betsy Baker in one of the axe scenes. I was a jack of all trades, helping out here, there, and everywhere. Those guys gave me a credit; I thought it was nice of them."

Down in the basement, Pierce and Sullivan contended with gallons of bile, stop-motion puppets and the bugs and snakes they bought for the meltdown sequence. Everyone connected with the movie mentions the huge Madagascar roaches that hissed when picked up.

Raimi and Tapert were very happy with Sullivan's work, and Sam says that if *The Evil Dead* had granted anyone a Production Designer credit, it would have gone to Tom Sullivan: "We simply could not have done the film without him."

After the reshoots, and when the effects sequences were finished, the Renaissance partners had a good deal of film that needed to be cut down to feature length. "The truth is," Tapert admits, "we had mountains of film. We had over 100,000 feet of 16mm, which was a lot of film at that time, and we had it all printed — we had no selects." With features, if a director films, for example, five takes of a scene, he might have takes two, four and five printed — his selects. Therefore, lots of the footage remains in negative form and is never printed, but there are no selects in 16mm.

First, they turned to Image Express, a company in Michigan that cut commercials. The Renaissance team knew they needed help to synch-log the huge mass of film, and suspected they might need an editor. Image Express suggested they look up Edna Ruth Paul, who was coming out to Michigan in the summer to cut car commercials for them. Edna Paul was a New York-based editor working primarily on low-budget films (the Lenny Bruce pastiche, *Dirtymouth* was one of hers) and After-School Specials. At the time, she was editing Frank LaLoggia's first commercial feature, *Fear No Evil*, so she knew the demands of horror movies. "We didn't know who LaLoggia was," Tapert admits, "but she was cutting the film. She had also cut a whole bunch of After-School Specials that we really liked. Sam decided she should cut the relationship material in *Book of the Dead*, but he knew how he wanted the action cut himself. So that's how we ended up with Edna Ruth Paul." This was now April, and they managed to get the film logged on their own.

The decision to hire Edna Paul gave them leverage in another area. "We knew when we were done shooting," Rob recalls, "that it was going to be harder to get more money from our investors to keep going. We thought that in going to a professional editor, and telling the investors we needed a bunch of money to do that, we would be more credible, and get enough money for that as well as other things we needed to do. And people did say that it made sense, so we were able to dig up more money to continue on the post-production process. Little did the investors, or we, know that what we thought was going to be eight to ten weeks of editing turned into twenty weeks. It was just a lot of film, and after that, we shot even more and added to it."

They bundled the film together and took it to New York, where Edna Ruth Paul began working on it, trying to turn it into a releasable film. For *Book of the Dead,* her assistant was future director Joel Coen.

The Renaissance team stayed with friends in New York while Edna was cutting the film, Tapert says: "Sam has a bunch of stories about staying different places, because at first, we crashed on other people's floors for a long time. We stayed with John Gallagher, a writer who used to write quite a bit for *Film Comment,* and with David Goodman, who had worked on *Evil Dead.* Finally, we got our own apartment.

"It just became a cutting and screening process, intended for ourselves, but the editor invited some other people to screenings. I always remember this one screening because one of the people we invited was a psychiatrist, and she was very offended by the idea of the violence, and she was also offended at Sam." But they continued to be practical, says Rob: "The first thing we did when we got back to Michigan was to cut a four-minute trailer to raise money; we used John Cameron to narrate it."

Edna's final version was about ninety-seven minutes long. Raimi gives her full credit for cutting the movie. He admits that he and Joel Coen did tighten it up by ten minutes, but says that Edna Ruth Paul was principally responsible for the editing of *The Evil Dead.*

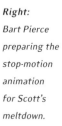

Right:
Bart Pierce
preparing the
stop-motion
animation
for Scott's
meltdown.

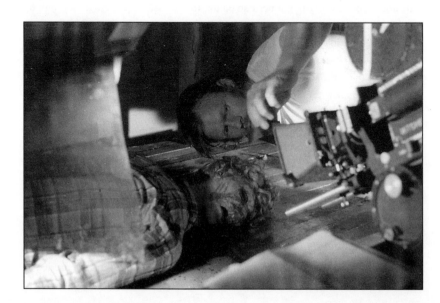

When making their Super-8 movies, Bruce and Sam had discovered the value of interesting, evocative sound effects, and were determined that their movie would have appropriate ones. Edna Paul had suggested they contact Joe Masefield, a demon sound editor, and Sound-1, the Foley lab operated by, as Bruce describes, "Elisha Birnbaum, a crazy Israeli guy who recorded the Arab-Israeli war in '67. This very adventurous guy came to New York and started this sound company. At night, he would do Foley by himself; he would turn the projector on, run into the recording room and do the Foley, footsteps, door slams and stuff."

As for Joe Masefield, Campbell says he's, "super-anal; he taught us how to label every sound effect — he had numbers for every sound effect he wanted to do through-out the film. We didn't know you could hire Foley walkers who would do all that stuff for you, so we just did the sound effects. We knew from our Super-8 movies, when we started to dabble in horror, that there were certain vegetables that were good for sound effects. Carrots were good for breaking necks; you had to get a real fresh bunch of cel-ery, usually the stuff that's too green to eat — that would make for good shredding and tearing. Cabbages are good for knife stabs. We got a turkey baster that gives you that SPLUSH SQUITCH SPLORK kind of sound; Joe Masefield referred to it as 'Kandarian plotzing'. Whenever bile spurted out of someone's neck, we had to do a plotzing sound. We also bought a meat cleaver and several chickens at a local market in New York, because they give you the sounds for when tendons break and twist and snap.

"We brought all kinds of cutlery and enough food for a banquet into this Foley stage," Bruce goes on, "and proceeded to basically trash the stage. We got reports later that the Foley stage had become renowned for the *Evil Dead* session; we had left a cer-tain aroma, since there were chicken parts buried under the sand for a year or more. We left our mark." And achieved a certain underground notoriety for the ingenuity of their sound effects (while on location in Tennessee, Sam recorded the sound of the wind, and this has since turned up in movies made by other people).

In fact, when Bruce Campbell appeared on the *Tonight* show in 1993, he expect-ed to talk primarily about his TV series *The Adventures of Brisco County, Jr*, but instead... "Jay Leno had me demonstrate the sound effects from *The Evil Dead*. I tried to tell him this was old, I don't do this any more. 'Nah,' he said, and the producers said they wanted me to make the wacky sound effects. I had to audition for the producers; 'Okay, this is a neck break.' I'd bite into a carrot, and they'd go, 'No, no, no, try the celery.' 'Oh, okay. This is a breaking bone,' and I'd bite into the celery. 'Celery is bet-ter,' they'd say, 'do the celery.' I had to audition through every sound effect we had used. The prop guy stood there with a pencil and paper; 'Let's see, I need some wal-nuts, I need a cabbage...' It was all coming back to me, like a Vietnam flashback. So on the show, I demonstrated with celery while Jay played a screaming student. I had the audience close their eyes. We chopped the chickens, my segment was over, and the singer was on. Ten years later I was still doing the same thing for no good reason."

MUS RICH'S HAND AND FACE, FIRST LAYER OF SKIN DISSOLVING. RED BLOOD LEAKS FROM THE RIPS. RICH'S EYES HAVE BEEN GOUGED
PROD. BUILD-UP SKULL + WIG / BUILD UP HAND. — SPLITSCREEN MATTE FOR HAND — STOP MOTION
6/4/80

MCU RICH'S FACE BEGINS TO ROT, REVEALING MUSCLE TISSUE AND THE BEGINNING OF BONE. THE SKIN SPLITS OPEN AND OOZES BLISTERS FORM AND EXPLODE MORE OOZE.
PROD + BOILD UP HEAD WITH BLOOD TUBES. SPLIT SCREEN AND STOP MOTION

In addition to sound effects, the movie needed a score. The team had prepared what's known as a temp (for temporary) track using music from other movies, to give an idea of what they wanted, but of course that would not do for the release print. They turned to Joseph Lo Duca, who pleased them so much he ended up scoring all three *Evil Dead* movies, *Crimewave*, all their *Hercules* TV movies and more, right up to *Jack of All Trades* (and even Rob Tapert's fishing videos).

Today, neither Lo Duca nor Sam remember who put them in touch with one another. "I wish I could call him up and thank him," Lo Duca says, "but I can't remember his name. He was a young man who worked making films for the state of Michigan traffic department, and was producing a black female vocalist at the time. I had produced and arranged some demos for her. One day, he asked me, 'Joe, you know you're really good at this music thing; what do you want to be when you grow up?' Not really thinking too much about it, I said, 'One of these days, I'd really like to do films,' thinking that's something you do when you've got all the playing and touring and whatever else out of your system."

Lo Duca had studied at the University of Michigan in Ann Arbor, and Michigan State University (MSU) in Detroit, seeking the best classical guitar programmes: "A person who had come up playing a lot of guitar could pursue music on a more formal level with a programme [like the one at MSU]. I was playing in a lot of jazz bands and writing music for those I played in, and had pretty much just got out of school when the opportunity for this film came along."

Although he'd seen his share of Vincent Price and Hammer horror movies, Lo Duca wasn't a fan.

What attracted him to Raimi, Tapert and Campbell was "the tremendous chutzpah these guys had; they had no office, but they had set up a business and they were really going to do this. I was impressed with their efforts, whatever the film looked like. These guys were just hell-bent on being film-makers from the ground up, and I was really hell-bent on being a film composer from the ground up."

The Renaissance partners interviewed other composers, but when Lo Duca played them a demo tape of the kind of music he intended to use on the film, they were convinced. With just a few instruments, it had a big, rich sound, both particular and ominous. Lo Duca was their man.

"I was very serious about taking on the commission," the composer says. "The budget for the first feature enabled me to hire five string players, which I doubled and sometimes tripled, and to get percussion instruments and a little bank of synthesisers together. I kind of crudely put together a score."

Lo Duca is too modest; his score for *The Evil Dead* is crisp and imaginative, matching and supporting the images perfectly. He did incorporate some themes reminiscent of those on the temp track, mostly from Bernard Herrmann scores, but that was at the request of the Renaissance team.

Only a few people have worked with Sam Raimi as often as Joe Lo Duca has, and no other composers, which puts him in a unique position to comment on Raimi's approach to film-making. "Sam," Lo Duca says, "is very musical. He has a musical soul. You can play a cue to him and he can hum it back after hearing it once. While he's not a musician, he can express himself very well in musical terms, as well as in terms of what is supposed to happen with the story. Sam's pictures have a lot of music, and it plays an important role; of course, sound effects are very important, with Bruce's input being important there.

"Sam is one of the most deferential people I know, and at the same time, inside he's so restless that there's many levels churning while he's working on a project. I don't think things really come to fruition until he gets to a final mix. While he'll be able to express a feeling he wants [a scene] to have, sometimes you don't know until you get to a final mix whether the music was supposed to deliver it, or the sound effects are. Making a film with Sam is very much a process of exploration."

Below and opposite:
Tom Sullivan's storyboards for Scott's meltdown sequence.

Sam, Rob and Bruce had finally finished *Book of the Dead*, but had no idea how much it would change their lives. Of course, they weren't the first young film-makers to successfully realise their ambitions. In Southern California in the mid-1960s, for instance, a group of college-age friends joined together to make *Equinox*, also a horror film about teenagers lost in the woods who encounter monsters and sorcery. Written by Mark Thomas McGee and directed by Dennis Muren, the film was shot on weekends and during vacations over a long period of time, and several of the people who worked on it went on to forge significant careers in the industry, just as the Renaissance partners would. The cast was mostly unknowns, although co-star Frank Boers, Jr later changed his name to Frank Bonner and co-starred in the TV series *WKRP in Cincinnati*. Great horror/fantasy writer Fritz Leiber made his first screen appearance since *Camille* in 1937 and other professionals, including Jim Danforth, helped out as well. Stop-motion animator David Allen made his feature film debut, while director Muren later went into special effects himself, and has worked for George Lucas' Industrial Light and Magic ever since. To date, he has won more Oscars than anyone else in his field. Eventually, Jack H. Harris (of *The Blob* fame) bought the film, and had established director Jack Hill shoot some extra scenes for theatrical release in 1971.

The *Book of the Dead* production team scheduled a grand première for investors, friends, local teenagers and others on 15 October 1981, but the fourth reel was out of synch. Would the show go on? It did, just barely — that very morning, a new print of the fourth reel was struck at Technicolor in New York and flown to Detroit in time for that gala première.

Apart from the title, the movie shown that night is the movie you see today, with only one other difference — Sam had composed the film for a 1:1.66 aspect ratio (that is, the image was 1.66 times as wide as it was high; 1:1.85 is today's standard), but 16mm occupies the full 1:1.37 'Academy standard' aperture, the way films were projected up until the early 1950s. The Redford Theater accommodated the old ratio, so that's how *Book of the Dead* was projected for the première, and it's never been shown that way again.

The crowd was festive, but no one knew quite what to expect. The investors in particular, Tapert admits, really "had no idea what was coming. This big theatre in Detroit, the Redford, has the largest pipe organ in the Midwest. It was a big house, eleven hundred seats, with a lower foyer balcony; we got about a thousand people to show up for it. When people arrived, we had searchlights and an ambulance out front, all that stuff. We brought in a bunch of high school kids from middle income families around this theatre, probably three or four hundred of them, and packed them into the balcony, and it turned into something like an ice hockey game — literally, the reaction was like you get at a hockey game. Before the film started, we said a few words, and then the pipe organ came up playing Toccata and Fugue in D flat minor. We gave them the full show going in, and then a party afterwards; it was a lot of fun, a great one-night event."

Ellen Sandweiss agrees: "It was wonderful. It was very exciting, and my parents came, and everybody came — and I had to sit through that one scene [the vine rape], which is always kind of the downer anytime anything comes up with this movie. When they did another première in Morristown, Tennessee, where we made the movie, I was already living in Asheville, so they flew me in by helicopter from Asheville to Morristown."

"In terms of premières, you couldn't ask for anything better" than the one in Detroit, Tapert says. "The audience was subdued at the beginning, and the tree rape scene so horrified the people that by the time the pencil went into the ankle, they were close to numb. But then the hockey fans were coming out, and there was that element of the crowd that was really with it. In an industry screening, you don't get a true reaction, but we did there. It started to come out of the balcony in this ice hockey-game-like fashion.

"I think it was the first time many of these people had seen a movie of this nature, because afterwards they were all charged up, as it was so visceral. The daughter of one of our investors, who was in *Within the Woods* herself, was so shaken by the movie that she couldn't stop crying. I mean, she was in *Within the Woods*, but she just didn't take it seriously. Her father thought, I'm sure, 'Oh my God, have I invested in something that's gone beyond pornography?' But at the same time, inside he went, 'Well, it works. I can't imagine people going to see it, but it wasn't a total loss.'"

For Sam Raimi, the main virtue of making *Book of the Dead* was as a learning experience: "I was realising why certain techniques had been employed in movies only when I was trying to employ them myself. I suppose I could have learned these things through more study, but sometimes it's best to learn them on their own. You learn why not to make a jump-cut, (because it's disorienting to the audience) as opposed to just reading about it. When they watch your movie, you see them lose it for a moment. By making the mistake myself and seeing it, seeing how they're upset and disoriented, not only will I not do it in a dialogue scene where I don't want them to be disoriented, but I *will* employ it in a sequence that's supposed to affect the audience in a very startling way. Now I'll actually change screen direction — though you're not 'supposed' to — because of the effect it has on the audience."

And so, finally, lessons learned, the movie was done. Really done. Shown to the investors, mentioned in the newspapers. It wasn't just an idea cooked up by some ambitious amateur movie-makers — it was a real movie, as real as *Lawrence of Arabia* or *Plan 9 From Outer Space*. The only thing left to do was sell it...

CHAPTER 5

BLOOD ON THE SCREEN

So, armed with a print of their *magnum opus*, the Renaissance partners began hitting the bricks, making the rounds, knocking on doors and handing their film to bored, disinterested distributors, many of who undoubtedly didn't even sit through the entire film. In fact, they had begun this process even before the première in October 1981.

This activity led to some interesting encounters. "When we were all done with *The Evil Dead*, and trying to find a distributor," says Rob Tapert, "we came out to Hollywood, our first trip here. It would have been May 1981. We were staying at the Park Plaza Lodge, a motel over on Third or somewhere. We ate at the Copper Penny, then wandered up to Hollywood Boulevard for the first time. Wow, stars, all the glamour." Unlike most who come to Hollywood for the first time, the Renaissance partners really did run into a movie star.

"Now I realise the chances of that happening are one in ten thousand, one in ten million," explains Rob, "but a woman walked by us, and with her was Charlton Heston. Walking down Hollywood Boulevard at five o'clock on a Sunday afternoon. Bruce turned around, and said, 'Mr Heston? Mr Heston?' Finally Charlton Heston turns around. 'I just wanted to congratulate you on your great career,' Bruce says. 'Oh, thank you,' says Heston. They shook hands, and he left. It was the coolest thing."

However, Tapert admits that, by October 1981, "we had been unable to get a distributor, which became a long and arduous process, because nobody wanted it. Out here, it was turned down by everybody." They screened the film for Paramount, for Charles Fries, for Avco Embassy and others in Los Angeles, but concentrated on distributors in New York. They went to distributor after distributor, but almost no one showed any interest, not even World Northal, which had profitably released the low-budget horror movie *The Children*, besides which *The Evil Dead* looks like, say, *Rosemary's Baby*.

The Renaissance partners weren't allowed to stay in the screening room when prospective buyers looked at the film. "They don't want anybody in there," says Rob, "so they can take phone calls, and be late and leave early, and do whatever they like. I'm positive not all of them sat all the way through it. We even had people not show up for screenings we had arranged — and we had to pay for booking the projection room."

At the time, New Line was just moving out of 16mm distribution. "They really needed product," Tapert points out. "They didn't have anything, they were still pretty much doing 16mm rights to old AIP and Corman pictures, plus some arthouse movies. They had some John Waters movies, and I think they were doing Jack Sholder's *Alone in the Dark*." New Line, whose executives saw *Book of the Dead* around November 1981, wanted to buy world rights to the picture, but offered no advance money at all, and the Renaissance team was discouraged.

While they were trying to sell the movie, Sam, Rob and Bruce had little income. Mostly, as Rob says, they lived with their parents: "I have no sympathy, and Bruce has less, for all these people out here in Hollywood who have development deals and have to work until ten and eleven at night — because they're getting paid. I graduated from college at twenty-three, then started grad school but dropped out to make movies, and didn't see a pay cheque until I was twenty-nine years old. So I had to sponge off my parents, although they aren't wealthy by any means.

Below:

The actual Book

"Between the time we made *The Evil Dead* and sold it, we had to take odd jobs as production assistants here and there; all three of us had to work. Bruce drove a cab. *of the Dead.*

We worked a lot for Bill Dear, who came to Detroit all the time to shoot commercials, because he's from there. We worked on commercials for the Maysles brothers, too. We ended up doing a lot of goofy production work to feed ourselves.

"It was a long haul, and it was difficult. I think all of us were fortunate that our parents were pretty much behind us from the beginning; if they weren't behind us, they got aboard anyway, although I don't think it was what any of them would have chosen for us. I know that Sam was planning to go to film school the following year — he had been accepted to NYU — but we went and made a movie."

And finally they got lucky, very lucky. "The name Irvin Shapiro came up because he had handled Scorsese's and Romero's and other guys' first movies. We got to Irvin at last. He came out of the screening room and said, 'It's your lucky day, boys. It's not *Gone with the Wind*, but I think I can make you some money.'" Their initial deal with Shapiro was for foreign release only, but eventually he handled the domestic deals, too. In fact, he went with New Line, who had previously wanted such a killer deal. Thanks to Shapiro, though, New Line only got North American theatrical rights; they shared ancillary rights — such as television and video release — with the Renaissance partners. Shapiro also ensured that Renaissance retained foreign rights and collected the cheques directly, without having to have any of the ancillary rights filtered through New Line.

In 1982, Irvin Shapiro demanded some production stills, but they didn't actually have any. Childhood friend Mike Ditz had come down to Tennessee for a couple of days, but all he shot were behind-the-scenes photos. So about eight 'production stills' were shot long after production wrapped; these are the familiar ones of Campbell with a chainsaw, the hand from the grave clutching the woman's throat, and so forth. The other photos were taken from the internegative — the printing negative — and used to print stills. The model in the photos with Bruce was Bridget Hoffman, who continued to have an intermittent connection with Rob, Sam and Bruce. She was a nun in *Crimewave*, provided a computer voice in *Darkman*, worked behind the scenes on *Army of Darkness*, played Echidna, 'the Mother of All Monsters', in several episodes of Renaissance's *Hercules* TV series and appeared with Bruce in Josh Becker's movie *Running Time*.

One advantage they had in Irvin Shapiro was that the canny old distributor knew and liked horror movies. In an article in the 14 January 1981 *Variety*, Shapiro cited *Dracula, The Rocky Horror Picture Show, Martin, Night of the Living Dead, Frankenstein* and other thrillers as examples of good product worth promoting. And he recognised the same values in *Book of the Dead/The Evil Dead*.

It was Shapiro who suggested the title be changed; his first suggestion was the outlandish *The Evil Dead Men and the Evil Dead Women*. Rob Tapert was holding out for *Fe-Monsters*; other titles toyed with were *Blood Flood, A Hundred and One Percent Dead* and *These Bitches Are Witches*. Can you imagine a book called *The These Bitches Are Witches Companion*?

Shapiro was one of those wonderful behind-the-scenes players in the movie business that people outside the industry rarely hear about, but who's a legend to those who deal in films. He was born in 1906, and became thrilled with movies when, as a teenager, he wrote film reviews for the *Washington Herald* and later took over management of the Wardman Park Hotel Theater in Washington, DC. Shapiro began his association with independent and foreign films early. The first movie he showed at that theatre was the 1922 film *Nanook of the North*, which he promoted to the hilt.

He moved to New York, hoping to get into the production side of the movie business, but that didn't work out, and eventually he wound up involved in the distribution of foreign films in America, and non-studio American films overseas. Shapiro also made deals in America with distributors on behalf of independent film-makers, as he did with *The Evil Dead*. He was instrumental in getting *The Cabinet of Dr. Caligari* and *Battleship Potemkin* distributed in the US, and even wrote a biography of Sergei Eisenstein when the director was only twenty-nine.

In 1929, Shapiro began working in the New York publicity office of RKO Pictures, but only stayed for about a year. He managed a few cinemas in New York, and then in 1932 began the company that he headed until Parkinson's disease forced him to sell in 1985. He died in 1989. Shapiro's company was originally called World Pictures and later Films Around The World. Among the films he was responsible for bringing to America were Jean Renoir's *La Grande Illusion*, Claude Chabrol's *Les Cousins* and Jean-Luc Godard's *A Bout de Souffle* (*Breathless*), all immensely influential movies. Among the American directors whose product Shapiro was the first to handle were Stanley Kubrick, George Romero — and Sam Raimi. In the 1930s, he was one of the founders of the Cannes Film Festival.

Above:
Irvin Shapiro.

Shapiro also dealt in reissues of both American and imported films through his Film Classics company. He was one of the pioneers in the release of films to television; when he leased the 16mm theatrical rights to some MGM films in the 1940s, the studio threw in the television rights to the same titles, and Shapiro made a mint.

Despite his own financial interests in television, Shapiro never lost his love of movies, and especially of the showmanship required to turn them into hits. He deeply admired people like George Lucas and Steven Spielberg, and in a special tribute to Shapiro in *The Hollywood Reporter* (10 May 1983), the man himself said, "If I were a young man today, I'd rather be producer of *E.T.* than president." (The tribute section featured a big ad thanking Shapiro signed by Robert Tapert, Bruce Campbell and Sam Raimi, all of whom adored him, and were endlessly amused by him.)

Writer Stephen King also knew Irvin Shapiro, and was equally delighted with him. "He was, at the time I met him," King recalls, "approximately 179 years old... and having the time of his life. That isn't quite true... but he was very, very old. He was a real gentleman of the old school. The stories that he told...! He just bounced them out. You sat there with your mouth open. I would love to be able to say, when I'm eighty-five, that I had a life that spanned half the things that he remembered. But of course, he lived through enough extraordinary events to fill four novels by Herman Wouk.

"One thing I remember him telling me was that he owned six or seven Picassos — sketches that Picasso had sold him for, basically, the price of six or seven good drunks on the town, when Picasso was down in his scuffling days. I have no doubt that story was true, but it was the sort of detail you'd expect to come across in a Judith Krantz fuck-and-shop novel. I remember that he had this little tiny office papered with one-sheets for exploitation pictures. He was dressed to the nines in an old-fashioned three piece suit."

Below:

Sam Raimi and

Rob Tapert take

The Evil Dead to

Europe.

Other movies handled by Shapiro in one way or another include: *Arrowsmith, Bang the Drum Slowly, The Brides of Fu Manchu, Cocaine Cowboys, Creepshow, Dawn of the Dead, Dona Flor and Her Two Husbands, Eating Raoul, Knightriders, The Lady Vanishes,*

The Little Girl Who Lives Down the Lane, *Louisiana Story*, *Man of Aran*, *Mean Streets*, *Pixote*, *Rust Never Sleeps*, *Le Testament d'Orphée* and *Tunnelvision*. But, apparently, his name appeared on only two movies — *Crimewave* and *Evil Dead II*. (He's thanked in the end credits of *Army of Darkness* because he was the first to suggest that Sam, Rob and Bruce make a sequel to *The Evil Dead*, and because he came up with the title *Army of Darkness*.)

At Irvin Shapiro's suggestion, they took *The Evil Dead*, as it was now called, to film festivals in Europe, where it was greeted with some enthusiasm. "At Alain Schlockoff's annual horror, fantasy and science fiction film festival at the Rex Theatre in Paris, the audience just went crazy," Tapert says with a smile. "It was the first day of the Beaujolais Nouveau in Paris," — when the year's new wine of that variety is brought to the city — "and everyone had been drinking the new Beaujolais, coming into the theatre stinking drunk. It's a main floor and three balconies, and the people on top are throwing stuff on the people on the bottom. They got into the film, too. They were chanting 'Sangre! Sangre!' ['Blood! Blood!'] and cursing. At the end, in the meltdown as the guy is gloppified, there's this green worm that tumbles down his face. They started chanting 'Allez les vers! Allez les vers!' I don't know what that means, but it had some kind of soccer reference." (It's acually a French pun. At the time, one of the most popular soccer teams was from the city of St Etienne, and they wore green jerseys. Fans of the soccer team would yell "Allez les verts!" — Hooray for the greens! When the green worm appeared in *Evil Dead*, the crowd cheered "Allez les vers!" Which, in French, sounds exactly like "Allez les verts" but means "hooray for the worm!")

It was at Cannes in 1982 that Stephen King first saw the film and what he had to say about it turned out to be as influential as the deals that Irvin Shapiro was making. "I saw it by chance at the Cannes Film Festival," says Stephen King, "when Richard Rubinstein and I were there on a junket to publicise *Creepshow*. And it blew me away. Totally. Blew me right through the back doors, through the lobby and into the street, figuratively speaking. I was registering with like one peripheral corner of my mind that there was a lot of shit going on in the picture that was so amateurish that you could hardly believe you were seeing it on the big screen. There was a matte of the full moon that looked like a postage stamp on a letter, if you imagine the screen as an envelope. But at the same time, even that they would try to put those shots in there with what they had was amazing.

"Then the larger part of my mind was registering things that I had never seen before in a movie, ever, that were working perfectly. These shots that were like insane Steadicam shots that were going on. Later, Sam told me how they were done, and I thought to myself that it worked because nobody in the organised film establishment would even *think* about trying it this way."

The movie dazzled King, and he still talks about it in amazed, admiring terms. "It wouldn't stop. It was over the top, it was like a thunderstorm in a bottle, just relentless. It was really scary, and I think that maybe Sam is the only person who ever realised that you could never go back and repeat that, ever. And so when he did the other movies — *Evil Dead II* and *Army of Darkness* (which up here in Maine we call Ahmy of Dahkness) they're just as good, but they're doing different things."

King met Sam Raimi at the Cannes festival (Rob Tapert got to go the next year) and thought Sam looked like a fifteen year-old waiter or busboy (not far removed from the jobs Sam was doing between *The Evil Dead* and *Crimewave*). King came back to the United States still reeling and grinning from the impact of *The Evil Dead* and wrote a review of it for the November 1982 issue of *Twilight Zone* magazine: "That [Sam Raimi] is a genius is yet unproven; that he has made the most ferociously original horror film of 1982 seems to me beyond doubt... *The Evil Dead* has the simple, stupid power of a good campfire story — but its simplicity is not a side effect. It is something carefully crafted by Raimi, who is anything but stupid... It doesn't sound like much. Well, neither does *Hansel and Gretel* nor *Bluebeard* in the hands of an untalented teller. What Raimi achieves in *The Evil Dead* is a black rainbow of horror... Mostly what's going on is Sam Raimi, who is so full of talent that somebody unable to get it together might be tempted to wonder if gobbling the man's fingernails could possibly do any good.

"In *The Evil Dead* the camera has the kind of nightmarish fluidity that we associate with the early John Carpenter; it dips and slides and then zooms in so fast you want to plaster your hands over your eyes. The film begins and ends with crazily exhilarating shots that make you want to leap up, cheering. (At Cannes, French cinema-freaks did exactly that.)"

King's review turned on *Fangoria*, and *Fangoria* turned on the horror movie fans. Not only did interest in *The Evil Dead* build, but suddenly, Bruce Campbell, Sam Raimi and Rob Tapert were names. Raimi had arrived as a director in a way that none of them expected. King is still a big supporter of Raimi and his movies: "The thing was it deserved to be released, and if I had a part to play in it, I'm just delighted. And Sam's still doin' it!"

England would prove to be a crucial market for *The Evil Dead*. Stephen Woolley and Nik Powell of Palace Pictures bought the British rights at the American Film Market in March 1982, the film's first sale. And in 1983, it was the highest-rented video in the UK. One of the first places *The Evil Dead* was released was Scotland, which was, according to journalist Alex Sutherland, "a traditional home for the guts and gore horror movie." In early February 1983, the film opened to "uproarious audience reaction and more than £100,000 in box office takings." It performed so well that the planned London opening was delayed a week in order to crank up interest; when it

*Left:
Sam and Rob
hold a press
conference.*

did open, it was on a 'day and date' basis, meaning a simultaneous theatrical and video release. *The Evil Dead* was, in fact, only the second theatrical release for Palace, but they soon had their tails in a ringer.

Scotland Yard declared the violent movie to be *obscenely* bloody, and Nik Powell was arrested for violation of England's Obscene Publications Act (OPA). This didn't happen until early 1984, however, and by that time, the film had played to delighted and squirming audiences for more than a year. During that year, "numerous OPA cases" (John Hazelton, *Screen International*, 3 August 1985) had been brought against video dealers in the United Kingdom, even though the film had been given a British Board of Film Classification certificate 18, passing it as suitable for people over eighteen.

Trials on these charges began in November 1984 — and five of the seven brought acquittals for the dealers. Nonetheless, the Crown persisted in its persecution of the movie, and this led to Powell's arrest. However, even before his case could be brought to trial, the judge dismissed it decisively. According to Hazelton, the judge felt that such frivolous prosecutions "bring the administration into disrepute. In my judgement, these proceedings ought not to have been started." A relieved Powell was set free with an apology.

Sam Raimi didn't even get the apology. As Rob Tapert says, "They flew Sam all the way over there; he flew all day, took a train to, like, Liverpool, got to court after being awake for forty-eight hours. He was sitting in court, and the defence said, 'We'd like to call Sam Raimi, the director of the film.' The magistrate said, 'The intention of the film-maker is not in question here. We don't need his testimony.'" And a relieved, if very tired, Sam Raimi returned to the United States.

On the other hand, in October 1984, *The Evil Dead* was seized by the German Department of Public Prosecution, and the film could no longer be shown in West Germany — even though it had been in distribution since February of that year without any noticeable increase in the dismemberment of demon-possessed girlfriends. It was reissued theatrically in 1992, and performed well.

New Line distributed the film in the United States, but when they submitted *The Evil Dead* for a rating by the Motion Picture Association of America (MPAA), it received the dreaded X.

A bit of history: in the late 1960s, the spectre of government censorship loomed over the movie business (again), so to offset this, the MPAA established CARA, the Classification and Ratings Administration. A group of anonymous citizens (lately, apparently entirely parents) watches movies and applies ratings to them, as advisories to — nowadays — parents. Originally, the advisories were for everyone, but that's slowly changed. These ratings are a good idea in theory, and did free movie-makers to tackle more adult stuff, but in practice, there have been big problems.

Even though two X-rated movies, *A Clockwork Orange* and *Midnight Cowboy*, were major hits (with the latter even winning the best-picture Oscar), because the MPAA had trademarked all their ratings *except* the X, makers of hardcore sex films, such as *Deep Throat*, were free to apply the X to their films — and in fact, it became a designation for such films. (To indicate that their films were especially sexy, distributors of hardcore films increased the number of Xs, finally settling on triple X, which is still used.) Many newspapers refused to carry advertising for X-rated movies, whether the X-rating was granted by the MPAA, or self-imposed by the distributors. No advertising resulted in fewer customers, so some cinemas refused to play X-rated movies (and some still refuse to play NC-17 movies, too).

While violent horror movies were initially seen as essentially harmless (the 1968 Hammer horror *Dracula Has Risen from the Grave* originally received a G), in time, if violent enough, they got an X, and that's what *The Evil Dead* received. The option remained for New Line to release the film without any rating at all, and that's what they did.

The movie finally opened in New York in April of 1983 on the same weekend as the smash hit *Flashdance*, and in Los Angeles in May the same year. At one point, Bruce, Rob and Sam were in Los Angeles (before all three moved there permanently), and went to see *The Evil Dead* on a double bill with the first *A Nightmare on Elm Street*, also a New Line release. "At the end of the movie," a slightly embarrassed, but amused, Tapert admits,

"Sam stood up and said, 'Ladies and gentlemen, I want to announce that the star of *The Evil Dead* is with us here today.' And he pointed at Bruce. All these people kind of look at him, and go, 'Yeah, it is that guy,' and Bruce is going, 'Oh, man.' It was pretty funny." Campbell enjoyed observing audiences as they reacted to the film: "It was fun to watch; a couple in a theatre had a coat over themselves, a guy and a girl, and they were looking through the sleeve of their jacket, and they were just sort of scanning the screen and if it was too horrible, they'd look at another part, or they'd close it off."

You are cordially invited to a screening of
The Ultimate Experience in Grueling Terror...

EVIL DEAD

AVCO III, WEDNESDAY, MARCH 31st, 11:00 A.M.

Worldwide representation, Irvin Shapiro, FILMS AROUND THE WORLD
At the American Film Market, Westwood Plaza Hotel (AFM Headquarters)
Room 1018, 1020, 1022, (213) 475-5296
FILMS AROUND THE WORLD, 745 Fifth Avenue, New York, New York 10151
Telephone (213) 752-5050, Telex 420572 FILM UI

Eventually, the partners made enough to pay off the investors in the picture, and to provide a small profit for them besides. "It took a long time," Tapert admits. "Even with a success, everyone is slow to pay. But it dribbled in over a period of time. When we started to make *Evil Dead II*, that prompted a lot of overseas distributors who owed us money to pay us." They broke even after six years; it was the fees for the rights to the sequel that put the Renaissance partners into profit.

Sam said, "I realised that the most important thing after pleasing the audience was to make our investors' money back. We had to go to individuals to raise money to make a picture, and we had to promise that their money would be returned, and hopefully with a profit." There are very few directors who consider returning a profit to their investors to be one of their main goals.

"That's where we came from," Rob points out. "It's a different way than most people come into Hollywood, because we sat at those darned kitchen tables with doctors and their wives saying, 'we promise we'll get your money back out of this.' We always saw their faces looming up in the background. So there was a definite incentive — people had trusted you."

Dazed, pleased and now Real Movie-makers, the Renaissance partners had begun to put *The Evil Dead* behind them. Sam Raimi had hit it off well with assistant editor Joel Coen and his brother Ethan, and they wrote a script together, first called *Relentless*, then *The XYZ Murders* and finally *Crimewave*. It became Raimi's second film as a director, but Sam, Bruce and Rob weren't yet done with those demons from Kandar, the Book of the Dead, and poor, tormented Ash...

BLOOD WILL TELL

Low-budget horror movies by new directors with unknown casts, released by lower-echelon distributors, as New Line was in 1983, are rarely reviewed by the likes of *Time* and *Newsweek*. When they are reviewed at all, it's usually by a newspaper's second- or third-string critic, the guy assigned the latest kung fu pictures, gross-out teen fodder and especially obscure foreign imports. And for the most part, that's just who reviewed *The Evil Dead*. But the reviews themselves were different.

For example, in *The Village Voice* of 3 May 1983, shrewd critic Elliott Stein not only spotted a lot of Sam Raimi's influences, he pinpointed much of the appeal of the film: "The Anthology Film Archives would have been the ideal place for the world première of *The Evil Dead*. It cannibalises *The Exorcist, The Night of the Living Dead, The Day of the Triffids, The Texas Chain Saw Massacre* and Three Stooges classic *A Plumbing We Will Go*." (He's one of the few who recognised the Stoogieness of the movie.)

"The script is balderdash," Stein says; "most sane adults, if they sit it out, will be revolted by the splattery climaxes. Why write of it? For three good reasons — three new, young, impressive talents: Tom Sullivan... Tim Philo... and twenty-one year-old director Sam Raimi." He relates the plot, then adds, "The survivor is played by Bruce Campbell, who is not only star but co-producer, and therefore seems entitled to dismember the rest of the cast."

In an international publication, Alex Sutherland said that "It is violent and shocking, amusing and disgusting... the plot is so implausible and the violence so excessive and fantastic, staged with such stylish camera work and special effects, that no true horror buff could deny its appeal."

David Chute, in the 27 May 1983 *Los Angeles Herald-Examiner*, compared *The Evil Dead* to *Night of the Living Dead*: "it achieves a similar claustrophobic intensity on a microscopic budget. It's a shoestring *tour de force*." Chute described Raimi as displaying "a ravenous, precocious talent." He also sensed a certain tongue-in-cheek quality which others have claimed to spot as well. But Raimi, Campbell and Tapert all admit (rather ruefully) that they didn't intend to make a comedy. Campbell says, "We played it absolutely like we felt it should be played. Our young sensibilities just wound up being overly dramatic about everything, and became ridiculous. Everyone says, 'Aw, they've got their tongues firmly planted in their cheeks.' No, I was just an inexperienced actor."

Chute liked the gore effects, noting that "when the zombies crumble and die in this movie, their runny flesh is rainbow coloured, like melted ice cream." But he also felt that the movie "can't be touted as a must-see work of art. In fact, whenever Raimi slows down and zeros in on the dim characters, you stop shuddering and start giggling." Chute's most telling point is one that others missed: "In horror movies, recklessness is often a virtue. When high-tech directors such as Stanley Kubrick (*The Shining*) or Tony Scott (*The Hunger*) set out to 'redeem' the horror genre by pumping it full of art, they end up killing it. They're too fastidious to deliver the grisly goods."

No one will ever accuse Sam Raimi's horror movies of being fastidious.

'Lor' in *Variety* admired the film too, saying it "emerges late in the horror film cycle as the *ne plus ultra* of low-budget gore and shock effects... [They have] built a better horror picture [which] should clean up in the fright marketplace." Abbie Bernstein in *Drama-Logue* called the film "one of the best-executed graphic gore horror films to come down the pike in quite awhile... [Raimi] knows a lot more about pacing, tension and camera placement than many of his more experienced, studio-backed peers." (Bernstein, a lifelong horror fan and writer, knows whereof she speaks.) Bill Krohn's *Boxoffice* review pointed out the limitations of the film, but also concluded that *The Evil Dead* "is by far the best horror entry of the year."

Vincent Canby's bemused commentary on the film in *The New York Times* (27 April 1983), not really a review, pointed out one of the major reasons for its success: "It's a great audience participation show... just intriguing enough to grab the audience and then... absurd enough to invite the audience to talk back to it." Which they always do, mostly to point out how much of an idiot Ash is being at any given moment.

Gerry Putzer in *The Hollywood Reporter* wasn't as impressed. His review is almost vengefully negative, as if he'd overdosed on graphic horror movies and wanted to get back at one of them. "The only thing distinguishing *The Evil Dead* from the mass of explicit horror films," he said in the 14 March 1983, issue, "is that its writer-director, Samuel M. Raimi, was twenty-two years old [sic; he was twenty] when he made the movie in 1980. The production... is nothing more than an amalgam of the most obvious (and popular) aspects of other successful films of the genre... Raimi's film makes these shockers look like paradigms of narrative technique. Initial business, however, should be brisk due to an effective mixture of gore and high camp." He found the plot to be "hackneyed" — a charge, it must be admitted, that's hard to disagree with. "The actors are more convincing as disgusting zombies than as honour students," Putzer sneered, adding that Campbell is memorable solely because "his sincere face remains on screen the longest in its natural state. A long box office life for *The Evil Dead* is unthinkable, but it may benefit from sporadic engagements on the weekend midnight-show circuit."

Aside from Stephen King's rave in *Twilight Zone*, the most favourable — and one of the most intelligent — early reviews of *The Evil Dead* was that by Kevin Thomas, in the 26 May 1983 issue of the *Los Angeles Times*. Thomas has seen just about everything; he's hung on at the newspaper for thirty years, while reviewers above and below him come and go; he always gives honest insights on all the films he's assigned. And he's been assigned a lot of horror movies.

He began his review: "*The Evil Dead* arrives on its way to becoming a cult film, having opened last month in New York amidst furore and long lines. Unquestionably it's an instant classic, probably the grisliest well-made movie ever. It's the work of Sam Raimi, a Michigan State University *wunderkind* (and comic book collector)... Raimi is one of those film creatures who unerringly knows where to put the camera and at what angle and how to assemble images for absolute maximum effect. He gets away with more gore than anybody else because of two crucial reasons: He has a hilarious sense of humour and he knows when to cut away." Again, Thomas thought that Raimi was aiming for laughs when he was actually being very earnest, but so be it if that's what leads to his declaring the movie a classic. He concludes, "*The Evil Dead* is wholly a product of the vivid imagination of Samuel M. Raimi, for whom this film is clearly just the beginning."

New Line's decision to release the film unrated created a real notoriety for the modest (but in-your-face) movie, and it got more notice than it probably would have if it had been released rated R. After the New York engagements, in fact, they had planned to make enough cuts to get the R, but as Kevin Thomas pointed out, the brassy assurance of this début feature made by unknowns had stirred up the jaded New York movie audience, so New Line bit the bullet and went for that unrated release.

Despite the marketing problems associated with the X-rating, the audience for *The Evil Dead* found it anyway. It was by no means a hit, but it did reasonably well; it opened in New York in seventy-two cinemas and pulled in $685,000 at the box office, making it the third highest-grossing film of the week in the city, but the Los Angeles release (fifteen cinemas, $108,000) was disappointing. (It has consistently done well on video the world over, however.) Nonetheless, it established Sam Raimi and Rob Tapert as names to be watched in Hollywood.

It did something else for Sam Raimi — it exposed his ego to nation-wide criticism: "The first time my movie was discussed on television was on the Siskel and Ebert show. I got my whole family around the television set; it came on, and out waddled this skunk, or this dog, some small animal, and they called *The Evil Dead* 'the dog of the week'. They talked about how awful it was, but because it wasn't me, just images from the movie, it wasn't as shocking as it might have been.

"Until *Darkman*, I didn't do much publicity because the movies I made then usually appealed to a very small audience. I think the thrill for me

was seeing Bruce's face or an image from the movie in an article in *Fangoria* magazine, a very good magazine that helped us a lot in getting going. I felt we were being accepted by the *Famous Monsters of Filmland* of our time; it was speaking to the audience for whom we were trying to make the movies, and the magazine seemed to accept our movies. That, I think, was one of the biggest thrills for me." Raimi continues to support the magazine, and *Fangoria* readers continue to regard him as one of their own.

Seeing *The Evil Dead* for the first time today simply cannot have the impact it did back in 1983. There have been too many rivers of gore to cross, too many mountains of entrails, too many gouged eyes, lopped-off heads, hands and legs for it to bug eyes and gag throats the way it did back then. Yet there's no doubt that the intensity of its violence is what gave the film its initial reputation as one of the great dare movies... did you have the nerve to sit through it without squirming? It was a fun-house ride, a spook tunnel, all the Halloweens of all time wrapped up into one movie. The carefully-calculated shocks worked like audiences were wired directly into the film — gasps and shrieks erupted on cue in cinema after cinema.

Seen today, as violent as it is, the movie seems relatively tame in terms of the volume of gore, although the Sullivan and Pierce meltdown sequence is still impressively revolting, and the sheer persistence of the demons and their cackling, gloating personalities are still fresh and surprising. You'll notice the uneven acting and the story holes, one of the biggest of which is this — if it takes a reading from the Book of the Dead to rouse the demons of the forest, what's that unseen force watching the car at the beginning of the film? The characters are not well drawn; Linda and Shelly are interchangeable, attractive female victims; Cheryl's a little spunkier, but it's easy to miss the fact she's Ash's sister. Ash himself has little personality beyond Bruce Campbell's own; he's a quiet survivor. The characters are clearly there just to be killed off and we spend very little time getting to know them. The scene with Ash, Linda and the necklace does stand out, if only because there's nothing else in the film quite like it.

The script is simply an efficient way of getting people isolated so that horrible things can happen to them. Raimi does try to extend it a little beyond that, but his intention was to make the movie 'the ultimate experience in gruelling terror'. And at that, he very nearly succeeds — perhaps because horror movies scare him. There is, however, more to it than that; *The Evil Dead* is greater than the sum of its parts.

What will pop your eyes and spin your wheels is the exuberance of Raimi's work — Sam is a born director. There are occasional impressive moments in his Super-8 movies, but they're essentially amateurish and unformed. *Clockwork* and *Within the Woods* unexpectedly revealed a new Sam, however, which might have surprised even him. They show a kind of cold-blooded ferocity that certainly has nothing to do with the Sam you'd get if you met him in person. He's a joker, true, but he's unfailingly polite, warm and open, friendly to a fault, honest and good-hearted — an all-American boy if there ever was one.

But like those other all-American boys Robert Bloch, Stephen King and David Lynch, when he's actually creating his art, Raimi can reach inside himself to pull out, snarling and clawing, a dark and demonic force infused with tremendous energy. It's not something he seems entirely comfortable with, though — after all, his only whole-hearted, all-out horror movie remains *The Evil Dead*. *Evil Dead II* edges towards comedy, though it still has moments of horror, and *Army of Darkness* is an entertaining adventure with some horror elements. Raimi enjoys directing comedy, but his one full-fledged attempt, *Crimewave*, doesn't really work. However, like all of his movies, it is full of his signature all-stops-out dynamism.

People have tried to imitate the content of *The Evil Dead* trilogy, but what they copy are the gore and some of the story elements. And those are, when you get right down to it, not really all that important to why this movie works. Raimi's style is bravura, relentless, and yet good-humoured; aggressive, but not hostile. He wants you

EVIL DEAD I   ©1992 Renaissance Pictures LTD.

to have fun while he's dragging you pell-mell through the story — Sam loves movies deeply, and that goes right back to those Super-8 shorts with Bruce Campbell, Scott Spiegel and the others, flinging pies, driving through boxes and running down alleys in Birmingham, Michigan.

Above: A publicity still, taken from the movie itself — none were actually shot during filming.

Like all horror classics, *The Evil Dead* succeeds not because of its excesses, not because of its content, but because of the person behind it. *Frankenstein, The Invisible Man, The Old Dark House* and *Bride of Frankenstein* could only be the work of James Whale; it was John Landis' playful personality that turned *An American Werewolf in London* into something special; Joe Dante's love of old movies and awareness of what makes things scary turned *Gremlins* into an unexpected hit. And it was Sam Raimi, his energy, imagination and sense of humour, that made *The Evil Dead* into something far more than anyone would have expected from a bunch of college students struggling to make a movie in the wintry hills of Tennessee.

CHAPTER 7

STRANGE BLOOD

Sam Raimi became close friends with Joel and Ethan Coen, who understand Sam's work very well. In Rebecca Mead's *New Yorker* article on Sam, Joel said, "Each successive *Evil Dead* becomes purer and purer, more like esoteric art films. Getting closer and closer to, like, Tarkovsky." Ethan added, "Sam was going to do an *Evil Dead* which just consisted of Bruce alone in a cabin. One actor, one set. Very arty. It would have been a really good movie; you know, the inner and the outer. Just Bruce, man. A contemplation of Bruce... Sam, you know, he's misunderstood. Even by himself."

They understood each other well enough that the Coens and Sam wrote the script for a movie first called *Relentless*, then *The XYZ Murders*, and finally *Crimewave*. Rob Tapert says that Sam "wanted to go for more entertainment for everyone, with action and suspense and this and that, and it had moments of brilliance, though it's not a good movie overall."

When they took *The Evil Dead* to the Festival Internacional de Cinema Fantastic de Sitges in Spain, they met Edward Pressman, a very active producer of medium-budget movies, with occasional expensive ones thrown in (*Conan the Barbarian*, for example) and a predilection for oddball projects (*Phantom of the Paradise* is one of his), through director Harley Cokliss (now Cokeliss). Raimi and Tapert impressed Pressman, and so he and Irvin Shapiro began pushing for the production of *Crimewave* in early 1983. Pressman arranged for financing through Avco Embassy, and became so involved in *Crimewave* that he actually played a supporting role in the film.

There were production problems, though. First, Embassy and Pressman didn't like the intended idea of Bruce Campbell playing two roles in the film, and insisted on casting Reed Birney in the lead, with Campbell relegated to the lesser (and unexplained) role of Renaldo. Rob Tapert considers this recasting the biggest problem with the film: "The guy who was cast couldn't do comedy, really, and Bruce can; it was written, in fact, for Bruce's style of comedy. He's handsome and charming at the same time that he's kind of goofy."

When the Renaissance team turned in their version, Avco Embassy weren't happy. One thing they didn't like was Joseph Lo Duca's score. "The person at Avco Embassy in charge of hiring the composer," Lo Duca says, "was worried that if the music didn't tell the audience it's a comedy, they won't think it's funny, and we bought a comedy, and it had better *be* a comedy. I actually only scored the last three reels of the movie." He does have one satisfaction, though — in one shot, the camera goes into Louise Lasser's mouth as she's screaming and out comes a trombone, and Lo Duca is the trombone player.

The story of *Crimewave* centres on Vic Ajax (Reed Birney, in the role written for Campbell), who is about to be executed for murder. As a carload of nuns roars across Detroit to save him, we see Vic's story in flashback. On a stormy night, he meets shy Nancy (Sheree J. Wilson). She is being pursued by Renaldo (Bruce Campbell), who has some vague connection with the security firm Vic works for. The firm is run by Trend (Pressman), who has hired two exterminators (Brion James and Paul Smith) to kill his partner. After a series of mix-ups and misunderstandings, there's a big chase across town — the exterminators have kidnapped Nancy, and Vic is in hot pursuit. Somehow, Vic ends up in jail, to be rescued by Nancy and the nuns with just seconds to spare.

Sam says, "Embassy Pictures pulled me aside when they saw the rough cut, and said, 'Sam Raimi, what you've given us is another *Evil Dead* movie, and we don't want that. What we want is a movie that will appeal to the mass audiences of America. So what we're gonna do is cut out everything that is wild and over the top, that general audiences won't want to see. And then we're going to release it as *Crimewave*.' I said, 'But that's what it is, it's a movie about being over the top, and if you cut that out, you'll end up with nothing, a hulk, a shell, neither fish nor fowl.' Nevertheless, they butchered it, and what's left is that movie called *Crimewave*, like a bastardised version of what I really wanted to do. It ate four years of my life. It was really a traumatic, turbulent experience, that I never want to go through again."

Probably the most significant aspect of the movie was the teaming of Raimi with the Coens — they went on to write *The Hudsucker Proxy* together, and the name 'Hudsucker' first turns up in *Crimewave*, then again in the Coens' weird and wonderful *Raising Arizona*. Sam and the Coens wrote the *Crimewave* prison scenes (which were shot long after the rest of principal photography, along with the

Below:
Bruce Campbell
as Renaldo the
Heel.

footage of the nuns careering across town), while they were already writing *The Hudsucker Proxy*. They also began work on *We Saps Three,* a comedy intended for Bruce Campbell, but never finished it. Additionally, Frances McDormand, who later starred in Raimi's *Darkman* and married Ethan Coen, has a small role here as a nun.

Crimewave doesn't really work, as Rob Tapert says, partly because it's simply misjudged in so many areas. Gags that probably convulsed Ethan, Joel and Sam while writing the script just don't have the right impact on screen. It has some bravura sequences (though Sam's camera is less mobile here than usual), with some spectacular stunts and imaginative scenes, particularly the one in which Paul Smith chases Louise Lasser through an infinity of pastel doorways, but basically it's a mistake.

Sam Raimi acknowledges this, too. "Sure, I blame myself. To oversimplify, I give it a D overall. I don't give it an F, because it has some moments in it. The picture I delivered was a C. That's the best way I can put it. I had a picture that was a whole letter-grade better. I'm not even saying the picture I gave them was good, but it had four times as many great moments. Now there's maybe one great moment and two good moments, but I had five great moments. The movie was never really good, but it would have been a hell of a lot better if Embassy had left it alone."

Rob Tapert feels it suffers from a problem common in the movie industry: "It doesn't know exactly what it wants to be. It wants to be entertainment, but is it an action movie? Is it a romantic comedy? It doesn't really fit into any genre, so you don't know how to respond. We always said we were going to make great entertainment, dancing and comedy and scares — but it fell between all those stools."

During the production of *Crimewave*, Shapiro began suggesting a sequel to *The Evil Dead*, since the original was doing great business overseas. "Ha," said Rob and Sam. "We're never going to do a sequel. We're doing *Crimewave*. It's going to be a huge hit." But Shapiro took out some ads announcing *Evil Dead II: Army of Darkness*.

At the time, Tapert dismissed the idea, but now he realises how shrewd Irvin Shapiro really was: "We were off doing something — who knows how that's going to turn out? — while he was setting up our next deal. So when it became clear that *Crimewave* was never going to come out, and Hollywood was never going to come beating at our door handing us all these projects, there was that ship to jump to. And having had Bruce tossed out of the movie, we wanted to go back and do a movie together. And we decided that while *The Evil Dead* was a physically incredibly ridiculous and hard experience, at least we were all kind of having fun doing it."

Opposite:
One of
Crimewave *'s*
bravura scenes
– exterminator
Crush (Paul
Smith) chases
Mrs Trend
(Louise Lasser)
through count-
less doors.

CHAPTER 8

BLOOD FLOOD

After *Crimewave*, the partners needed something to restore their confidence (and bankability), and they agreed with Shapiro's idea of making a sequel to *The Evil Dead*. Dino De Laurentiis had already approached Sam Raimi to direct a movie version of *Thinner*, one of the novels Stephen King wrote under his 'Richard Bachman' pseudonym, but by that time they had pretty much decided to do *Evil Dead II* on a big scale with a medieval setting, so Sam turned De Laurentiis down. "We were dealing with Avco Home Entertainment, André Blay and some other guys, trying to get *Evil Dead II* going, but they stalled us for something like four months," says Sam.

Around this time, they started interviews with potential crew members, one of whom went down to North Carolina to do some additional work on Stephen King's *Maximum Overdrive*. "For whatever reason," Bruce Campbell explains, "she ended up having dinner with King, who asked her what she'd been up to. She said she had been meeting with Sam Raimi up in Michigan, who was having a hard time getting *Evil Dead II* financed." King had a deal for several films with De Laurentiis, and phoned Dino to tell him that he should make *Evil Dead II*.

Horror and science fiction movie fans tend to regard Dino De Laurentiis as something of a controversial figure, who produced a disappointing version of *Flash Gordon* and a remake of *King Kong*. "Dino produced one of my favourite films of all time, *La Strada* by Federico Fellini," said Sam. "I just love that movie, and when I work with De Laurentiis, I get an incredible sense of history from him. I'm honoured to work with this guy. The positive point about Dino is that he's in control of his own destiny, unlike most people in Hollywood. If he says 'yes' it means 'yes' — you can skip the whole corporate substructure, you can skip all the people in marketing who don't want your picture to be made vs the people in distribution who do vs the people in the creative affairs department who think 'maybe.' Dino says 'yes,' your picture's going; if he says 'no,' it's not going. It saves the film-maker a lot of headaches. If he said no to a project — and he said no to a lot of my projects — I suffered for a night, and I woke up the next morning, thinking 'Okay, what else can I do?'

"But with the studios, sometimes, by their very nature, being a collective group who make decisions, you are caught in the middle many times, and you don't have a definitive decision for months. So as a film-maker, I really appreciate Dino's decisiveness, and that he's put himself in a position where he has the power to make decisions and carry them through instantaneously. And I really respect him for his ability to be so concise, and not to have to rely on a body of people to make decisions for him because he's afraid. Obviously, he's had a lot of pictures that aren't successful, but only because he's trusted in the film-makers. For all the right reasons, he's been unsuccessful. But for the most part, Dino is a man who believes in vision, and does everything he can to carry that vision out."

De Laurentiis was born in 1918, and educated at the Centro Sperimentale di Cinematografia in Rome. His first significant credit was as the producer of *L'Amore Canta* in 1941. During his years in Italy, he was producer or co-producer (often with Carlo Ponti or Fellini) of many international successes, but De Laurentiis had visions of being a producer of colossal, star-laden movies, like De Mille before him. However, large-scale productions like *War and Peace* and *Barabbas* didn't achieve the reputation of his smaller films, such as Godard's *Pierrot le Fou*, and audience-pleasing entertainments like Roger Vadim's *Barbarella*.

*Above:
Sam Raimi,
filming* Evil
Dead II.

He started a huge studio in Rome, immodestly named Dinocitta (to rival Cinecitta), but it collapsed under the weight of financial failures like *Waterloo*. De Laurentiis relocated to the United States where, for ten years, he produced or executive produced films of varying quality, ranging from *Serpico* and *Three Days of the Condor* to *Ragtime*. Again he began drifting toward gigantism, and *Hurricane* and *Flash Gordon* were flops, but that didn't stop De Laurentiis from building sound stages and an entire production facility in Wilmington, North Carolina, and elaborate offices in Beverly Hills. These housed his distribution company, De Laurentiis Entertainment Group (DEG). Though DEG had some successes, most of its films didn't do well, and it folded in 1988.

De Laurentiis was sceptical about financing a sequel to *The Evil Dead,* but agreed to talk about it. "We were smart," Tapert claims. "We got all the Italian grosses for *Evil*

Dead, because I knew it had been a huge hit in Italy, and we took them in with us when we saw Dino." Sam, Rob and Bruce met with Dino De Laurentiis in December 1985, during the time he was setting up DEG. Tapert outlines the climax of their meeting: "Dino said, 'You go down to North Carolina, look at my studio' — he clapped his hands twice — 'We do it.' Just like that. We wanted four million dollars, but they reduced it to $3.6 million, and we said, 'okay.'"

Tapert admits that, "Dino was always a little upset that we weren't in Wilmington, though. A week or two before we were going to shoot, he calls: 'Bob, I want you to come see me.' 'Okay, Dino, do you want Sam?' 'No, just you.' 'Oh. Okay.' Well, I got in the car and drove to the studio. He keeps me waiting for half an hour, finally walks in and says, 'So how long does it take you to get here?' That was his first question. I said, 'Three hours.' He says, 'I don't have three hours to come and see you. Nobody from my company is going to be able to come to see you, too far away. Why you do this?' 'Well,' I said, 'we really like this location best of all.' 'Okay,' he says, and leaves. He dismisses me, and I realise that all this was about him making me know exactly how long it took to get to Wilmington, and that he was never going to make that drive."

"Dino [can have] very bad taste," Tapert says, "but he's a mogul, and he's got *such* a passion for the industry, for the business. Really, his passion is for making money, but he's able to disguise it, that pure passion for money, behind everything else. Because with Dino, that's the only thing it's about: money."

"But Dino was great. We feel very fortunate to have been able to deal with Irvin Shapiro, and, for better or worse, with Dino De Laurentiis. They're great film characters from eras that are gone forever. Both, in their own ways, had very innovative and interesting approaches and ideas about film and film financing and all that. Both those guys taught us a lot of lessons."

With the amount De Laurentiis gave them, they had to scale the sequel way back; it wasn't going to have the intended medieval setting, because that was simply too expensive; the setting had to be the cabin again, or something equally cheap. But one thing was definitely different from *The Evil Dead*: the sequel was going to be at least partly a comedy. Although Rob Tapert likes horror movies, Bruce Campbell has never really been a fan, and, by his own admission, Sam Raimi is actively scared of them. The Super-8 movies had virtually all been comedies, and Sam and Bruce wanted to head in that direction, if for no other reason than to make a movie that was different from the first one.

So, they built the unusual half-comic, half-serious approach into the script from the earliest drafts. It isn't a spoof, though some have regarded it as one; it's not making fun of any conventions of the horror genre. It doesn't contain overt, verbal jokes, and all the characters are essentially straight, not clownish. Instead, it treats straight elements for laughs, which is something more novel. It's the comic aspect of the movie that makes it unique — that, plus Raimi's astonishing style.

Sam turned to his old friend Scott Spiegel to collaborate on the script for *Evil Dead II*. "Sam was concocting a story which was essentially *Army of Darkness*," Spiegel says, "The Deadites, the castle and the time travel idea, but the problem with it is that it was a high-budget sequel to a low-budget, somewhat successful movie, which did just well enough to warrant a sequel." But not an expensive one.

Although Sam Raimi argues against this viewpoint, *Evil Dead II* can be seen as something like a remake of the original rather than a sequel. The action begins earlier, different things happen, and the extra characters show up midway rather than being in the cabin from the beginning, but like *The Evil Dead*, the sequel is primarily Bruce Campbell in a cabin battling the forces of darkness.

At first, they planned to include all five characters in the recreated *The Evil Dead* scenes, but Sam decided to reduce the cast of that segment of the movie down to just Ash and Linda. "We're just trying to get a shorthand look at the thing — we want to

Below:

Sam's medieval storyline was relegated to one scene at the end of Evil Dead II.

Above:

Ted Raimi and Rob Tapert.

get the audience up to speed to start *Evil Dead II*," Sam said. He decided that they would actually "just show that Ash went up to the cabin with someone, they found the Book of the Dead, it possessed her, and he learned the only way to stop them is through the act of bodily dismemberment — and then we're off and running." He admits with a sigh that those fans who like to see exact continuity between sequels "are probably very upset with us."

It's true that the stories of the three films don't quite match: in *Evil Dead II*, only Ash and Linda come to the cabin; the other characters are ignored. At the end of *Evil Dead II*, Ash, trapped in the thirteenth century, blows away a winged Deadite and is cheered as a hero by men in armour. At the beginning of *Army of Darkness*, even though footage from the previous film is used, there are some differences. Yet another actress plays Linda; when Ash ends up in the past, there's no winged Deadite, and he's taken captive rather than hailed as a hero. This blurring of the idea of sequels in the second two films is strange and unusual, but it manages almost perversely to reflect Raimi's style as a director in a way that a faithful, letter-perfect sequel wouldn't have.

"We tried to get the rights to the footage from *Evil Dead* to use at the beginning of *Evil Dead II*," Sam explains. "Unfortunately, because the picture was sold by Irvin Shapiro to so many different countries, and different distributors in each country, we would have had to go to each one — there were probably around fifty — and gotten clearances to use it in their territory. It was a very weird situation — some of the distributors had even gone out of business. So we decided that since we couldn't use the footage, we'd just have to reshoot it, to tell the audience what happened, because most people haven't seen *The Evil Dead*."

Just like when they were in high school, Scott's sense of humour meshed with Sam's while writing the script for *Evil Dead II*. "He wanted to make it wackier, weirder," Scott explains, "because while Rob and Bruce were saying, 'it's got to take place at the cabin, keep them trapped there, that's all we ask,' Sam wanted at the same time to take it in a different direction." Spiegel himself wanted to have more sequences set outside, an idea at first rejected by the Renaissance partners. But they changed their minds — as long as there were still enough scenes inside the house.

At first, they began writing in the house in Silver Lake, Los Angeles where Sam lived with Joel and Ethan Coen, Frances McDormand, Kathy Bates and Holly Hunter, but there were too many distractions, so they finished the script elsewhere. Sam wanted Hunter to play Bobby Joe in the sequel, but Rob grins at this suggestion; he says that Hunter hated *The Evil Dead* when she saw it, and is sure she would have never taken the role. True enough, she appeared in the horror movie *The Burning* in 1981, but by 1987 had moved up to the much more respectable *Raising Arizona*, made by the Coens. Sam wanted to cast Holly because she had dazzled him with her talent. One evening in Los Angeles, he went with Hunter to the airport to pick up McDormand, and while waiting for her plane, Sam asked Holly to help him out. Another producer had offered Sam, "a terrible script; I said, 'Holly, you want to read this with me and see how it goes?' So she started reading it with me while we were waiting, and I began to think that this was the best script I'd ever read because it came to life. Later, when I got home and continued reading it by myself, all the magic had evaporated. It was all in her, and I realised what a great actress could do with a bad script."

Wherever they were writing it, Sam "wanted to be the guy at the typewriter," says Spiegel, "which is fine with me; he wanted to write in 'low angle' and to suggest lenses, which is the way he writes scripts — which was okay since he was going to be directing it. This freed me up to be the pacer and throw tons of ideas at him. He obviously came up with a ton of ideas, too, but he was also trying to formulate it into something."

The script took quite a while to write, because Sam was still working on *Crimewave*, and Scott was involved in a film he'd helped to produce — *Thou Shalt Not Kill... Except*, an idea Josh Becker originated while he was working on *The Evil Dead*. But they kept going. One thing Spiegel wanted to bring to *Evil Dead II* was logic, which he felt was notably lacking in some parts of *The Evil Dead*. In that movie, he grouses, "somebody can be under a trapdoor for forty minutes, and then arbitrarily decide, 'Oh, I can break out of here.' Well, why didn't you do that forty minutes ago?"

He also wanted to establish some kind of rules and regulations (*a la* those for vampires and werewolves) for possession by the evil Force, one reason that early in the film, Ash can become temporarily possessed. He's cured by "the cleansing rays of the sun," as Spiegel puts it, but when the sun goes down, if he lowers his guard, he's subject to possession again.

Raimi and Spiegel had a few ideas they ultimately discarded; for example, they gave some thought to including a few escaped convicts. "In a pre-credit sequence," says

Spiegel, "we would have seen the convicts escape and bury their loot right near the cabin, and then run away because the sheriff's on their tail. Then Bruce would arrive with his girlfriend and that whole thing happens, ending with him burying her. The convicts would come back, and dig up Linda's bloated, severed head instead of the loot." This didn't exactly seem funny to their collaborators, so they dropped the idea.

Spiegel was very fond of a spectacular sequence that was deemed too expensive. In person, though, he describes it so colourfully, with sound effects and gestures, that it's easy to envision. "Sam really thought it was cool, too," says the enthusiastic Spiegel. The first part of the story, he says, had to be an exact recap of the original film, including the scene where the wheel drops through a hole in the bridge. The beginning of the scene as Scott wanted it is in *Evil Dead II*, "with Bruce realising, 'Oh my God, I've been hit by the Force, the sun's going down, I've got to get out of here.' He starts driving across the bridge, which would be kind of a cheat, because in the first one the bridge was destroyed. He's going across the bridge cautiously. The sun is setting. It's getting dark... Then from the other side of the ravine comes the evil Force, NRRRRRRRHHHH, knocking down things. All of a sudden it's heading for the other end of the bridge, and

Below:

Sam and friend.

Bruce sees these trees being ripped by this invisible Force. Then it hits the bridge! The wooden slats of the bridge rip up! PTPTPTPTPTTPT!" Scott makes tight little waves with both hands, showing how the boards are torn up. "Bruce puts the car in reverse, but he gets stuck in the exact same hole we saw earlier. In the meantime the Force is barrelling down on him, and the bridge is going NNEEEEE, and the boards are going GHGHGHH! It's right on top of the car! He pulls the car out at the last moment and gets to the other side as the whole bridge collapses with the evil Force on it. I thought that would have been epic," he says, sinking back in his chair, "but I guess the budget wouldn't allow for that."

Also jettisoned was Spiegel's tentative suggestion that the movie be narrated by Ash. "'I tried with each passing moment to keep my sanity while this unstoppable evil...', you know," Spiegel describes, "but that would have been corny, too. By not doing the voice-over it's probably less annoying, and you have more of a suspicion that

Ash might not survive the night." The lack of narration, of course, does require Bruce Campbell to mutter and yelp to himself a lot, but it's all part of Ash's charm.

Spiegel loved the idea of including a quick shot during the Evil Ed sequence where Ash would be raised off the floor by a hand at his throat. You think it's Ed's hand until the camera pulls back to reveal it's Ash's own severed hand, up to more tricks. They shot this one, but it slowed down the action at that point, and couldn't be worked in. At one point, Sam suggested that the hand return in giant form, knocking on the front door, but this was too wacky an idea even for Spiegel.

The bizarre idea of the living, demented hand comes from a Super-8 short Scott Spiegel made — but it was Sam's idea to adapt it for *Evil Dead II*. In Scott's comedy short, *The Attack of the Helping Hand*, a woman battles with a rambunctious white glove with a happy face and a big red nose, a spoof of a series of commercials for Hamburger Helper airing on television when Spiegel made his film. Of course, crawling hands appeared in earlier movies, including *Dr. Terror's House of Horrors*, Oliver Stone's *The Hand*, *The Addams Family* and, most famously, *The Beast With Five Fingers*. In Stanley Kubrick's *Dr Strangelove; Or, How I Learned to Stop Worrying and Love the Bomb*, the hand of Peter Sellers (as Strangelove) occasionally tries to throttle him.

Sam continued to try and find ways of using that hand. On the set, he wanted it to fly after one of the characters — Greg Nicotero says someone suggested adding a little Superman cape to the hand — but when Rob Tapert saw the scene on the video monitors, he immediately vetoed the idea.

Scott Spiegel points out that he didn't complain about the ideas Sam proposed, "because when you have ideas and you're collaborating, you can't always articulate them fully, and you hope that the other person might understand what you're saying and run with the ball. Sometimes it happens, and sometimes it doesn't, but that's the chance you take in collaboration." (Spiegel is *not* fond of the odd-coloured blood, if that's what it is, that shoots out of the wall and from under the trapdoor, but, as he says, he was a co-writer, not the director.)

Before they decided that Knowby's daughter would have a boyfriend, she was going to head for the cabin alone, on a train. The spirit of her father, which does turn up in the finished film, was going to manifest itself here, but when she acquired Ed, plans were changed. Scott came up with an idea for a different ending to the film, one that hearkens back to the silent *The Cabinet of Dr Caligari* — at the end, we would learn that Ash was really insane all along, and that all of the supernatural stuff was in his imagination.

The sequence in which the room comes to life and laughs at, then with, the near-demented Ash does indeed look like the ravings of a madman. It grew out of a

silly gag Scott would play with a gooseneck lamp while he and Sam were writing the script. The lamp, which had already been in *Thou Shalt Not Kill... Except*, wound up in the finished film. (And the clock from the original film returns, having also done a guest spot in *Thou Shalt Not Kill...*) "I learned," Scott says about the lamp, "do not joke around with Sam or it's going to end up in the movie."

Even though Scott Spiegel was busy playing a role in *The Dead Next Door*, he managed to visit the set of *Evil Dead II* frequently, and he's one of the knights in armour at the end of the film (so is Josh Becker). *Evil Dead II*, he says, "was the smoothest-running shoot I think I've ever been on. And everybody was so nice. It was like this little family unit making a film, everybody was so together and so into it."

The finished film is very close to the script as originally written, although the script itself is less overtly comic. There was an opening scene in the thirteenth century, with the ground breaking open much as it does in *The Evil Dead*, freeing the evil Force, but that was dropped for pacing, and the scene with Professor Knowby and his colleagues finding the Book of the Dead moved later in the finished film. Raimi wrote the opening scenes of Ash and Linda alone in the cabin on location, again primarily because of time.

Spiegel is very grateful for the opportunity *Evil Dead II* afforded him. The movie, he says, "helped me very much. Sam was coming to prominence in Hollywood, and since I was looking for an agent, that film really helped out." He's also pleased that

Raimi is well aware of the influence that Spiegel had on his career, since Scott turned Sam on to horror movies in the first place.

De Laurentiis' office was in Wilmington, North Carolina, but Sam and the others felt a bit nervous about being that close to the powerful producer. He also wanted to charge them the cost of studio rental and equipment, when they knew they could get that stuff cheaper elsewhere. So they went out to a location Bruce scouted, Wadesboro, also in North Carolina, but those three hours from Wilmington. It's where Steven Spielberg made *The Color Purple*, and the big white farmhouse seen in that movie became the production office for *Evil Dead II*. Locals soon learned this, and would-be writers sent Rob Tapert several scripts that the writers assumed were sure-fire money-makers; perhaps the most notable was *Legend of the Pit Bull Dog*. Local entrepreneur Harry Huntley owned the property, and he thought at first that this new movie was going to be the financial windfall Spielberg's film had been. It wasn't, not by a long shot, but Huntley did alright, because, as Bruce explains, "Anything we needed to do from then on had to be through him." Huntley would find out what they needed, what they intended to pay, and then do it for that price, no matter what it might have cost him.

Making *Evil Dead II* wasn't anywhere near the bizarre marathon of madness that production on the first film had been; by now, the Renaissance team had two movies under their belts, and they knew how to do things. "We just went and huddled in Wadesboro," Rob explains, "took a little school [the J.R. Faison Junior High School] and turned it into a studio. It's a very small movie, really; it's all in a cabin." Rental on the school was only $500 a month.

Of course, there were certain *costs* in getting a price that low. Bruce met with the school board, and by a miracle of coincidence, it turned out that most of the members of the board ran companies that were just perfect for doing some contracting for the *Evil Dead II* production team. There were some benefits to being in touch with the neighbourhood power structure, too. The production company couldn't afford to put up the cast and crew at hotels and motels, so a local woman rented them bank-foreclosed homes for the duration of the shoot.

The location was still rural, but less so than the Tennessee locale of the first movie. The *Evil Dead II* company was integrated into the life of the movie-wise community, it wasn't the dead of winter, and things simply went more smoothly and more professionally. However, it's also worth noting that everyone involved in both films talks about the making of the first one with more enthusiasm and nostalgia (however ironic) than they do about the second — or about any other movie they've made since. There were no drunken locals demanding roles, no stolen power tools, no brothels setting up in their quarters, no cast and crew defections. Like *Army of Darkness* after it, *Evil Dead II* was, in terms of how it was made, basically Just Another Movie. One of the ways it was a more ordinary production was that the press covered the film. Genre journalists were invited down to North Carolina and given the royal treatment by Rob Tapert and the rest of the *Evil Dead II* crew. *Fangoria* fielded two writers, Will Murray and David O'Malley. (O'Malley had ambitions of his own; he had already directed several films, beginning with the 1976 release *Mountain Man*, and eventually directed 1989's *Easy Wheels,* based on a screenplay by Sam and Ivan Raimi which O'Malley rewrote, and which was executive-produced by Bruce Campbell and Rob Tapert.)

Sam Raimi set new challenges for himself as a director with *Evil Dead II.* "When I was on location," he says, "I would try to come up with a different filmic approach to each sequence, so that it had a consistent look within the scene, but each appearance of the evil that was raised by the Book of the Dead would be new filmically, and hopefully fresh to the audience. I remember that's how my days were spent, just thinking about the approach, what would be an interesting visual attack on the scene. I still think it was some of the most rewarding time I've ever spent in my life. Nowadays, it's hard to just think about the visual look of the movie for days at a time, but I had the luxury of that in North Carolina because it took so long to build the set — we had a very small crew.

"It's hard to explain to others, 'Well, I'm going to be thinking how the movie looks for the next three days.' Now, I get phone calls, and people don't really take that idea seriously — they need your time for what they consider important things. On the next picture, I should set aside days just thinking about the visual look of the film. I don't even mean storyboards, or specific shots, just the approach. Why would I have a close-up here? Because everything that we're doing is supposed to be very claustrophobic in this scene, so I never want the camera to get back far. That's the type of conceptual thinking I would do, if I had the time."

As he says, on *Evil Dead II*, Raimi did have the time to think about individual sequences in detail. For example, at the climax, "there's a scene where the trees are attacking the house; I really wanted to show the violence and power of a tree as it hit the house — I wanted to make that clear visually. In other movies, I'd seen them shake the camera; I knew what that was like. I needed something different, I wanted it to be still more violent, and yet to have a residual effect (once the camera shaking stops, you're back to normal).

"So I decided to zoom the camera on each hit and do a very hard Dutch [a sudden, pronounced tilt of the camera angle to one side], so in the course of about twelve frames there might be a snap-zoom and a Dutch, and that would seem like a hit, if I had the right sound effect, as opposed to a shake. And it would create a feeling of violence on film without showing any blood or gore. It would leave their world unsettled, because they started on right angles in the frame, and now they're ending on a Dutch angle. On the next shot, I'll counter that, zoom in and Dutch to the left. I'll keep leaving them unsettled in new ways throughout this sequence. It'll be, I thought, a proper way to show the impact of the violence of the attack on the house. That's one example of a sequence that I tried to work all the way through in my head before drawing a shot of it."

Above:
Tom Sullivan,
working on the
new Book of
the Dead.

Sam explained a little of his strategy to the *Los Angeles Reader* (20 March 1987): "Instead of just building the suspense, peaking with the scare-point when the audience would jump (which we certainly did quite a bit), we would sometimes peak the suspense and then hit 'em with a gag. They're so edgy, they're either gonna scream or laugh. So we gave 'em a laugh once in a while, just to play with the dips and heights of the suspense — which was really our only goal: to give 'em a great ride... They'll have a great time with their dates."

Since the decline of the studio system, the most important person on a movie set is the director, with few exceptions. Not only are the visual and performing styles of a movie shaped and guided by the director, but the mood of a set stems from him, and how he (or she) deals with the cast and crew. There are two factors involved here: personality and professionalism. An obnoxious personality can be offset by sheer professionalism, but no matter how nice a guy the director is, if he looks like a babe in the woods, the cast and crew won't feel any respect for him. Sam Raimi is a nice guy, but he also comes to the set thoroughly prepared, with full storyboards and a clear idea of what he wants to achieve each day. And he's also flexible enough to change those ideas if necessary, and open enough to listen to good ideas from other people.

On the set of *The Quick and the Dead*, Sam explained more about his ideas of what a director really does: "The job of any director is to convey the ideas he has for the picture to all the cast and crew. That's really his only job. It is many times very simple, and many times very difficult. It's very exciting, though, it's a great job. The tough part is when other people have ideas, and they're right. That's when you really have to think, as you spend late-night hours [and] plan where the character's going to go, the shots, how you plan to present them — and stop what you're doing, and recognise the truth

of what *they're* saying. You really have to go for it; they won't give a good performance unless they believe it. The tough part is not [in] letting them do that, but figuring out how it impacts [on] everything else, both what comes before it, whether you've shot it or not, and the stuff that follows chronologically. This includes stuff that you have already shot and are locked into, and how you'll change the stuff yet to be shot. You have to think about all this."

The *auteur* theory is frequently wildly misinterpreted by many, often by directors themselves. The original idea wasn't that the director was the sole author of a film, but that the director was the principal shaping force. Sam feels that's true, "but it is definitely a collaborative art form. I've never seen anything as collaborative. A big movie takes eighty-five people, and everybody contributes — if they're doing their job properly. The director's job is really to be the conductor of the symphony orchestra, who knows he needs a violin not there, but later. The director has his sheet music, his plan; he has to stick to the basic sheet music and understand that his job is to make all the instruments work in harmony and to make something that is greater than the sum of the parts."

The reconstructed cabin (the exterior, at least) was just a short drive from *The Color Purple* farmhouse. In his article in *Fangoria* #62, Will Murray described arriving on the set: "In a nearby hollow stands the familiar cabin from *The Evil Dead*. Beside it is the scorched-earth graveyard where the Evil Dead themselves lie buried. Not seen in the first film are two *Wizard of Oz*-like trees, the Mean Tree and the Gnarly Tree, which stand guard in front of the cabin, woodsy faces subliminally visible in their bark." In the finished film, while these trees are seen, the faces are only rarely visible, and we never see the originally-planned smoke pouring from their mouths, although they do advance on the cabin. This idea came from Shakespeare, of all places; it's Sam's take on Birnam wood coming to Dunsinane, from *Macbeth*.

Murray quoted Sam Raimi on the subject of the cabin itself: "We've taken some artistic liberties with it... We've given a little *Dr Caligari* tilt to the windows and made the doors a little askew. Sometimes we'll be tilting the camera in accordance with the lines of the set, when our characters fall into angles and things start getting real hairy in the cabin, to throw the audience off more."

Some critics mistakenly thought the interior of the cabin in the first movie was far larger than it could really be. However, except for the basement, what you see actually is the interior of the cabin. In *Evil Dead II*, however, not only were the interior and exterior of the cabin two different sets, miles apart, but the interior is indeed much larger than the cabin could be, particularly in the sequence in which the Force POV from the woods pursues Ash back to the cabin, and he gallops along within the walls of the building. Cabins rarely have three-foot gaps between their interior and exterior walls...

David O'Malley visited the interior cabin set in Wadesboro for *Fangoria* on a sound stage in the gym of the disused J.R. Faison Junior High School: "A sprawling, rustic cabin fills the abandoned gym, weathered and authentically detailed [because it was made of wood from old buildings], perched on a solid form of two-by-tens. Beneath the cabin, an appropriately dank and ominous fruit cellar has been created. The cabin interior changed over the course of the film; as the horrors increased, so did the angles and dimensions of the cabin. At the end, the windows are no longer perfect rectangles... On this particular day... the fruit cellar contains a huge plastic blood pool. Above it, inside the cabin, the crew stands by patiently, trying to ignore the smothering heat. Sheets of transparent plastic are draped over cameras and props and people, giving the impression of an oddly grotesque hillbilly mausoleum."

The set was built on two levels to make filming easier; at one point, it was even planned that the camera would follow the action directly, in one take, from the main floor of the cabin down into the cellar, but this was never done. However, the two-level construction did make many of the effects much easier.

On the exterior location, Sam said, "We're going into a little more depth with this story... What really happened with the discovery of the Book of the Dead, how it got here and what its true origins are... We follow it through the ages as different civilisations find it and are destroyed by it. The spirits are awakened every century or so, until it comes to this small cabin where the Professor brought it so he could study it undisturbed." This rather grand idea of following the book through the centuries does appear in the movie, but it's only implied in dialogue.

Some of the ideas that Raimi outlined to Will Murray were in Raimi's mind, and never on screen at all, such as what the real intent of the Deadites is: "Their goal is not just to wreak chaos but to test the mettle of man, to find out whether he is strong or weak, if he is good or bad, so they will know if it is time to walk and rule the Earth.

So, they use Ash as that measuring stick of goodness. How far can they push him until he blows?" In the movie, of course, the goal of the Deadites seems to be to kill as many people as possible, as colourfully as they can.

Ash, though, remained the central figure. In *Fangoria* #65, Bruce offered some thoughts on the changing character of Ash: "Ash is no longer the whimpering moron he was in the first one. He progresses from being sort of 'with it' to being more of a movie hero, 'I'll save you now,' that sort of stuff. It's a whole new character. I tried to lose a little bit of weight and get a little gauntness back that I had when we made part one... Up until about halfway through, it's very difficult for me to watch [*The Evil Dead*] in a theatre... Audiences are really abusive because Ash is so dumb. You know, shouting, *'Cut her up, you stupid idiot!'* Ash is being a nice guy, but he's not functioning."

Of course, Campbell created Ash under Raimi's guidance. When an actor and director work together often — Robert De Niro with Martin Scorsese, for instance — they often develop a kind of shorthand method of communicating, and this is true of Bruce Campbell and Sam Raimi. "Sam would say, 'Bruce, do a Number Twenty-nine,' or whatever, and Bruce would fling himself against the wall," Rob Tapert explains. "They did a gazillion movies together, and have the routines down."

When they were filming the impressive, not to say alarming, sequence in which Bruce batters himself with dinnerware, Sam was on the set, calling out to him. "Okay, now bang your head on the floor real hard," Rob Tapert reports. "Take the plate, and smash it on your head, *now*, take another plate — *now!* Grab the knife, look at your hand..." It helps, of course, that Bruce trusts Sam. (Maybe he shouldn't — the prankster in Sam leads him to insist on being the one to whack Bruce in the face with a branch as he's driving away from the Force.)

Bruce Campbell said, "Rob and I might pull out our red pencils on anything we didn't like or didn't think worked. Sam would do a draft, and we'd submit our notes and try to be as specific and helpful as possible, rather than say, 'This scene stinks.'" Campbell had some scenes cut from the early script that featured his character: "There's a long section in this movie where I'm the only one there. Because of our last movie, we're really aware of bog factors. You want to really keep this going all the time. And if it means cutting down the part, even though from an actor's point of view it might be a really neat scene, you still have to forget that. Because if people are coughing or moving around in the audience, you *know* you're losing them." So Sam cut these Ash scenes.

Kassie Wesley (Bobby Joe), told *Fangoria* that: "Sam knows exactly what he wants and exactly how to get it... It's wonderful to work with someone so creative and helpful... Sam is real patient and protective. He makes you feel comfortable... Some directors, when you get emotional, don't know how to handle it or they can't deal with you in a gentle way. He's very good about that." Of the actors from *Evil Dead II*, the one who's been the most successful, other than Campbell, is Wesley, with guest-starring spots on prime-time television and roles in daytime soap operas. She played the good-hearted Chelsea Reardon on *Guiding Light* from 1986 to 1991, then, in 1993, became the scheming Blair Daimler Manning on *One Life to Live*. She married a co-star, becoming Kassie DePaiva, and has several websites devoted to her. You have to wonder how many of her soap opera fans know she swallowed a flying eyeball...

Danny Hicks, who played Jake (and who also appears in *Darkman*), said Sam was "Like a little kid, enjoying himself too much... He's so funny. He keeps everything light. I'm having a hell of a good time... Sam is wonderful with actors. He's one of those great directors. It's never wrong, but it can always be better. He gets good work out of you through encouragement rather than intimidation."

Vern Hyde, in charge of mechanical effects on *Evil Dead II*, was amazed by the variety of camera rigs required. "We've built some real strange things," he told *Fangoria*. "[Raimi] comes up with the weirdest contraptions. We've had the Sam-o-Cam, the Splash-o-Cam, Camel-head/Samel-head, Ram-o-Cam, Torso-Cam, and so far they've all worked."

Make-up maestro Howard Berger told Will Murray, "Sam Raimi kept adding more things that we weren't prepared for, but we still dealt with it. We were looking

Left:
Bruce Campbell
as action hero.

forward to getting home after six months. It was a hard film to make, like being in a war... Sam really gets into it. This was one of the first experiences I've had where the director knew *exactly* what he wanted, like with my test make-up on Bruce. Usually, they say, 'Make it scarier.' What does that mean?"

Mark Shostrom, the make-up supervisor on *Evil Dead II*, said that Sam, "Talks in percentages to tell you what he wants. He'll say, 'make this element twenty per cent less and punch up this other element fifty per cent.' He's so enthusiastic sometimes that you have to be careful about suggesting an idea to him. If you suggest an idea as a joke, he can take it seriously — which has happened a couple of times."

Because of the problems *The Evil Dead* faced through being released unrated, everyone connected with *Evil Dead II* was concerned that however gory it might be, it had to get an R-rating. (This is one reason there's even more emphasis on bizarrely-coloured bodily fluids in the second film than there was in the first. The stuff doesn't look as gruesome when it's not red.)

Below:

The Ram-o-Cam advances on Denise Bixler as Linda.

Bruce Campbell said, "You don't see as much spouting from its origin, but it's there, like when the walls of the cabin bleed. The bile and all that stuff is there, although you don't see it oozing from people. There are many reaction shots when you splatter it. You see someone get sliced and you cut away real quick. One of the main creatures spews all over Ash. The violence in *Evil Dead II* is treated as being very

unpleasant. The only people who are enjoying it are the monsters. The whole idea is that they're punishing these people for awakening them from an ancient slumber. They're groggy, like bears from hibernation. They like hurting people. And they're going to have fun while they're doing it."

At the time, Sam said, "We had to cut our blood flow from 500 gallons to five gallons. I'm positive we'll get an R-rating." As it happened, *Evil Dead II* was also released unrated, but more on that later.

Make-up and make-up effects cover a broad range, or at least they did when *Evil Dead II* was made: straight greasepaint make-up, appliance make-up, full body suits, articulate dummies, etc. All of these were used in the film. Tom Sullivan, returning for a second *Dead* outing, told Murray, "It's a much more accessible film. The first film just dwells on goop coming out of eyeballs and being pulled out of bellies; I find that stuff humorous myself. I don't think the intensity is going to be different. We've distilled various things out of the first film and amplified them, and that's going to overshadow the lack of blood and violent stuff. This is much more of a horror monster film than a horror splatter film. It's a worthy sequel. When the audience comes out of this film, like the first one, they're going to feel they got more than their money's worth. They're going to want a third *Evil Dead*."

Mark Shostrom sculpted several of the most striking make-ups, but there was a huge crew working with him. In fact, there were three crews; Shostrom was in charge of the main make-up team, which included make-up artists Robert Kurtzman and Howard Berger, sculptors Mike Trcic, Shannon Shea and Aaron Sims, and assistants Greg Nicotero and Bryant Tausek. Tony Gardner (now running his own company, Alterian Studios), was in charge of the foam used extensively to create appliances and suits, and Dave Kindlon managed the mechanical effects used in the make-up. The experience was so gratifying to three of those involved, Robert Kurtzman, Greg Nicotero and Howard Berger, that they formed their own company, KNB EFX Group, one of the busiest and best make-up effects companies in the business.

The genesis of their company was the main thing Nicotero got out of *Evil Dead II*, he says: "It was the first chance Howard, Bob and I had to work together, and gave us a little taste of what the three of us were capable of. Mark Shostrom was the person who gave us that opportunity; he was the boss, a great person to work for. Half the reason we had as much fun as we did was because of Mark Shostrom. He's an incredibly funny person."

Nicotero told Murray, "Preproduction of *Evil Dead II* was a blast. We had the best fun because we had ten weeks of preproduction. By the time we left for North Carolina, we had everything done... Each crew person was in charge of a certain character, just so each character's style would remain consistent throughout the entire film.

Right:
Deadite Ed,
played by
Richard
Domeier, a
long-time
QVC host.

Mike Trcic, Shannon Shea, Howard Berger and Mark Shostrom each handled a character. It was my job to co-ordinate everything and make sure things ran smoothly."

Shostrom said, "Sam and I sat down and discussed each character's possession, and the thing Sam came up with was that whenever a character is possessed, the evil Force can do anything it wants. So we took a little artistic liberty in designing a different look for each character. We had four or five major characters that get possessed, and different things happen to them. They get weird, get their heads chopped, their hands cut off. They have to keep going through changes, so we have to keep changing the looks as we go along."

The initial Deadite Ash make-up included thick eyebrows, with very different extensions of his nose and chin. (Nicotero says this was called the 'Sid Caesar' make-up.) Dead Ed has several rows of teeth and a distorted face. This was an especially good make-up, sculpted by Shannon Shea, both very dramatic, and thin enough that the actor's face didn't seem enlarged. Shostrom's lab also prepared a dummy of Dead Scotty, created before the flashback cast was reduced to just two.

Bruce had to wear soft scleral contact lenses for the first time in *Evil Dead II*. The lenses, white with little red veins, left Bruce essentially blind, but it was painful to have to keep re-inserting them, so often he kept them in between takes. "There was one instance," Nicotero remembers, "where he had to use the rest room, and we were out in the middle of the forest. There was no toilet nearby, so I took him over to a tree, and came and got him when he was done. The next day, one of the transportation guys tells me they'd found a rattlesnake in the woods, right over at the base of the same tree. And I had this horrible image of Bruce, completely blind, peeing on a rattlesnake."

Working on the film was a pleasure, Nicotero says, as he thought *The Evil Dead* was: "A cool movie that was so scary and really fun; it hits on a lot of levels." On the first day of production of *Evil Dead II*, shooting the first scene, of Henrietta in her rocking chair, he got a chill, realising, "Oh, man, we're really doing it. This is it." Like everyone else interviewed, he remembers the sequel as one of the easiest shoots he's ever been involved in, something no one could ever have said about the first movie.

Nicotero's first impression of Sam and Bruce was that they were very serious fellows, but he changed his mind once Bruce was into the trial make-up, and the two old friends started goofing around. Nicotero shot a lot of Beta footage in Shostrom's lab at this time, and the minute he got out the video camera, "They were performing; I didn't really know how to take them — they took so much delight in being in front of a camera; as soon as they had an audience, they were on."

Virtually every time Nicotero aimed his camera at Sam Raimi, the ham in Sam emerged like a genie from a bottle. "Hi there!" he would say genially, explaining how the miracle of special effects is about to bring this particular terrifying scene to life. Sam, clearly having a grand time, often hides from the camera, flat-out lies about what he's doing, or launches into elaborate but unrehearsed comedy dialogues with Bruce. It's a shame Nicotero wasn't able to finish this making-of documentary — it demonstrates clearly how much fun everyone had. The tape includes a spoof of the necklace scene from *The Evil Dead*, mock gun battles in the green-painted hallways of the school, a cute dog and running gags.

When he read the script of *Evil Dead II*, Nicotero initially thought it was going to be a straight horror film. "One of the most interesting things for me," he says, "was seeing the change of how I thought it was going to be, and watching Bruce's physical comedy and realising this wasn't a straight horror movie any more." At first, Nicotero was disappointed by the shift, but eventually he came around to liking the comedy.

During much of the movie, before each shot, someone — usually Campbell himself — spritzed Bruce in the face with water to make him look sufficiently sweaty. Also, fans beside the camera blew at the faces of the Evil Dead, causing their hair to swirl and move. In the film, the effect is eerie but almost subliminal.

Greg Nicotero filmed some of the most complicated effects, revealing that, for example, Ash's crawling hand was done many different ways. A robot-controlled hand scuttles by a live rat (called Señor Cojones) on its way to the hole in the wall, then for

Above:
Sam, filming
in the cabin's
fireplace.

some shots, they cut a slit in the floor with the side toward the camera slightly raised. Beneath the floor, one of Shostrom's crew — usually Nicotero — donned a prosthetic wrist stump, then ran their hand along the trench, followed by the camera. The raised area blended in with the floorboards in the background, and effectively hid the trench. When Ash puts the bucket over his five-fingered opponent, that's Nicotero's hand sticking up through the floorboards.

The hilarious, disgusting flying eyeball shot, so impressive on screen, was actually a very simple rig. The crew fastened a squared-off U-shaped rod to the camera, with the eyeball on one end. The camera whip-panned in a circular motion with the focus tight on the eyeball. The rod, painted flat black, was hidden by being out of focus and blending in naturally with the background.

Tom Sullivan returned to do several kinds of effects for *Evil Dead II* — primarily stop-motion animation. At the beginning of the film, over a shot of the vortex, various stop-motion creepy-crawlies scuttle or fly by; these were sculpted and animated by Sullivan, as well as the winged Deadite that appears at the end of the film (Doug Beswick animated the dead, dancing Linda, the other major stop-motion sequence in the movie). After *Evil Dead II*, Sullivan moved to the San Francisco Bay area, where he worked as a professional illustrator, largely for Chaosium, who produce role-playing games. He has also illustrated books, his favourite being *Petersen's Field Guide to Cthulhu Monsters*, depicting creatures from the stories of H.P. Lovecraft. He worked on *The Fly II* for director (and effects expert) Chris Walas, then returned to Chaosium, and has set up his own website, Dark Age Productions, selling items he has created.

Henrietta Knowby, the Professor's possessed wife, was one of the most elaborate, complicated effects creations for the movie. The make-up team poured lentils into the sculpted polyurethane and foam-rubber suit to give weight and mass to the body. The suit was worn by Ted Raimi, who suffered a lot in the heavy outfit; at one point in the film, about a cupful of sweat pours out of 'Henrietta's' ear. Each night, when he took off the suit, the make-up crew poured more sweat out of the 'boots'. Greg Nicotero cheerfully adds that because Ted's body had been thoroughly dusted with talcum powder, the stuff they poured out of the boots usually resembled spoiled cheese.

Below:
Ted Raimi,
modelling
Henrietta's
latex costume.

All this despite the fact that, to keep Ted as cool as possible, Henrietta's scenes were shot at night. "We had oxygen on the set for Ted," Bruce says. "We used to prop him up between shots. On top of putting the suit on, the make-up, and the white contact lenses, he had to be hoisted and spun several times. He was hanging in a harness that really grabs into your crotch and under your arms and is horribly uncomfortable and you can't breathe, but other than that, and the heat, it was an easy gig for him." The suit presented a lot of problems; the head was a fourteen-piece prosthetic, and the polyurethane foam suit was in thirty sections; after the six-hour application process, the only part of Ted left uncovered was his fingertips.

In other effects sequences, Henrietta transforms from her regular, Deadite head to what was called the 'Pee-wee head' (because of Large Marge's transformation in *Pee-wee's Big Adventure,* done via clay animation). Mike Trcic told Murray, "Raimi wanted a total on-screen transformation from one character to a totally different one... Given time and money, the only way I could see that being done was with

Above:
Henrietta is
hoisted into
position.

replacement heads. I sculpted a bust of Henrietta down to the middle of her chest, and the first two heads, but had to leave... Rick Catizone finished the stop-motion on it."

Mark Shostrom also described Henrietta's transformation: "The neck grows longer via stop-motion animation. We have our character in the suit rigged with a very long neck and a cable-controlled head with large teeth and Evil Dead eyes." When Ash blows away Henrietta's decapitated head, what sprays across the screen is a mixture of bananas, stewed tomatoes, rotten peaches, green Ultraslime and black methacyl, the filling for the gelatin heads.

Another spectacular sequence features Ash being propelled through the forest, way off the ground, by the Force POV. Screaming and hollering, Ash occasionally rotates like a propeller — which, essentially, he was. Campbell was strapped to a big metal X, mounted on a rig that allowed it to slowly rotate. The camera was under-cranked; that is, it shot fewer frames than normal per second, so that the action, when projected at twenty-four frames per second, is greatly speeded up. Bruce's boots were bolted to the crosspiece, and the arms of the X went into his oversized sleeves and pants legs. They drove him slowly down a three-quarter mile stretch of road chosen for its overhanging trees. It took about twenty minutes to do a complete take, and they did several.

When the trees attack the house, some of them are miniature hand and rod puppets created by Bob Dyke and manipulated by Gary Jones, but some are full-size rod-and-foam puppets. (Dyke and Jones were special effects experts living in Michigan.) One was the 'Baaaah Tree', thirteen feet long and operated by three people in the trunk. The huge head in the doorway at the climax of the movie was done full-size, but it never worked quite right, which is one reason why you rarely get a good look at it; Raimi used anamorphic lenses to distort the image, and in general cut around the huge, peeled-looking head.

There were also some elaborate effects scenes that had to be cut from the finished print. For example, after Ed's head is whacked in two, initially his scalp and eyeball crawled about the floor as Ash dismembered the rest of his body. But "it was too wacko of a shot" to be left in, Rob Tapert says. Sam says that "it was a very good effect, but the scene had already climaxed when his head was lopped; that was just an afterthought, an additional shot we didn't need to tell the story, and wasn't thrilling to the audience in terms of pacing."

Nicotero videotaped some shots of Ash's face reverting from Deadite to normal — thanks to air bladders under his 'skin', wounds closed up and the bony extrusions shrank. Berger and Nicotero puffed air into tubes running under the make-up to inflate the bladders. However, this effect wasn't used in the finished film. Another cut scene was an exterior. After flinging a body against a tree, Deadite Ash lurched through the forest, catching sight of a cute little chipmunk. With a roar, he grabbed the animal (a small prop) and bloodily bit it in two, then flung it away. On Nicotero's tape, the effect is much more comic than horrific, which is probably why it wasn't used.

One of the most astonishing, bravura aspects of *Evil Dead II* is Bruce Campbell's energetic (to say the least) performance. Though he's handsome in a film star way, he acts like a silent movie comedian caught up in a horrifying nightmare. His reactions are big, and his stunts awe-inspiring; if you don't blink, at the climax you can see him being swept *sideways* through the forest, actually dangling from a Peter Pan-type flying rig that moved on tracks. Bruce's stunts range from lying face down in a puddle of water longer than you'd think possible to grabbing himself by the scruff of the neck and flipping himself over onto his back. He goes through more violent suffering than anyone else in the history of horror movies — and he does it all at top speed, while doing his best to maintain a characterisation, too.

As Campbell told *Fangoria*, "You have to take a lot of abuse... I think it's great, I really do, because you never have to do all this stuff continuously. You just might have a hard day every so often, where you have to do five things over and over and over. To me, I'd much rather have that than sitting around waiting for one shot during the

Above:
Sam, Rob and
Bruce film Ash's
flight through
the woods.

course of a day. That's the stuff that drives me crazy. Any actor just wants to work. I'd almost rather be injured than be idle." He's certainly never idle in this film.

On *Evil Dead II*, Campbell did have a stunt double, but wanted to do his own as often as possible. As things turned out, "I did as much as Sam would let me. There weren't many times when the stunt co-ordinator/stunt-man would say, 'Oh, let the actor do it.' They'd say, 'Let me do the stunt.' And I was off in the corner, saying, 'I can do that.' So I got a few. I did do all my harness shots; I was more than happy to do them. I think audiences feel more for the character if they see the guy knocked around. I'd like to see Jack Nicholson knocked on his butt a couple of times."

Campbell's energy impressed Howard Berger, as he explained to Murray: "Bruce got really, really into it... He eats this stuff up. He bit through the denture for his possession make-up. He went 'Rarrrh!' and the denture broke in half, and those things don't break... When his hand got possessed, he really put it through hell. We shot for twelve hours. By the end of the night, it was completely destroyed, with pieces of latex hanging off."

Overall, the shooting went smoothly and professionally, but there was a problem. Eugene Schlugleit was hired as cinematographer, and brought his own crew and equipment (at a fair rental price) along with him. However, Bruce claims, Schlugleit's crew "were starting to hassle us about moving the camera so much, and moving the lights and set-ups, and became picky about when they wanted to move them and where. Finally, we told them that while we had no problem with their equipment and we'd continue to rent it, 'we just don't want *you*.' So over a weekend, we pretty much had the Night of the Long Knives, and got a whole new camera and electric crew." The replacement cinematographer was Peter Deming, who ended up being credited as 'Director of Photography'; with Schlugleit billed as 'Director of Night Exterior Photography'.

Sam admits he became angry enough somewhere around this time to get imperious, announcing to the crew that *he* was going to make a movie, and anyone who wanted to join him should follow him to the location. He drove off in a huff, and waited on the set for the *real* film-makers to show up. Only Bruce Campbell arrived, and Raimi was so irked that he fired him. Things were more or less back to normal the next day, though.

The shooting in North Carolina wrapped, and the company was dispersed. But there were problems with the finished version; some replacement scenes needed to be shot, and these were done back in Michigan. If you watch the film carefully, you can usually spot them, as the lighting on the sets is much bluer than in Wadesboro; details of make-up and costume vary, too, but the sets themselves are an excellent match.

Most of the Michigan footage appears in the early moments of the film, as Rob Tapert says. "The girl driving up in the car, and some weird things we needed in order to shorten the front set-up. Originally, we were going to have voice-over, just join him at the cabin, but then we realised we needed to set up the girl, and the bodies, and all that — the 'Recap of the Decap' in order to set up the body that will later attack him with the chainsaw. We never got that figured out quite right."

"We fixed some sequences up that weren't working," Tapert says. "We reshot the 'Blood Flood' where the room gets flooded with gore three times, maybe more, down in North Carolina. One time it didn't work, once it looked lame, and so we shot it a third time. It was a nightmare to do, because we had something like fifty fifty-five gallon drums full of coloured water in this school gymnasium. The different coloured blood was jet-pumped through this piping out into the room. We had a thousand gallons of coloured water on the floor, running down a sandbag trench. But finally, at the end of it, we still didn't have all the shots we needed."

In Michigan, they tried a new technique for really battering Bruce Campbell with the 'Blood Flood'. The camera was turned sideways, he lay on a hidden plank a few feet above the floor, and the bottom of a huge garbage bag full of phoney blood was ruptured right above his face. "He was blowing red and black snot for months," says an admiring Rob Tapert. "Bruce has suffered more for his art than most actors."

CHAPTER 9

BLOOD ON THE SCREEN II

When *Evil Dead II* was completed, it was obvious that, despite precautions and deletions, it would get an X certificate (just like *The Evil Dead*), and De Laurentiis was reluctant to release it rated that way through his DEG distribution company. Instead, the film was released by the Rosebud Releasing Corporation, which only released that movie. An attractive logo of a rose blooming in time-lapse photography (designed by Sam Raimi) was created and added to the film, with the fly sound effect used on *The Evil Dead* (most people presume it's a bee buzzing around the rose).

The business of the rating and Rosebud Releasing was curious enough that it prompted an article by Jack Matthews in the 13 March 1987 *The Los Angeles Times*. He noted that *Evil Dead II* had originally been scheduled for release by DEG, which had access to hundreds of cinemas nation-wide, but was instead released unrated by the new Rosebud Releasing Corporation. Small independent companies can't usually release movies in 340 cinemas across the country.

Matthews asked Alex De Benedetti, the executive producer of *Evil Dead II* and titular head of Rosebud, just what had happened. De Benedetti, said Matthews, told him that, "DEG sold the American rights to the film to him when DEG executives and Sam Raimi could not agree on cuts that would be necessary to get an R-rating. The movie was never submitted to the movie ratings board, but everyone involved in the making of the film and in the marketing of it agree that there was no question that it would have gotten an X in its current form."

De Benedetti told Matthews that Rosebud managed to place the film in so many cinemas because, "DEG's distribution people booked the theatres before the movie was sold to Rosebud, and the advertising material had already been prepared by DEG's marketing department." Matthews tried to find out if Rosebud was really just an arm of DEG, but was unsuccessful. It was. Other studios did the same thing with X-rated or unrated movies; there was nothing new or, for that matter, illegal about this practice. It was a way the big distributors had of more or less covering their corporate asses in case the movies drew a lot of complaints. But there's an additional *legal* reason for doing this, too. Distributors are signatories to the MPAA contract that prohibits them from releasing unrated movies; by forming a separate, even if temporary, corporation that is *not* a signatory, they're able to release unrated films.

The fact that the film didn't have a rating did present some problems for De Laurentiis later on, when the movie was part of a package of DEG films scheduled for showing on one of the pay-TV movie channels with which the mogul had a deal. Rob Tapert explains, "To make that sale, *Evil Dead II* had to get an R-rating. But when they finally cut it to fulfil that contract, they realised the result just wasn't worth releasing. The cut version did get an R, but the movie was undone, and no one ever did anything with that cut. What's weird is that *The Evil Dead* played uncut on The Sci-Fi Channel."

Sam Raimi has firm views on censorship, which *Evil Dead II* ran into, not just in America, but in several countries around the world: "I believe that it's more dangerous for citizens to let the government decide what they can or can't experience or see than it is to have a movie like *Evil Dead II* available for distribution in a particular country. I would rather live with whatever dangers a movie like *Evil Dead II* may stimulate than the dangers of a government that determines what is too much for me. I think I'm an adult and I can decide. I'm certainly against censorship in any form. I think you can make a movie that could present violence and terror in a way that the viewer would want to emulate the actions; that's certainly possible. But the whole nature of a horror movie, or certainly the kind of horror movie I make, is that the violence or the monsters or the spirits or the ghosts are frightening to the audience, and you laugh at them. It's not something that makes the audience want to go out and become monsters or attack demons. It's hard to relate to anyway, the fact that the government would ban a movie with ghosts and spirits and creatures of the woods, and flying time warps — it's frightening to me. It's frightening that the people of the country allowed this to happen. That's the real horror to me."

As David J. Schow, award-winning writer of horror short stories and screenplays, points out, "Peter Kurten, who hacked up all those people in Germany around the turn of the century, worked himself up into a frenzy by listening to the Catholic High Mass."

Below:

Rob, Bruce and Sam attend the Detroit première of Evil Dead II.

In any event, the film finally opened in American theatres in March of 1987. As he had with *The Evil Dead*, Bruce Campbell enjoyed checking out the audience reaction: "I was promoting the film in the South, in New Orleans. In the scene in which the possessed Henrietta's head is slammed in a trapdoor, her eye pops out and flies into a girl's mouth. At this screening, two guys got up, they screamed, they ran out of the theatre. I thought, 'Is it that scary?' But out in the lobby they were laughing so hard they were hitting each other on the back. It just goes to show you whatever you can say about horror — it doesn't get a lot of respect, it's like a rung above porno on the respect scale — there aren't many films that can do that, that can make people go nuts.

"At another screening, [there] was a family who couldn't decide whether to stay or go. So they stood at the exit door, and when a horrible scene would happen, they'd go, 'Aaaaah!' and run out to the lobby. You'd see the exit door open a little bit, and the dad pokes his head in the door and says 'It's okay now, it's all clear,' and the family would come in and sit in the back row, and then the next, 'Aaaah!' Someone else would get decapitated and they would just run out, but they were too fascinated, and kept coming back, which I thought was amazing. There was still something in the movie that kept them coming back, determined for more. I think it's a kick."

Though he enjoyed being an actor and a movie executive, in 1987, just before the film opened, Bruce Campbell had news for his partners. One day while he, Rob and Sam were driving somewhere together, he told them that he was withdrawing from Renaissance Pictures as a partner: "It kind of dawned on me that Sam was going to start getting other offers, and I could tell, based on the offers, that there wouldn't always be a part for ol' Bruce, and I didn't want to feel compelled to stuff myself into anything. I guess I always wanted to be invited, rather than assume anything. I felt it was best to sort of launch off, hoping we'd always work together, while Sam would be pretty much freed up to do whatever he wanted to do. Then I proceeded to starve, thank you very much. It was a launch into the great unknown, which proved to be just that. I figured I'd come out to California; I had a script I was finishing up, I'd get it written, and we'd be shooting by that summer. That was my great awakening to the land of California, where they don't give a shit whether you're in California or not." But Bruce did eventually begin landing jobs in other movies, slowly building a reputation as an actor on his own.

Scott Spiegel is proud of his involvement in the project, but added, "I'm surprised at how many people dig the movie. What's really cool from my point of view is how many more people may have seen it than [saw] *Evil Dead*, or who like it better than *Evil Dead*. And now the verdict's coming out that they pretty much like it more than *Army of Darkness*, too; it may be the popular favourite of the trio."

The reviews started coming in and, if anything, they were even more favourable than for *The Evil Dead*. For instance, Steve Swires in *The Hollywood Reporter* said, "The unwritten law that sequels must invariably be inferior to the originals that spawned them is once again broken with *Evil Dead II*. Superior in every way to the lively but tacky *The Evil Dead*, *Dead II* is guaranteed to gross out even the most jaded lovers of gratuitous gore... [Sam Raimi] exults in joyously demonstrating the mastery of his craft. Deftly combining shocks and yuks, he punctuates the more gruesome moments with an outlandish sense of humour straight out of the Three Stooges' brand of broad slapstick... Raimi seems poised on the verge of a major genre career."

John Powers, in the *L.A. Weekly*, said, "No movie this year has made me laugh half as much as Sam Raimi's whirligig sequel to his cult classic, *The Evil Dead*." Jimmy Summers, in *Boxoffice*, said, "*Evil Dead II* — a cheerfully demented horror spoof — comes off as an extremely funny movie."

Kevin Thomas, one of the strongest champions of the first film, liked the second one, too, as he said in his *Los Angeles Times* review: "[The film is] at times a kind of ballet of dismemberment... There are images of satanic grace that actually recall Bosch, thanks to the darkly mischievous power of Raimi's bizarre imagination... But just when things start getting too grisly, Raimi rushes in with a hilarious, send-up joke to remind us that all this blood and guts is meant in spooky Grand Guignol fun... As

Left:
Sam and Scott
Spiegel on the
Evil Dead II set.

a film-maker, Raimi is a dynamo who knows how to make a movie as cinematic as possible. [*Evil Dead II*] is a terrific trip, though admittedly not one that everybody would enjoy taking."

And not everyone did. The fact that the picture's funny stuff was funny on purpose almost eluded Deborah J. Kunk, whose review appeared in the *Los Angeles Herald-Examiner:* "Some of the gross-out stunts are amazing, occasionally even funny... [But overall] the result is a relentless, non-stop nightmare of primordial dread that boasts an elegant, albeit disgusting, single-mindedness."

The movie annoyed Kirk Honeycutt, then the film critic for the Los Angeles *Daily News.* He admitted that "Raimi has a distinctive flair for pirouetting camera movements and outrageous special effects. But story, character and acting fly out the window along with the eyeball. Nothing holds your interest other than the comical gore. Even then, Raimi's humour is fleeting: it springs out of a momentary absurdity or incongruous line. It is never organic to the picture." The sound of a man who just doesn't get it, and never will: "By mocking his characters' plight — the chief source of his laugh getting — [Raimi] undercuts the terror."

But though the favourable reviews far outnumbered the negative, the picture didn't do well at the box office in the US. Rob Tapert admitted, "*Evil Dead II* was not a success here in America. Theatrically it died; video-wise, it did *fairly* well. But *Evil Dead II* was a huge, huge, huge hit in Italy and Japan. Our pictures have never done that well for us here."

In 1993, *Spin* magazine did a list of the 'Top 100 Films of the SPIN Years' — that is, the 100 best movies released during the years of publication of the magazine, which began publication in 1985.

And the top, A-number one movie on their list? *Evil Dead II.* Their description: "Ah, the beauty of a disembodied eyeball springing loose from its socket and shooting into the open mouth of a surprised bystander. Sam Raimi has never been smarter, Bruce Campbell has never been stupider. Endlessly inventive and utterly idiotic, this moronic, malevolent movie is a triumph on every conceivable level." (The list and notes seem to be the work of Jonathan Bernstein.)

The next few films on their list included: *RoboCop, GoodFellas, Blue Velvet, Terminator 2: Judgment Day, Die Hard, Reservoir Dogs, Beetle Juice, Bullet in the Head, Aliens, Re-Animator* and *Near Dark.* Lower on the list you'll find movies with greater critical reputations, like *Unforgiven, JFK, The Crying Game, The Silence of the Lambs* and *Cape Fear* (1991), as well as other disreputable but worthy titles like *Bill and Ted's Bogus Journey, Gremlins 2, Hellraiser, Tango and Cash* and *Ferris Bueller's Day Off.*

De Laurentiis was happy with the film overall, and wanted Sam to do another movie for him. He again raised the possibility of having Raimi direct an adaptation of

Stephen King's novel *Thinner*, but Sam eventually backed out. "I couldn't figure out how to make the guy believably go through that process of emaciation," he admits. "It was so central to the story, and always on screen, and always the point of the thing, I thought it would be under too much scrutiny. I didn't want to take what I thought was a great book and make it into a less-than-great movie." Which is just what happened when *Thinner* was finally filmed in 1996 by director Tom Holland.

Sam had also been offered a script called *Star City*, a thriller about a small-town cop and his involvement with two policemen from Los Angeles who are looking for a trio of fleeing murderers. Turning that down, he confessed, "was the biggest mistake I ever made in my life," since the film was finally made by director Carl Franklin, and retitled *One False Move*, one of the highest-praised medium-budget movies of its time. "I thought it was a very cool picture," Sam says. "Carl Franklin did such a great job of it, and so did Bill Paxton [the lead actor]. I think that was one opportunity I blew." Of course, Raimi later worked with Paxton on *A Simple Plan*.

Below:

Pete Ferry as 'Raimi' in The Dead Next Door.

In the meantime, Sam generously invested money in J.R. Bookwalter's interesting straight-to-video horror movie *The Dead Next Door*, but chose not to take any credit on the finished film — although one of the central characters is named 'Raimi'. (The names of other prominent horror movie directors are also used for character names.) Scott Spiegel has an acting role in the movie, as a cop victim of a zombie attack, and Bruce Campbell supervised the post-production audio for the film.

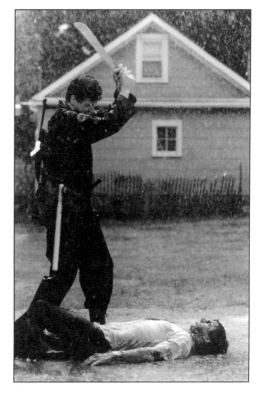

In 1988, he also directed his only rock video to date, 'Cold Metal', with and for Iggy Pop. The video is unexceptional, really, shot on a short schedule, and for the most part is a straight presentation of the song, though Sam's inventiveness turns up sporadically, and the vortex from *Evil Dead II* makes an appearance.

But something new was on the horizon for the Renaissance partners. Sam Raimi had sold a story idea to Universal, who also entered into a production deal with Sam and Rob. The result was Raimi's most successful movie to that date: *Darkman*.

CHAPTER 10

DARK BLOOD

The Renaissance team, now primarily made up of Sam Raimi and Rob Tapert with a small, permanent staff (including some people, such as Sue Binder, they knew back in Michigan), had completed another *Evil Dead* movie, and sought to head on into new territory. Sam had come up with the idea of a man who can change his face; he pitched the idea to Universal, and Renaissance entered into a production deal with them. The Renaissance partners cheerfully acknowledged the similarities between the plot of their proposed new movie, *Darkman*, and films of the past. Sam Raimi said, "It has a lot of elements of a lot of pictures and stories that have gone before, that's for sure. *The Phantom of the Opera, The Elephant Man, Batman, The Shadow.* And standard American revenge pictures, too. The movie came from the idea of a man who can change his face to become other people. It was originally a short story I wrote; it segued into a longer story, then a forty-page treatment, and then it became the story of a man who had lost his face and had to take on other faces, a man who battled criminals using this power. And then, because he lost his face, the idea of what would happen if he'd had a relationship before became important. It became a more tragic story, similar to *The Hunchback of Notre Dame.*" Others have pointed out similarities to the 1930's movies *Doctor X* and *The Walking Dead* in the film, which Sam wrote with his older brother Ivan.

"As he became a crimefighter, it became more like *Batman*," Sam went on. "A non-superpowered man who, here, is a hideous thing who fights crime. As he became that hideous thing, it became more like *The Phantom of the Opera,* the creature who wants the girl but who was too much of a beast to have her. While it's similar to many other stories, I think it's unique."

Rob Tapert points out that the project was "developed by the studio," which meant the hardest time for him and Sam was "that period between turning in the scripts and trying to get the green light. The whole nonsense that goes into trying to get a movie made. Once they said 'make this movie,' that was a joyride, that's what you live for, that period of time when you're actually doing something creative."

Sam Raimi wanted to work with Frances McDormand, who took the starring female role in *Darkman*, but they almost cast Julia Roberts in the part just prior to the release of *Pretty Woman*, the movie that made her a megastar. They also tested Bridget Fonda, Sam says, "but she was just a little too young for Liam. She gave a great audition; I was crying and everything, but she looked a little too young." Fonda did say she liked Raimi's movies, though — she was happy to play the cameo role of Linda at the beginning of *Army of Darkness*, and later still was the co-star of Sam's *A Simple Plan*.

The major difference between *Darkman* and the earlier Renaissance films, in terms of production, was the increased budget — around $16 million this time. This meant a longer schedule and more effects. As Rob said, "This picture has an incredible amount of miniatures and effects, a tremendous amount. A lot of things we were doing weren't safe to do full size — blowing guys through a roof, blowing up factories, helicopters that come crashing down into moving traffic."

During post-production on *Darkman*, Sam talked about the kind of director he is: "I don't shout. I see the script in a particular way, and I envision the movie from the script, and it's really just a matter of talking to people. 'No, no, he doesn't exit at *that* point, he exits at *this* point. The wall's gotta be blue, not green. The explosion takes place here, and it's a much smaller explosion, and it's all sparks, no fire, because of the electrical quality involved.' It's really just a question of explaining to people on the set what it is that has to take place, of losing as little as possible of the vision you have of the picture. It's a question of recreating in three dimensions what you have envisioned the movie to be. To me, it's really a communications process. I try to explain to the whole crew and cast before we start what the movie is. On a moment-to-moment basis, it's creating those beats in the movie that have to take place in order to tell the story, as I see it."

It's hard to believe from watching the movie itself, full as it is of bravura camera effects and movements, but with *Darkman*, Sam was really trying to reign himself in. As he said at the time, "The style is very different in this picture. My main goal is to create real characters in something of a fantastic situation. I'm trying to keep the camera

Below:
Liam Neeson as
Darkman.

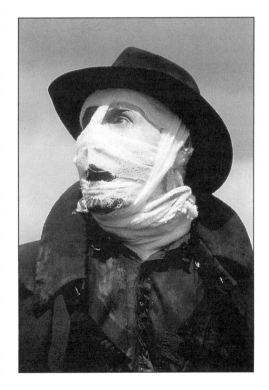

movement to a more realistic level, as opposed to a wild level, where I take on the point of view of spirits, or unnatural, or supernatural things. I'm trying to make this take place in the real world."

The result was his most widely accepted movie so far, which pleased Raimi despite the problems inherent in working with a major studio. As he said, "I've never been able to make a hit picture, but that's never been my goal. It has always been to make the best movie possible, to entertain the audience. I thought they were synonymous — and maybe they are."

Below:

Julie Hastings (Frances Mc-Dormand) and Peyton Westlake (Neeson).

The plot revolves around scientist Peyton Westlake (Liam Neeson), who is researching a substitute for human skin, for burns victims and the like. He's very close, but his synthetic flesh dissolves smokily after ninety-nine minutes. The evil Durant (Larry Drake) and his henchmen take Peyton by surprise, killing his assistant and setting fire to the lab. It explodes just as his fiancée Julie arrives, and Peyton is left severely disfigured, prone to violent rages and no longer able to feel pain. He escapes

from hospital and resumes his experiments in an old factory, this time hoping to restore his own face.

Julie has an affair with millionaire property developer Strack (Colin Friels), whom she later learns is Durant's boss. Using his ability to replicate faces, Peyton sets out to destroy Durant. Strack, meanwhile, orders Durant to kill Julie and Peyton. After an astonishing, innovative helicopter scene, with Peyton — Darkman — dangling from a cable beneath a chopper zooming through downtown Los Angeles, he manages to kill Durant. The climactic battle between Darkman and his arch-enemy ends in Strack's death. Peyton accepts that he's changed too much to return to Julie now — adopting a new face (briefly played by Bruce Campbell), he disappears into the city.

Darkman's combination of straight super-hero adventures, horror and comedy, presented in Raimi's blazing, imaginative style impressed most audiences, but turned some off. He was dealing with dark material in a light way with the theme of a man who loses his face, his identity and, in a sense, his soul. Raimi was at the top of his form to that date in *Darkman*, and actor Liam Neeson was more than capable of capturing the character. Despite the clumsiness of the story and the occasional odd mood shifts, *Darkman* is a dynamic, fascinating film that improves with each successive viewing.

Darkman succeeds thanks to the intensity of Raimi's style, the astonishing stunts and the outstanding performances of all four leads. Rob Tapert says Universal felt that *Darkman* was their best-reviewed film of the year, but admitted, "The experience on *Darkman* was very difficult for Sam and me; it isn't the picture we thought it should be, based on the footage we shot and all that. The studio got nervous about some kind of wild things in it, and made us take them out, which was unfortunate. We fought until the very last minute to get some of it back in, and a lot of it was what the audience really liked."

Nonetheless, they kept their offices at Universal, and continued to work with the studio on more projects, while still being able to make deals off the lot. And one of those deals was *Army of Darkness*. Though the film was a Universal release, it was essentially an outside production, made with Dino De Laurentiis, and had already moved into active pre-production before *Darkman* was a sure thing. "Hollywood's a funny place," says Rob Tapert, master of understatement. "After *Evil Dead II*, we had this tough time getting *Darkman* going. Sam had offers to do this and that, and Dino offered *Army of Darkness* — here's the money, here's the money. We actually had the script and the whole thing ready to go while Universal wouldn't give us the green light on *Darkman*. We finally drew the line in the sand, and told Universal we were going to make this other picture. That was what we needed to spark it, to get it to go."

CHAPTER 11

ANCIENT BLOOD

Even after the moderate success of _Darkman_, Universal didn't exactly flood the Renaissance offices with scripts. "I think they figured me as a weird film-maker," Sam sighs. Meanwhile, Dino De Laurentiis had given them the go-ahead for _Army of Darkness_ back when Universal was dragging its corporate heels getting _Darkman_ going.

Rob Tapert explained that they returned to De Laurentiis, "because we made a deal with Dino a long time ago, and we had to honour it. Plus, Sam and I love them. We did _Evil Dead II_, and Dino left us alone. We delivered Dino an X-rated picture when we had to deliver an R; he said he liked it as it is. He released an X-rated [actually, unrated] movie and took a beating at the US box office. Dino's been very good to us on this picture, too. He says, 'That's all the money you have,' and you can go back and ask for more until you're blue in the face, and he won't give you any more, but he leaves us alone, he's supportive in every other way. And you don't have the studio interference on a day-to-day basis, making your crew jittery. Sam and I have enjoyed working for Dino very much."

Sam agreed. "This movie was a lot of fun to make," he said, "mainly because of the involvement with Rob and Bruce, and because we were allowed a very free hand creatively, like on the first two _Evil Deads_, so that made it a very good experience for us. That was due to Dino De Laurentiis, and the fact that he trusted our creative vision."

Army of Darkness had a lower budget than _Darkman_, but Tapert and Raimi viewed it as a trade-off — less money but more control. It was "a step back toward more independent film-making, away from the studio structure," Tapert says. "You don't have ten different execs with ten different opinions deciding what's wrong with your movie based on what they see in the dailies."

Because their script for _Evil Dead II_ had turned out so well, Sam invited Scott Spiegel to co-write _Army of Darkness_. However, Spiegel was involved in rewrites on _The Rookie_, the Clint Eastwood movie he co-wrote with Boaz Yakin, as well as with _The Nutty Nut_, a movie he wrote and intended to direct. (That project was later taken out of Spiegel's hands, and directed by Adam Rifkin under the title _The Nutt House_. Spiegel,

Left:
Bruce Campbell
as Ash.

Bruce Campbell, Ivan Raimi and Sam Raimi had all worked on the script, and they all used pseudonyms in the credits when it was released in 1992.)

Spiegel was flattered, but his other jobs were pulling him away. Also, "I felt I had already done one of those films," he explained. "It was kind of neat to be brought on board again, but I could do it only if we did it quickly, which I knew couldn't happen. I love working with Sam, though, and I'd like to do more of it." Not only was Spiegel involved in his own work, but Raimi was still finishing *Darkman*, and Renaissance

Pictures had other projects starting up as well.

Around this same time, Sam had collaborated with his brother Ivan on a script finally called *Easy Wheels*. "That was a story originally written by Ivan, which we scripted together," Sam says. "It was called *Women on Wheels*, a story of women motor- cyclists who steal babies and sell them for drugs. It was a horrible tale, but a comedy; the script we wrote needed a lot of work, so when David O'Malley, who directed the film, got the script, much of it changed — some for the better, some for the worse, but it was basically different. I didn't think it reflected any longer the work I had done on it," so he replaced his name on screen with his official pseudonym, Celia Abrams, his mother's maiden name. While not a Renaissance Pictures production, it was executive-produced by Rob Tapert, with Bruce Campbell, and Ted Raimi appears as a bartender.

Tapert says, "The original script was very interesting; it was riding a razor's edge, it never once winked at itself, but the whole time it was way out in left field. David O'Malley introduced that whole element of dumb comedy, singing in jail cells and all this other stuff, so the insane purity of vision I liked in the original script got fucked up. It was originally a much harder story, and was called *Women on Wheels*, but we weren't allowed to use that title. I liked parts of it. For lack of anything else, it's *Hercules vs the Amazon Women* set on bikes." The movie had scant distribution, even on video, though it has some virtues, particularly a good, if odd, lead performance by Paul Le Mat, playing, as Rob describes him, "this wandering guy with a steel plate in his head, and a vision he's seeking."

Collaborating with his brother on the script had gone well, so Sam brought Ivan in to co-write *Army of Darkness*. "Ivan has a good sense of humour," Sam says, "and he's got an interesting eye for characters that I really admire. He'd brought a lot of char- acter to the Darkman and the villains; mostly I think he brought a sense of humour to *Army of Darkness*, and I appreciate it very much." As with Scott Spiegel, when Sam col- laborates with Ivan, he does the typing. "Sam won't let me sit on a certain side of him," said Ivan, "but I won't reveal which side." They worked either at Sam's house in Los Angeles or in Ohio, where Ivan worked at the time.

"Sam and I have worked together since he put me in his films in unflattering roles in high school," Ivan said. "Put this dress on, you're going to get hit with a pie... I went the wayward route, to medical school. Sam encouraged Rob to drop out of col- lege and make films. I'm the one who went wrong. Why am I still working for a liv- ing?" Ivan liked the challenge of starting the third film with Ash trapped in the past; "I thought that was such a unique place to be, it wasn't right to bring him straight back. Sam and I have always been influenced by this concept that was in *Ghostbusters* — but I thought they didn't develop it — which was technology vs the supernatural.

I wanted to take it seriously, [and] I thought how cool, all those machines. We wanted
to make some movies idolising technology, saying it can defeat the supernatural. It
always seems to be the reverse, with evil galactic empires defeated by the spiritual side
of The Force, or a wizard or something like that. So the reverse is an interesting Devil's
advocate argument."

Above:
Bruce and Sam
Raimi on set
between takes.

The idea of hauling Ash back to medieval times went back as far as Irvin
Shapiro. As Bruce Campbell explains, "*Evil Dead II* was originally designed to go back
into the past to 1300, but we couldn't muster the money at the time, so we decided to
make an interim version, not knowing if the 1300 story would ever get made."
However, the worldwide grosses for *Evil Dead II* pleased Dino De Laurentiis, and he
approved the medieval setting. This script was mostly written in 1988, but *Darkman*
intervened, and De Laurentiis was willing to wait. So when they got the go-ahead, Sam
hauled out the 1988 draft, and he and Ivan worked on it for some time, bringing in
new ideas and scaling it to the budget that they had.

The initial budget of $8 million was clearly too small. As Campbell says, "It
became drastically real during the course of preproduction that there was no way in
hell we were going to make that script for $8 million, based on how Sam likes to make
movies: he likes a long time to shoot." De Laurentiis had a multi-picture deal with

Universal at the time, so *Army of Darkness* became one of the films in the deal, with De Laurentiis putting up half the money and Universal the other half. "We figured we needed $11 million," Campbell goes on, "but the finished budget was around thirteen; we needed another couple of million in there for enhancements and changes. Once they opened the movie back up and made cuts, there was more technical expense incurred, as well as paying us a back salary. We knew that in dealing with studios, a back-end deal usually means you'll never get your net profits, so we had an arrangement with Dino De Laurentiis where we would retain England as a territory, because we knew from the first two *Evil Dead* movies what it was worth." Raimi, Tapert and Campbell knew they could always sell rights to that territory back to Dino if they needed the money.

Ash and the Deadites aside, *Army of Darkness* has more differences to the first two *Evil Dead*s than it does similarities. As Sam claimed, "This picture is not so much a horror film as it is an adventure film — there's no gore in *Evil Dead 3*, I mean, *Army of Darkness*. The old policy was 'the gore the merrier,' but now we're trying to make it in a different vein. While there are still horrific effects, it's played more for comedy

Below:
Ash's customised
medieval
Oldsmobile.

and adventure than to elicit a horrific reaction from the audience. The effects are slanted toward skeleton animation, and the magic and terror created by the Book of the Dead, vs the effects slanted toward the dissection of the human form. It's more fantasy rather than horror oriented. We've told more of an old-fashioned kind of story with this film, vs the first two *Evil Dead*s, which are modernistic types of films, [with] minimalistic stories, all effects. This one actually does have a story and more expanded characters. I think in this picture Bruce Campbell's character, Ash, is more fully expanded upon than it was in the previous two *Evil Dead*s, which is not a tough thing."

Bruce Campbell added, "We all decided, 'Get him out of the cabin.' There were earlier drafts where part three still took place there, but we thought, 'Well, we all know that cabin, it's time to move on.' The three of us decided to keep it in 1300, [because] it's more interesting. I think when you get into sequels, you had better make sure that you are entertaining yourself as well as the audience, otherwise you get kind of in a rut. Hopefully we'll never get in a situation where you can cut any of the sequels together and it doesn't matter. This one is a chance to really get out and have it become a fun adventure story [rather] than a hardcore, in-your-face horror film. Rob and I generally read drafts and compile extensive notes, turn 'em in to Sam, and he acts as the editor. He says, 'That's a good idea, let's do this,' or, 'No, I think we need to do this.' We always defer to Sam, but he's pretty good about taking our notes."

As Bruce says, the changes in the story and the character of Ash, "go back to the point of us trying to stimulate ourselves as well. Do we just want to go from one slice-and-dice movie to the next, or do we want to get into other realms? Ash is definitely a loser in this one, though, I'll tell you. Actually, part of the beauty of the *Evil Dead* films is that everyone sitting in the audience is at least as smart as he is. If he did everything right, he never would have been in there in the first place. The first *Evil Dead* would have ended after about ten minutes. They'd get to this cabin and go, 'okay, it's time to go home now. It's getting scary, we're leaving. Let's go back and rent a video.'"

Although *The Evil Dead* did set up a romance for Ash, nothing paid off, and the romantic interludes in *Evil Dead II* are numbered in seconds of running time. In *Army of Darkness*, he gets to be a lover ("Gimme some sugar, baby") as well as a hero. (Sam shot a love scene before a fireplace, but cut it from the American version, although it did turn up in foreign releases of the movie and the extended video from Anchor Bay.) Campbell enjoyed the change: "It's actually a treat. Ash gets the chance at a little bit of tenderness. He doesn't handle that particularly well, either, but it's neat to keep it a mixed bag, so it's not just looking serious, it's not just looking afraid, it's not just screaming and yelling, you also get to have a semi-adult sort of conversation. But that's also handled in a stylised way. You won't see a scene with Ash and a woman that's straight from *thirtysomething*. It ain't going to happen."

In *Army of Darkness*, the plot not only provided Campbell with the opportunity for a little romance, but to play more than one role (technically speaking). First he rather inexplicably multiplies into numerous six-inch miniature Ashes, played by Bruce and some doubles. He actually manages to *act* tiny here, with giant leaps and exaggerated expressions. Sam keeps the camera high and at a distance, emphasising the miniature aspect of the rotten little Ashes. One dives into his mouth, and soon full-sized Ash splits into two. And, this being the kind of film it is, one is Good Ash and the other is Evil Ash, with a progressively ruined face, courtesy of Alterian Studios.

"I think they're both in a way comparable losers," Bruce says. Evil Ash might be a bit more competent in some areas, "but that doesn't necessarily make him a more qualified individual. So we've got some stuff [in which] he has some difficulties commanding his guys because he's frustrated — he's got a lot of confidence, so most of his men are fuelled by over-confidence." Unfortunately, most of Evil Ash's blunders didn't turn up in the final cut, although his lower jaw, held on by rope, does have the tendency to drop off from time to time.

"Regular Ash," Bruce continued, is "basically an idiot about seventy per cent of the time, but then when it comes to fighting, he knows what to do. Ash doesn't make many mistakes when it actually comes to battling the Evil Dead. He's a good quick-thinker and a bad slow-thinker. If he's got to sit and reason something, he's going to have trouble."

Bruce Campbell has taken direction from Sam Raimi more than anyone else ever has, or is likely to. "Over the years I've actually seen him become a little more open to input," he explained. "He doesn't feel threatened, he's comfortable with it. He knows lenses, he knows technique. I've seen him become much more confident behind the camera. He always was, in a weird way, which is great, but now he's able to turn to actors, and they're not as much chess pieces as they were."

On the other hand, as Sam himself admitted, at this stage of his career he wasn't yet entirely comfortable directing actors, and Bruce noticed it: "You get actors who come in and they're used to preparing a certain way that Sam doesn't know. He'll keep the camera rolling and he'll say, 'Go right back to one,' and I think it threw some of the other actors." That means to return to the positions you were in at the beginning of the take, and it applies to both actors and crew. Sam was unusual in keeping the camera running when going back to one.

The picture came together smoothly enough, within the budget's restrictions. South African actress Embeth Davidtz, making her first American film, had a satisfactorily medieval look — Ivan Raimi said you might find her on the cover of *Modern Jousting*. Dino De Laurentiis objected to her at first, but was satisfied with her performance in dailies. (So was Steven Spielberg, who later cast her as Amon Goeth's maid in *Schindler's List*.) Shooting began in mid-1991, and continued for around 100 days.

There is much more exterior work in *Army of Darkness* than in either of the previous movies, with a huge castle set (or most of it, anyway) built on a hill near Acton, California, on the edge of the Mojave Desert. The Introvision special effects process, heavily used in *Army of Darkness*, was used to create the rest of the castle. Acton is about fifty miles from Los Angeles, a very isolated location; the castle set was way up on the side of one of those barren-looking but beautiful California hills. Nearby is Soledad Canyon, where Spielberg directed *Duel* years ago. Down in the valley below the castle location is Shamballa, the wild animal ranch run by Tippi Hedren and her husband as a retirement home for lions and tigers, whose roars spooked horses imported for the big charge of the Deadites at the climax of *Army of Darkness*.

Although most of the exterior filming for *Army of Darkness* took place in and around the castle set near Acton, other sites were used too. Vasquez Rocks, a very popular filming location between Palmdale and Los Angeles, became the path to the cemetery and the open woods through which Ash is chased by the Force POV. Bronson Caverns, in Griffith Park, Los Angeles, were also used for scenes eventually cut from the American release print of the movie.

Vasquez Rocks and Bronson Caverns are quite possibly the most heavily-used locations anywhere in the world — hundreds, perhaps thousands, of movies and episodes of TV shows have been filmed there. And both are open to the public, since they're on park lands. Vasquez Rocks has become quite a tourist destination, and clearly-marked signs will lead you to these highly recognisable slanting rocks, which served as the backdrop to countless Westerns and science fiction films.

Bronson Caverns are in a part of Griffith Park that most people overlook, down a dirt road on the east side of Bronson Canyon. They were part of a quarry at the beginning of the twentieth century, and have been used for movies ever since. No film is too big or too small to set up at the Caverns — the climax of *The Searchers* were shot there, for instance, and virtually all of Roger Corman's *Teenage Caveman*.

The author of this book visited the Acton set for *Fangoria* one afternoon and evening, and much of what follows is based on first-hand observations. At the castle, a massive portcullis hung above the entrance, and the drawbridge was lowered across the dry moat. As Raimi prepared to shoot the big battle, shadowy figures wandered about in the growing dusk, mostly extras garbed to play Deadites or defenders of the

castle. There were several degrees of Deadite-ness — those who stayed in the far distance simply wore tights with skeletons painted on them; those who were closer to the camera had more elaborate outfits of black, form-fitting garments with fake bones fastened to them, and detailed masks. Even closer to the camera were stuntmen adept with swords wearing suits to make them look like rotting corpses. The Deadites closest to the camera were played by articulated skeleton puppets, operated from below the frame line by operators from KNB EFX.

The Deadite Captain was played by Bill Moseley, who was very impressive as 'Choptop' in *The Texas Chainsaw Massacre 2*. His role, fairly large in the rough cut of *Army of Darkness*, shrank to just a few lines in the final version, but he was glad to work on the picture anyway. "Four or five years ago," Moseley said, "I took my then-pregnant girlfriend to see *Evil Dead II*. I had never heard anything about it, I had never heard of *The Evil Dead* or Sam Raimi or Bruce Campbell, and I went to see it during its very brief run at Mann's Chinese Theater on Hollywood Boulevard. I completely freaked out. Within the first ten minutes, I knew I wanted to work with Sam Raimi."

On the night of the charge of the Army of Darkness, everything slowly came together; Bruce's make-up was finished, Moseley and the other Deadites were in costume, and everyone gathered in the sloping field in front of the castle. Smoke pots were ignited, field 'artillery' (catapults, mostly) was in place, and the Deadite army, on foot and on horseback, were in position.

Sam stood in the middle of the field, an electric megaphone in his hand, as he exhorted his Army of the Dead on to really nasty stuff. He called them, "Evil, rotting hulks, creatures of the night, decaying monsters," and suggested that they should be "eyeing the castle, thinking about the plunder inside." When they'd been worked up to the proper fever pitch, the Deadite Captain and another skeletal horseman — so skeletal there was no actor, just a torso mounted on a saddle — galloped up to Evil Ash and the transformed Sheila to announce that the army is ready to charge. Moseley did his work well, but in take after take the skeletal torso never worked quite right. The army of skeletons regrouped and the whole elaborate take was done again. And again, on into the night.

After principal shooting, some of the skeletons were rendered in Ray Harryhausen-like stop-motion animation by Pete Kleinow. One of the most interesting stop-motion effects, however, was cut from the film for running time, despite the movie's relative shortness. When Evil Ash begins to emerge from Good Ash, they briefly have four arms and four legs, and a spidery puppet of this was built that scuttled through the forest on its back. This was another scene restored to various foreign releases, videos and DVDs.

Once they had completed the exteriors, the *Army of Darkness* company moved over to the Introvision stages in Hollywood, where Kleinow handled the stop-motion animation, and where the Introvision process added a lot to the film.

Introvision is one of those technologically-intensive processes that's very difficult to describe in words, but easy to understand when you see it demonstrated. What it amounted to was the ability to do matte work at the same time that you're shooting your actors. It involved front-screen projection of art or previously-photographed miniatures onto Scotchlite-coated screens that bounced back virtually all of the light they received. The images were projected through the camera lens, so the light reflected back at the lens itself. Standing on an Introvision set, you'd see actors and a few props, and large silver objects of no definite shape, but if you looked through the camera's viewfinder, you would see just what will be appear on the screen later on — the actors moving among the projected sets. The light wasn't bright enough to register on the actor's clothing, and their bodies blocked their shadows on the screen.

An early form of this process (not actually Introvision itself) was used in *2001: A Space Odyssey* back in 1968, which front-projected the African landscapes behind the actors in ape suits in the opening sequence. What Introvision added was the idea of placing smaller front-screen elements around the stage so the actors could move behind as well as in front of them.

As Bruce Campbell explained, "Usually when you're doing a matte shot or other optical, you have to wait a couple of weeks to make sure the matte works, and if it doesn't, you have to go back and reshoot. But with Introvision, you see your shot the next day at dailies. What you see through that lens while you're shooting — that's it. It was great for us, because we didn't have time to screw around with so many effects involved. [With] this movie it was almost like everything was an effect." Nowadays, of course, digital technology has largely superseded Introvision.

Introvision's Hollywood stages housed a miniature of the castle, elaborate not just in terms of fine detail, but in terms of the actual architecture. It had six towers, including a square one and another with a spiral staircase up the outside. There was also a separate miniature of the portcullis side of the castle.

Introvision was also behind the ruined twenty-first century city where Ash winds up in some versions of the film. "Sam clung to a fairly fatalistic version of the

Below:
Preparing the
Army of
Darkness.

script," says Rob Tapert. "At the end, Ash had slept a hundred years too long, waking up in a blasted, destroyed future." The movie's early scenes, set in the S-Mart supermarket where Ash works ("Shop smart, shop S-Mart!"), were also meant to be very different. "We originally had a much bigger scene at the beginning," says Rob, "with Charles Napier as Ash's mean boss, who was hollering at him all the time, but he got cut out completely." Bridget Fonda also had more screen time in the initial version. "We had a whole scene there talking about his banal life," Sam recalled. "How the boss was really mean to him, and how the stock boy was someone Bruce was mean to. But it took too long, and we want the kids to get to the goods, so there's now only a passing flash of him in his former element."

Elsewhere at Introvision was the pit where Ash battles both the back-flipping, highly limber Deadite and the big, grotesque Pit Hag. Spikes thrust out nastily from the walls, the floor was permanently flooded and the whole place had a suitably dank, dismal atmosphere. KNB EFX built the Pit Hag suit worn by Bill Bryan, who played the Stay-Puft Marsh-mallow Man in *Ghostbusters*.

They also built ten skeleton puppets, as Bob Kurtzman explained on the Acton castle set: "Eight of them are rod puppets with mech-anical hands which people control from underneath; two of them are the full upper-body, cable-controlled ones with radio-controlled heads. They're on dolly tracks." Some, heh heh, "Were cast from real skeletons. We took moulds off them and made fibreglass versions," Kurtzman said. "This project is a major group effort, and our guys on the show, when they weren't doing make-ups or sculptures, were putting armour together. All armour for the puppets was modified from vacuformed kit we got from the team who did the armour for the live actors." The Anchor Bay DVD of *Army of Darkness* includes a good, amusing documentary about KNB's work on the film.

While *Army of Darkness* had some of the routine difficulties every film faces, many of the problems stemmed from the kind of movie this was. The sheer number of effects was an obstacle that everyone had to overcome. "It's the most effects-heavy picture we've made," said Sam. "In general, I [had] less time [to spend] supervising each effect than if there were fewer effects, as in the past."

Another obstacle was shooting at night in the summer. "Most of the picture takes place at night," Sam pointed out, "and we were shooting at the equinox point, when the days were the longest and the nights were shortest. Our Director of Photography, Bill Pope, would light an area, and that could take an hour and a half to set up. So we'd only have about six hours left to shoot, and those six hours involved horses, make-up and other time-consuming elements."

Also, in those days they had no experience at all in dealing with animals (and the shoot used a total of forty-seven horses). "There are some big horse attacks in

Above:

The Pit Hag.

this picture," Sam added, "with explosions and a lot of animated effects all in the same frame. Horses don't care what the director wants; they're going to do what they want to do."

Overall, the biggest problem was one that almost all medium-budget movies face — money. As Tapert said, "It [originally] had about half the budget of *Darkman*. We had a lot of the same crew people working for a lot less money (but doing a better job, I think). And it took more time than we wanted."

Sam adds, "We didn't really have enough money to make the picture the way we wanted to, because it had a much bigger scope than any we've made. As it turned out, Rob, Bruce and I had to put a lot of our own money into the picture." They didn't have to deplete their bank accounts, but they did take less money in payment than the original contract said they would be paid — something like a million dollars less, among the three of them — and ploughed it back into the film. "That money was almost gone within a month of shooting," Campbell points out. "Just on paper, it was gone. When you get into the bowels of making a film, you don't always think rationally, you just think 'I gotta have it, I gotta have it.' We renegotiated some portion of a settlement, and that took some time."

The extra money was partly to cover the new ending and partly for a scene that the Renaissance team thought was crucial, but which De Laurentiis and Universal decided was superfluous. "It's the scene inside the castle where the old lady turns into a Deadite and goes crazy," Tapert explained. "The 'Yo, She-Bitch' scene. If you look carefully, you'll see the sets are so cheesy, they're ridiculous. It moves very fast, with good reason."

Greg Nicotero explained that, as originally storyboarded (like *Darkman, Army of Darkness* was storyboarded from beginning to end), the possessed woman was to push down some giant pillars that toppled into each other like dominoes, flattening one guy. "She gets partially crushed," Nicotero said, "then the head stretches open. Ash grabs a flaming log, shoves it down her throat — her mouth closes and then she spits the log out." The flying timber was supposed to knock off someone's head, before the She-Bitch was dismembered and her head thrown out of the ruins. The miniatures for the sequence were constructed before Universal vetoed this more elaborate version, which also involved several make-up effects.

Despite the restrictions, Sam Raimi enjoyed shooting the movie: "I find it a very exciting and fun experience to shoot a picture. The most entertaining thing was being able to play with soldiers on a big scale. Have fifteen horses come down through here! The catapults are launched, flinging flames through the air over here!"

Joseph Lo Duca, who'd scored both of the earlier *Evil Dead* movies, was brought back on board for *Army of Darkness*, although Danny Elfman, a hot movie composer who'd done fine work for Renaissance on *Darkman*, did compose the 'March of the Dead' theme. "I especially enjoyed working on *Army of Darkness* because we brought the benefit of our past experiences together," Lo Duca says. "We had quite a long spotting session — that's the official time when you sit down with the director and go over the movie scene by scene, discussing in broad strokes and short strokes where the music is going to be, and what it's supposed to do for the film at a given point. With the advent of synthesisers and my knowledge of working with them, I was able to present a lot of the cues in a mock-up form before I took them in front of an orchestra, and we could really hone in on specifics within a scene."

Lo Duca worked with Sam so often that they have developed a kind of formula, broken in one of the most memorable scenes in *Army of Darkness*. "In all of Sam's movies where I've worked with him, the formula had been 'the funnier the comedy, the more serious the music' — the music never commented on the comedy, and played against it. But the scene with the little Ashes was supposed to be this dark Warner Brothers cartoon right in the middle of the movie, and the way Sam spotted it with me was that there would be absolutely nothing wrong with taking a little diversion at this point and going with the comedy all the way." For once, reverting to a more standard approach to movie-making paid off for Raimi, as Lo Duca's score matches the extravagance of the sequence perfectly.

They delivered the film to Universal for release in summer 1992, when schools were out and the target audience, primarily teenagers, would be able to go back to a slam-bang action-fest like *Army of Darkness* again and again. Immediately, however, there was a problem with the rating. The MPAA's Classification and Ratings Authority (CARA) gave *Army of Darkness* an R, while Universal desperately wanted a PG-13. The Renaissance team plucked scenes here and there, trying to tone it down, but again it received an R. Universal even turned the film over to a non-Renaissance editor, who still wasn't able to get it trimmed to PG-13 status. The first two *Evil Dead*s were released without any rating at all, so it's possible that CARA was being more strict with the third than they might have been if it was a stand-alone original. "*Evil Dead* went out unrated," says Rob Tapert, "even though it was given an X. *Evil Dead II* went out unrated, flaunted in their face, even though they had given it an X. They were very aware about *Army of Darkness*. Having been to these appeals boards, it's a joke."

Universal finally bit the bullet and decided to release the film with an R-rating in, essentially, the cut that Renaissance had prepared, but many interesting scenes were sacrificed along the way, including the feature film acting début of the Happy Valley Kid. Bruce Campbell is, of course, the star of all three of the *Evil Dead* movies, and Sam Raimi has a line at the end of *Evil Dead II*, but apart from playing various Deadite rear-views, aeroplane attendants, hitchhikers and dismembered, twitching body parts, Rob Tapert hadn't really been seen on screen. So Sam gave him a small role in *Army of Darkness* — but don't look for him in it.

As Rob says, "The editing room is cruel." His scene was cut, but it is on the American extended video version. While filming it, Rob: "was in this whole medieval costume with a white contact in my eye, scars on my face, looking like an absolute idiot." A problem arose involving a complaint by a local woman about the picture, and Rob, outfit and all, had to sort it out. "What happened," he explains, "was that Sam wanted to shoot on the other side of some train tracks; the truck went down there, dropped off the camera, and did the shot. The truck was still sitting down there, with the camera and all that, when a kid came across the street and said, 'This is our property; get that stuff off there.' A crazy woman came out and said we had to pay her right now for shooting on her property — land which we assumed belonged to the railroad. I told the guys to drive the trucks out, so the woman put her head under the back tyre, and our location manager arrived just in time to stop the teamsters from rolling over her head. Sam needed the camera and that lens, but it was stuck by the tracks, so I went down there." Rob had to deal with the police and the annoyed woman, who eventually got the money that Rob still feels was simple extortion. "That was an amusing anecdote for a producer," he adds. "Funny how it's amusing to you *now*," says Sam.

As well as the love scene between Bruce Campbell and Embeth Davidtz; a variety of footage was cut, as Rob recalls: "A lot of Evil Ash and Evil Sheila stuff went. We lost probably a minute in that montage of building stuff. We lost them going to get King Henry to bring his men for the final battle, which he at first refuses to do. At the climax, there were two distinct attacks on the castle, with Greek fire [and] a lot of other things. It was much more elaborate." There was also considerably more by-play between Ash and his little clones. These scenes all had to go, and not just because of the rating, but to make the film shorter and punchier.

Then, they hit a snag that no one could have foreseen. In 1986, Dino De Laurentiis produced a film called *Manhunter*, an adaptation of Thomas Harris' novel *Red Dragon*. As is common practice, De Laurentiis retained certain rights to characters in the novel, and to future movies. This, of course, didn't stop Harris from writing something of a sequel to *Red Dragon* — the best-seller *The Silence of the Lambs*, which featured the same brilliant serial killer, Hannibal Lecter. Jonathan Demme's film *The Silence of the Lambs,* starring Anthony Hopkins and Jodie Foster (all of whom won Oscars), was released by Orion, with Dino leasing them his rights to the character of Hannibal Lecter.

When Harris began writing a *third* novel about Lecter, Universal quickly bought the movie rights. De Laurentiis was producing several films for distribution through Universal, and so the head of the studio, Tom Pollock, wanted him to release

Below:

Ash, a little the worse for wear.

the rights to Lecter to Universal. De Laurentiis refused, or so he claimed, while Pollock claimed there had been a handshake deal for the rights. Lawsuits followed, as reported in *Daily Variety* (18 May 1992): "The suit stems from a two-picture deal gone awry between Dino De Laurentiis and Universal. De Laurentiis claims that the studio is basically holding back the final leg of financing for... *Army of Darkness*, in an attempt to strong-arm him into giving Universal equal participation on any sequel to *Silence of the Lambs*."

Suddenly, *Army of Darkness* vanished from the studio's release schedule, while lawyers for De Laurentiis and Universal wrangled over the rights to Hannibal Lecter. There was nothing personal in all of this, nothing aimed at the Renaissance team, but still *Army of Darkness* sat on the shelf, even though De Laurentiis claimed they had been compelled to complete production early, declaring, "Universal has unilaterally required an arbitrary delivery date that it knows De Laurentiis cannot meet." (*The Entertainment Litigation Reporter*, 24 March 1992.)

"We finished it in the spring of '92," Bruce Campbell says, "and then it was on ice for six months while they battled it out and finally came to terms, and our film was done. We had to deliver it [early] because Universal was trying to force us to. Dino said we should finish the movie so we can say that we held up our end of the obligations — and we delivered. The scariest thing to me is when you make films for large companies, you realise that there is a level of business going on that is so far above the concerns of your movie that through various arbitrary decisions based on real estate or some legal deal or some financial thing that was started years ago, they're restructuring *your* movie. Or an executive gets washed out with his boys, and the incoming people don't want to deal with your movie because they feel like they're stuck with it, so you've lost all support — and that's more frightening than not having enough money." A far cry from making movies on the streets of suburban Detroit.

While Pollock and De Laurentiis struggled like giants far above Renaissance Pictures, Universal continued to fuss over the rating for *Army of Darkness* — as well as over the ending. "Universal didn't want that ending," Sam says, "with Bruce being royally screwed in time. So they demanded — and they had final cut — that a new ending be shot. We shot the new ending in two days just to kind of give them what they wanted. Actually, I kind of like the fact that there are two endings, that in one alternate universe Bruce is screwed, and in another universe he's some cheesy hero."

Campbell is just one of many who don't like the test screening method of arriving at a final cut of a movie. "When you get four or five or a dozen kids out of a huge audience complaining, they actually stop and listen to those kids. They start asking, 'What scenes didn't you like the most? Which ones did you like the best? Tell us.' It got to be very frustrating. We thought, this was our third [*Evil Dead*] film, and we

should be able to do this one just how we wanted, and it really wasn't so. We had more freedom in our $350,000 movie."

The unusual feature of these particular screenings was that the movie was virtually complete; running ninety-six minutes, with the effects and the music in place. The colour timing was completed and even the master negative had been cut. Ordinarily, test screening prints are incomplete. When Universal demanded that the movie be shorter, and have a different ending, "we had to go back in, open it up again, get into all the film elements, and drastically reduce it in length," Campbell sighs. "It went from our ninety-six minute version to eighty-one minutes in its present state. I think the cutting made some sort of sense overall. It was more drastic, though, than our cutting would have been — we'd have taken out maybe five or six minutes. After screening it in Europe at a couple of festivals in '92, I got a sense that the movie kind of beat up on the audience, and *then* this big battle started at the end. It was sensory overload. But we wouldn't have cut it so drastically, and we would have kept the original ending." As a matter of fact, the original, blasted-future ending remains on the film over-

Above:
Ash, complete with mechanical hand.

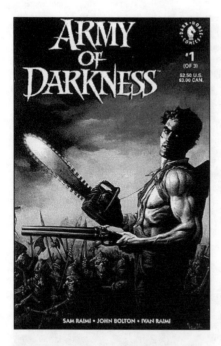

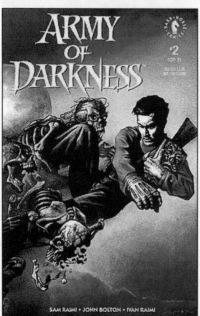

seas. And it's in the Dark Horse comic book version, which was scripted by Sam and Ivan Raimi.

The advertising campaign was, for those who had followed the series, surprising and amusing, with its central image of a triumphant Ash with a beautiful woman climbing his leg, his chainsaw at the ready, and a buffed-out body. Universal called Campbell in, "to take a couple of reference head shots," he recalls. "I had no idea what they were doing. I went into a studio, and they said, 'We need a kind of sly look on your face.' So I gave a whole series of stupid shots. Next thing you know, they show me a rough of this Frank Frazetta-like painting. 'We've got to approve it in a day,' they said, 'and if you don't approve it, we don't have an ad campaign.' So what were they telling me? Why did they submit it to me at all? It was frustrating because the lines of communication were not clearly drawn, and things got lost in the shuffle like crazy. They would bring us in and show us the thirty second [television] spots, and the ten second spots, but it's not like they would sit down with us and go through it frame by frame. Once you get into the studios, they adopt much more the attitude of, 'Thanks, kid. You did a nice movie. We'll take it from here.' This is not to take away completely from Universal, I don't want to paint that picture — they were fairly solicitous, but it's the system. *This* is the part of the company that makes the movies, *that* is the part of the company that promotes the movies. But this was the most removed we'd been from hands-on film-making. Dino deserves credit, though. He stayed involved to the very end, and he's the easiest executive we've ever had to deal with, because you go right to him. In studios, there's a whole flotilla of junior executives who are terrified to make any hard decisions, and if these two kids in Pasadena don't like the scene, it's in jeopardy."

Army of Darkness was released at last in January 1993, in an eighty-six minute cut that neither Universal nor Renaissance were completely satisfied with. But it was out there, playing in cinemas across America. Unfortunately, those cinemas tended to be on the empty side.

The hard-core *Evil Dead* fans, as it turned out, were somewhat disappointed by the comedy/adventure slant of *Army of Darkness*. Many felt they couldn't tell whether to take the movie seriously or laugh at it, as is often the case with Joe Dante's films, with similarly unfortunate box office results. In all of his films from *Crimewave* through *Army of Darkness*, Sam Raimi sought to make movies that were both funny and something else, usually exciting or frightening. American audiences often aren't prepared for this approach — they want their adventure more or less straight (wisecracks are okay); their heroes not only heroic, but sharp and sexy.

Audiences were confused, or even irritated, by Ash. This time out, he's *such* a jerk that he's somewhat hard to root for. On the one hand, this weakens audience identification with the leading character, but on the other, it was a courageous decision to fly in the face of conventional

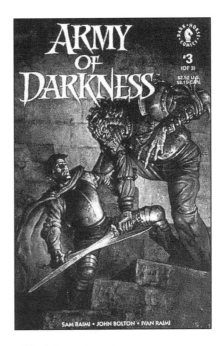

Hollywood wisdom and the pressure to come up with a more likeable, traditionally heroic figure.

Above and opposite: John Bolton's cover art for the Dark Horse comics.

Reviews were generally favourable, though like the hardcore *Dead* fans, critics often wistfully missed the over-the-top violence of the first two movies. Pat Dietmeier, in *Boxoffice*, said that it was like, "reading an expurgated edition of an EC horror comic, or watching a Sam Peckinpah Western that has been edited for television: you recognise the tone of voice, and there are flashes of inspired lunacy marbled throughout, but the overall feeling is that something critical is being withheld."

Virtually every critic who covered the film admired, even raved about, Raimi's visual style, but many felt the film lacked any real emotional content, seeming more like an adventure movie for teenagers plotted *by* teenagers. Some tried to read Raimi's mind and deduce his intentions, to see parody where none was intended, even though Sam is not actually a satirist. Injecting humour into situations where it isn't usually found is not the same as spoofing those situations. The problem is that Sam is a unique director, with a one-of-a-kind approach, who simply can't be pigeonholed.

In *The New York Times*, Janet Maslin's comments seemed on target: "[The movie] comes closer to comic book sensibility than many a real comic book does, thanks to Mr Raimi's broad, jokey visual style and his taste for pre-teenage humour... Taken on its own terms, [it] displays some ambition and wit, though not nearly enough to lend it a broad appeal. It is best watched as a string of wild visual effects... that take on a life of their own. *Army of Darkness*, a display of real if misplaced talent, has a crisp, punchy look and an energetic style. Mr Campbell's manly, mock-heroic posturing is perfectly in keeping with the director's droll outlook."

Andy Klein, in the *Los Angeles Reader*, was one of several critics who thought they spotted homages by Sam and Ivan to classic fantasy writers of the past, and was one of several critics who noted the plot's obvious similarities to Mark Twain's classic novel *A Connecticut Yankee in King Arthur's Court*: "It's utterly without sexual or emotional content — a heroic epic as written by adolescent boys to whom sex is still a vaguely icky abstraction... Despite nods to *The Wizard of Oz* and the L. Sprague de Camp/Fletcher Pratt *Incompleat Enchanter* books, what transpires is Mark Twain's *A Connecticut Yankee in King Arthur's Court* — the king here is even named Arthur... stripped of ideas, romance and complexity. What's left is action, plot and wit — which

should be enough to satisfy the target audience. It satisfied me, even though I'm a couple of decades past adolescence, and I long since stopped finding sex either icky or abstract."

Critic David Hunter not only felt he saw resemblances to fantasy writers, but to a whole legion of movies; he also singled out Bruce Campbell for praise: "The Hong Kong cinema of the Tsui Hark variety is evoked, along with at least a dozen other films in passing: *Excalibur, The Empire Strikes Back, Jason and the Argonauts, The Road Warrior* [Mad Max], *Robin Hood, The Day the Earth Stood Still, Gulliver's Travels, Monty Python and the Holy Grail, Alexander Nevsky* and, of course, *The Texas Chain Saw Massacre*... [The ending of *Evil Dead II*] sets up the continuation of the story in the best tradition of Edgar Rice Burroughs and Robert E. Howard. Rather than transporting the very effective scare tactics and relentlessly foreboding atmosphere, Raimi instead achieves the level of a Conan story as envisioned by Kurt Vonnegut Jr. An H.P. Lovecraft chiller envisioned by Hunter S. Thompson would have been more on the mark... [Campbell achieves] the dash and style David Lynch fave Kyle MacLachlan has always lacked. His modern-guy-in-the-land-of-the-boobs performance is a winner, even if the film's concept as a whole is extremely slim."

At the *Los Angeles Times*, Raimi supporter Kevin Thomas didn't review *Army of Darkness* — Peter Rainer did, and he liked the film, more or less: "It's the kind of concoction we've come to expect from Raimi: Goofball riffs crossed with cheesy/sophisticated horror effects. He's a gifted knockabout movie maniac who works on his own pop comic wavelength... [Ash is] so stalwart he's lunky — he's a parody of heroism even as he performs such amazingly heroic feats as staving off an army of galloping skeletons... Raimi wants to kid the genre but he also wants to demonstrate that he's able to do it straight. The film loses its prickly, nervy humour toward the end, when the skeletons launch a full-scale attack on a castle... Even here, Raimi's imagery... is a cut above the norm... But the film doesn't surprise us in ways that make us laugh anymore. It doesn't turn serious, exactly, but it loses its parodistic edge... Raimi, when he's really cooking, knows how to make the techniques of fantasy-horror seem funny all by themselves... [He] builds our awareness of movie technique into our response: he makes us laugh at our connoisseurship because, after all, it's really a connoisseurship of *schlock*."

The movie didn't pull in particularly impressive box office figures in the United States but, as usual with Raimi's films, did well overseas. Ultimately, even Rob Tapert wasn't as happy with the end result as he had hoped: "*Army of Darkness* went with kind of epic humour and no horror at all. Now, I wish it had been slightly more horrific." There was no way in the world Universal would ever release an *Evil Dead* movie on *Evil Dead* terms, and Sam himself wanted to pull away from the gallons of gore of the first two movies, so, as entertaining and smoothly made as it is, perhaps *Army of Darkness* simply wasn't the right film at the right time.

Army of Darkness may not have made as much money as everyone hoped, or even been quite the movie that its fans wanted it to be, but it was a fitting end to the *Evil Dead* saga, which began with Ash lurking shyly in the back seat of his own car, and concludes with him heroically blowing away one last Deadite and sweeping a gorgeous woman into his arms. If the movies are seen as Ash's epic struggle against the Darkness, they could not have had a better ending.

CHAPTER 12

BLOOD STILL IN THE VEINS

By the time *Army of Darkness* came along, Sam Raimi, Bruce Campbell and Ash had firmly established themselves in the minds of young film fans worldwide, and this meant there was a market for merchandise. So Renaissance Pictures started a merchandising arm, turning up at horror movie conventions with a dealer's table and selling their product through ads in magazines and from flyers. They initially offered three stills (Mike Ditz's post-production shots) and a photo of artwork from *The Evil Dead*, four monster-face stills from *Evil Dead II* and eight shots from *Army of Darkness*. There were also T-shirts and sweatshirts available, some aimed at a rock music-fan sensibility, others aimed at... well, others, such as a photo of Bruce Campbell saying "Groovy". They released several posters too, including a fine one by John Bolton.

Over time, an enthusiastic fandom grew up centred on the movies. There were several fan magazines — fanzines — devoted to the films, such as Sean McLaggan's *Raimi-Zine*, and even one (*Bruce on a Stick*) devoted solely to Campbell himself. In 1993, as the audience for merchandise continued to grow, the model kit company Screamin' issued a dynamic, impressive kit of Ash, complete with pained grimace and chainsaw, with the description of Ash in the kit written by Campbell. Another model kit, released in 2000 by McFarlane Toys, features Ash circa *Army of Darkness*, and was the cause of some legal wrangles between Renaissance Pictures and Universal's marketing arm.

The online auction company, eBay, often features *Evil Dead* merchandise for sale. Among items offered recently were publicity photos, a video workprint of *Evil Dead II*, the Renaissance-marketed T-shirts, an *Evil Dead* clock (no telling exactly what that was, but it was claimed to be "Hot!"), many posters, copies of magazines like *Starlog*, *Fangoria* (several issues of this), and *Cinefantastique* with articles on one or more of the *Evil Dead* movies, various videotapes, the Screamin' Ash figurine, tickets to the *Book of the Dead* première, postcards, laserdiscs, DVDs, a set of German stills from *Evil Dead II*, something described as 'The Making of *Evil Dead II*', a keyring, a mousepad featuring Bruce Campbell's picture, Japanese lobby cards, what claims to be the Necronomicon

Left:

Rob Tapert, Sam
Raimi, Bruce
Campbell and
Scott Spiegel,
circa Evil Dead II.

from *Evil Dead II*, an *Evil Dead* pin, and on and on and on. No one is getting rich off this stuff, but there is a lot of it. The Internet turned out to be fertile ground for *Evil Dead* fans, and websites proliferated. There are sites devoted to the films as a trilogy, some focusing on Sam Raimi's career, some even devoted to *Ted* Raimi, and a lot for Bruce Campbell fans, including an excellent official one Bruce runs himself.

After directing the Iggy Pop rock video 'Cold Metal', Sam Raimi photographed *Motivation*, a Playboy Channel short starring Ted Raimi, for director Bernard Rose. Like other major Hollywood directors, Sam also helmed several commercials, including a Virginia State Lottery ad featuring a caveman motif, and several for Jack in the Box (one starring a samurai chef). In 1990, he signed with Firehouse Films, a production company specialising in commercials. Three years later, Joe Mantegna, an executive producer at Firehouse Films, formed his own company, Zooma Zooma, and brought directors Peter Lauer, Ralph Hemecker and Sam Raimi in to work with him. Sam continues to direct the occasional commercial.

He was the subject of an episode of the British TV series *Son of the Incredibly Strange Film Show* in 1989, and is occasionally interviewed as an expert on horror movies and thrillers. One of his odder contributions to cinema history can be found on the video *Flying Saucers Over Hollywood: The Plan 9 Companion*. The late Mark Carducci produced this documentary about the making of Edward D. Wood's most famous movie, which features interviews with some unexpected faces. Scott Spiegel and Sam Raimi recreate Swedish wrestler Tor Johnson's appearance on Groucho Marx's *You Bet Your Life*, with Scotty playing Tor and Sam doing a very creditable Groucho, though they crack each other up before the end. On a different note, in 1993 Raimi married Gillian Greene (daughter of actor Lorne Greene), and they've since had three children.

If Rob Tapert, Sam Raimi, Bruce Campbell and the others had started with a comedy, it's quite possible they'd still be in Detroit, with Sam working in his father's business, Bruce an ad agent acting on weekends and Rob Tapert an outdoors executive. Instead, they stepped into a puddle of blood — horror, a genre scorned by critics and loved by its fans, mostly adolescents. However, even with the very first movie it was obvious to the more astute that Sam Raimi wasn't just another horror movie director. He was something new, someone with a fresh technique. Raimi thought he was modelling himself on John Carpenter, Wes Craven and Tobe Hooper, but his imagination took him in a different direction altogether. The fusion within him of a fear of horror and love of comedy resulted in movies like no one else's. Sam is a genuine innovator, and backs this up with superb technical skills — he knows the use of lenses and camera speeds, and the eloquence and excitement of camera movement like few of his peers.

It's hard to deny that Raimi's pictures, at least until recently, have been basically cult-favourite items — cleverly, sometimes brilliantly, made, but mostly movies *about* movies. Rebecca Mead's *New Yorker* article was titled 'Cheese Whiz' with reasonable accuracy. It can be hard to get people who don't much care for horror movies to look at a Raimi film as anything other than a kind of indulgence, however stylish and entertaining. Sam was running the risk of becoming a niche director, and nothing else — but things began to change, and he started gaining attention from people in Hollywood who don't necessarily want to confine his wild abilities, but to harness them to stories they're suited for.

One was Sharon Stone. When she was approached to star in *The Quick and the Dead*, the producers sent her a six-page list of approved directors for her to choose from. She sent back a page with one name on it: Sam Raimi. And she told the producers that if Raimi didn't direct the movie, she wouldn't star in it.

When asked on the set of the film, 'Why Sam Raimi? What did she like about him?' Stone replied, "Everything, but I particularly loved *Army of Darkness*. What I liked about Sam wasn't that each and every one of his pictures was so fabulous — because each and every one was *not* so fabulous — but in each and every one, you could see a film-maker taking the opportunity to become a better film-maker, to

stretch the limits of his technical and creative ability. So you know this is not a person who is running on ego, this is a person running on the desire
to be the best film-maker he can be. And I felt that
would be more exciting and more collaborative."
She referred several times to future projects she
had in mind for her and Sam to do together. So far,
though, they have not reunited.

Stone's performance in *The Quick and the
Dead* was one of her best to that date, even though
Simon Moore's script deliberately limited the characters to archetypes. Raimi's Western is a very conscious (though not self-conscious) attempt to
recreate some of the themes, style and appeal of
Sergio Leone's majestically operatic spaghetti Westerns of the 1960s, especially the 'Man With No
Name' trio that starred Clint Eastwood: *A Fistful of
Dollars, For a Few Dollars More* and *The Good, the
Bad and the Ugly*. There's an emphasis on trappings
and icons — very specific guns and garb, a taci-
turn gunfighter with a mysterious past, the town
boss of almost unlimited power and greed. But it's

Above:

*Sam on the set
of* The Quick and
the Dead.

brisker, more romantic and somehow more American than Leone's movies.

Raimi does include a few Leone tropes in *The Quick and the Dead's* visual style;
the staging of the gunfights, the emphasis on close-ups of eyes, the grubby townsfolk
(and the huge number of them), the sleazy flamboyance of some of the gunslingers
(the film centres on a quick draw contest), and the extravagant use of widescreen.
Sam's own style is unmistakable, however — the swiftly moving cameras, very high
angles, bone-lean editing and some goofy comedy work together with character and
theme. At the beginning, we see a ground-level close-up of Gene Hackman's spurred
boots stride across the floor; at the film's climax, when she gets the upper hand, we
see a matching close-up of Sharon Stone's boots striding purposefully down the main
street of the town of Redemption. Early on, a beam of sunlight stabs through her hat
and we see her shadow with a hole in the hat brim. At the end, the same thing happens to Gene Hackman's chest.

The story itself verges on the absurd. The only effective ways to film an idea
that's this close to going over the top would be to adopt a lean, cool Bressonian style,
with the actors underplaying everything and the camera distant and quiet — or to go

for baroque, as Sam does. At the same time, he's disciplined; conversations play out in restrained close-ups and two-shots. The balance between big gesture and low-key intensity in *The Quick and the Dead* isn't perfect, though, and a few gunfights are too laconic, while a few play out too showily.

It's with the actors and characterisations that Raimi makes his biggest advances. While it's almost redundant to say that Gene Hackman is outstanding as Herod, the town villain, Raimi did shape and guide his performance, and after *Unforgiven*, it's Hackman's best in a Western. Sharon Stone is as tight-lipped as Eastwood in Leone's Westerns — she's not a woman playing a man's role, but always a woman in a man's world. And she very effectively suggests a terrible secret that's tearing her apart.

The Quick and the Dead was a major step forward for Sam Raimi as a director. It was his first film with a substantial budget by studio standards, his first with major stars, his first Western, really, his first mainstream movie. And though the spareness of the story sometimes makes everything a little too stark (somehow there's both too much and not enough going on), Sam's grasp is firm and controlled. It's a bold, vivid movie, strikingly different to other latter-day Westerns. While it hearkens back to Leone, it's still fresh and vigorousy, a good movie by any standards.

Below:
Leonardo
DiCaprio, Gene
Hackman,
Sharon Stone
and Russell
Crowe in The
Quick and the
Dead.

The Quick and the Dead was released in 1995, and Sam's next film as a director wasn't until three years later, when he made *A Simple Plan*. This chilly, grim little piece was one of the most memorable films of 1998; no other movie that year had the icy conviction and steady gaze of *A Simple Plan*. Like the novel by Scott B. Smith, who adapted it for the screen, Raimi's film was direct, unadorned, suspenseful and deeply disturbing. A lot of movies want us to identify with the moral problems faced by the principal characters, but we rarely do so as inescapably as in *A Simple Plan*.

Ordinary people are handed the American Dream of wealth, and we see what it does to them, and by extension what it would do to us. In other movies, it's easy to see where the characters go wrong, to proudly conclude that in their position, *I* wouldn't do that. That comfortable position is undermined in *A Simple Plan*.

Sam Raimi completely dumped his characteristic stylistic flamboyance in favour of a cool, clean, naturalistic 'director-less' style. The only serious flaws are that it's somewhat too long, and features a scene near the end that veers unnecessarily (and unconvincingly) into sentimentality, which wasn't in the original book.

Bill Paxton plays Hank Mitchell, a quiet young man living in a small town in a northern state; he's happily married to Sarah (Bridget Fonda), who's expecting their first child, and has a solid, if modest, job at the local feed and grain store. His only living relative is his older brother Jacob (Billy Bob Thornton), a sad, unemployed loser whose only friends are a somewhat belligerent drunk, Lou Chambers (Brent Briscoe), and a dog. Lou, Jacob and Hank unexpectedly find a small plane, crashed in the woods. The pilot is dead, but there's a duffel bag full of money — $4.4 million, in fact. Hank at first insists that they take it to the police, but Lou argues that it's probably drug money, and that they should keep it. Uneasily, Hank finally agrees to hold the money until spring, when the plane is sure to be found; then they'll have better information about the source of the money. If it's marked, they'll burn it; if not, they'll split it up and leave town.

Above:
Billy Bob
Thornton,
Bridget Fonda
and Bill Paxton
in A Simple Plan.

From that point on, the plot of A Simple Plan develops with the inexorable doom of a car crash you watch but can do nothing to stop. One misstep leads to another; each decision seems to be the right one at the time, but they come from base, twisted motives. And yes, there are murders.

A Simple Plan is grim to the point of being desolate, not even relieved by ironic detachment, or jokes at the expense of the characters. It's an utterly realistic, completely authentic story of real people in a situation that gets out of control. The similar Shallow Grave was full of darkly comic asides, satirical moments and almost vicious irony. A Simple Plan takes the same story in a far more disturbing direction, striking directly at the heart of the classic American Dream of sudden fortune.

Sam Raimi knew what he was doing in taking on A Simple Plan. Aware that this story would not be enhanced by his usual showy camera techniques, he employed a cool, distant but not disinterested style; there's not a single 'Shaky-Cam' shot in the film, which is made in the classic Hollywood style: simple two-shots, close-ups, master shots, etc. This reticence and discipline on Raimi's part was the best decision he's yet made as a director, and at once took him from cult favourite to significant Hollywood player. Sam has established a *range* of styles — whenever he wants, he can go back to wacky camera moves, bizarre angles, flamboyant performances and so on, because he's now shown the money people that he can play the Hollywood game in the traditional style — and play it extremely well.

By the time *A Simple Plan* was released in America, Raimi was already directing his next film, *For Love of the Game*. This was about a Detroit Tigers pitcher, Billy Chapel (Kevin Costner), scheduled to pitch in a big game against the New York Yankees in Yankee Stadium, even though his pitching arm is causing him serious pain. He's also getting old for a ball player, but he isn't really considering giving up the game. Other characters include the Tigers owner Frank Perry (Brian Cox), Billy's on-again, off-again fiancée Jane (Kelly Preston) and his friend, Tigers catcher Gus Sinski (John C. Reilly). When Perry reveals to Billy that he's sold the club, he sadly adds that the new owners will be trading Billy, an eighteen-year veteran, to another team.

For Love of the Game, based on the unfinished novel by Michael Shaara, comes close to being one of the great baseball movies; in fact, as long as it sticks to the game itself, it *is* one of the great baseball movies. Raimi found new ways of filming the sport, some simple, some complex, that made it come alive on screen as never before, including varying the angles, so sometimes we watch it from announcer Vin Scully's box high above the field, sometimes from the level of the players. Raimi communicates the power of a major-league pitch — we see the crowds as the players do. And it's never merely trickery; every angle, every filming choice (including what seem to be CGI baseballs) adds something to the scene. Raimi deserves tremendous respect for what he achieved — re-envisioning baseball filming in a fresh, lively and engrossing manner. He found a way to combine his vivid film-making style and the demands of a studio movie. And yes, that is Ted Raimi in one scene.

The trouble is, however, that the sport occupies only half the movie. As long as we stick to the game, it's intensely suspenseful and exciting, as Billy is pitching a 'no-hitter'. That is, there are hits, but he's keeping the other team from scoring; in a great bit of the story, he doesn't realise this until late in the game. The rest of the movie is far more conventional. It's not bad, but we've been there before, even with Kevin Costner, and the personal stories in *Bull Durham* were far more interesting than the one here. Raimi tries to retain our interest, but we keep longing for the movie to return to the baseball.

The baseball in *For Love of the Game* is simply great sports movie-making, with Raimi at his peak to date as a director, but there's just not enough of it. Most baseball movies deal with trouble between the players, or between a team and their rivals, or between the players and the managers, coaches or owners. There are a couple of scenes in which, almost casually and certainly not with any thought of personal glory, Billy gives other players good advice, or is there when they need him, but *For Love of the Game* needs more of that; more warmth, even more sentimentality.

Kevin Costner made news by refusing to publicise *For Love of the Game*, claiming that Universal damaged the film by not releasing it in the R-rated cut he preferred. In the end, though, the difference is a matter of seconds. Interestingly, Costner didn't take his usual $20 million salary, settling for a share of the gross instead, which he felt made him a partner in the film. Universal didn't agree, and offered to give him his full salary — to his credit, Costner declined. He and Raimi also had some minor clashes, but both men reported having a lot of respect for each other, working their problems out in normal actor-director manner. Raimi emerged with his reputation not just intact, but enhanced.

Almost since his earliest days in Hollywood, Sam has been working as an actor as well as a director, making brief appearances in films and television shows, usually those directed by friends, including *The Stand, Innocent Blood* and *Miller's Crossing*

Below:

Sam's cameo role

in John Landis'

Innocent Blood.

amongst others, but his part in *Indian Summer* in 1993 deserves a lengthier mention. As a child, Sam often spent summers at Camp Tamakwa in Canada, and one of those he attended camp with was Mike Binder, who later became a director himself. In the nostalgic *Indian Summer*, Binder actually set his story at Camp Tamakwa, and in hon-our of their summers together, Binder offered Sam a role in the film (the impressive ensemble cast includes Alan Arkin, Diane Lane, Bill Paxton, Elizabeth Perkins, Kevin Pollak and Vincent Spano). Raimi was interested in learning more about the problems actors faced, and took on his largest acting role to date, apart from *Thou Shalt Not Kill... Except*. Sam is strictly the comic relief in *Indian Summer*, but he's very funny, get-ting laughs every time he turns up on screen. His performance is so good, so well-timed, that he deserves comparison with the likes of Buster Keaton and Stan Laurel, and he received favourable reviews.

"I've always been interested in acting," Sam said. "The original reason was because I was interested in entertaining people, and beyond that, nowadays, I'm inter-ested in learning about what it's like being an actor, what it's like performing in front of a camera, because I think it helps me be a better director. My real goal is to be a *great* director... But it's going to take a few decades of making pictures and a lot of time to master the craft, to make that happen."

As this book was being completed, Sam was on location with his next film, *The Gift*. Tom Epperson and Billy Bob Thornton wrote the script, and the movie, being shot in Savannah, Georgia, reunites some of the crew from *A Simple Plan*, but this time Rob Tapert is more directly involved, as one of the producers. The story concerns a woman with extra-sensory perception who becomes involved in a crime; presumably, with both Thornton and Gary Cole, who was in the Renaissance television series *American Gothic*, involved, it will have a strong regional flavour. The top-drawer cast also includes Cate Blanchett, Michael Jeter, Greg Kinnear, Keanu Reeves, Giovanni Ribisi, Chelcie Ross, J.K. Simmons and Hilary Swank.

Just before production began on *The Gift*, Sam Raimi was hired for his next film, the long-awaited *Spider-Man*. Sam is due to work on post-production for *The Gift* simultaneously with the pre-production for *Spider-Man*, scheduled to start shooting in late 2000. Many directors were vying for this high-profile job, but comics fan Raimi reportedly won the day because of his enthusiasm for the famous 'Death of Gwen Stacy' storyline. The combination of Raimi's intense, kinetic visual style and a comic-book story seems ideal, and the budget for *Spider-Man* is so huge that he'll almost cer-tainly be permanently elevated to the ranks of Hollywood's top directors.

Meanwhile, Rob Tapert became a major television producer. Renaissance had produced the features *Hard Target*, which brought John Woo to the United States, and *Timecop*, as well as two straight-to-video sequels to *Darkman* starring Arnold Vosloo as the scarred hero, but then something happened that changed not only the direction Renaissance was going in, but ultimately Tapert's life as well.

Universal came to Renaissance and asked them to produce several Hercules films for their 'Action Pack' series of television movies (which, in effect, were really pilots for series). Rob said they'd rather do movies about Conan, but those rights were tied up elsewhere — though this does explain why their Hercules was originally more like Conan than the Hercules of legend. The shows eventually found their own tone, which was broad enough that one week an episode could be starkly realistic, then the next might involve a lot of fantasy and the one after that be a raucous comedy. One episode even parodied the Australian movie *Strictly Ballroom*. Ted Raimi turned up frequently as Joxer, a clumsy, would-be hero in the mode of the early Jerry Lewis.

Furthermore, discovering John Woo (largely through the enthusiasm of Renaissance staffer David Pollison) led Renaissance to adopt an unusual approach for the action sequences in the *Hercules* and, later, *Xena: Warrior Princess* series. They (usually Pollison again) studied the action scenes in movies by John Woo and other amazing Hong Kong action directors, and adapted them to a lower budget. It was only fair, after all — several Hong Kong film-makers had studied Sam Raimi's hyperkinetic style in the *Evil Dead* movies, and adapted it to their own ends.

This resulted in a very, very busy couple of years for Rob Tapert and Renaissance Pictures. Both *Darkman* sequels began production in that period, though *Darkman III* wasn't released for another two years, and *Timecop* came out in 1994. There was also *M.A.N.T.I.S*, a super-hero series about a famous scientist who, though confined to a wheelchair, could gain mobility and some super-powers when he donned an exoskeleton of his own design. Meanwhile, the five *Hercules* movies were shot on location in New Zealand: *Hercules and the Lost Kingdom*, *Hercules and the Amazon Women*, *Hercules and the Circle of Fire*, *Hercules in the Underworld* and *Hercules in the Maze of the Minotaur*. Renaissance was justifiably proud when Oscar-winner Anthony Quinn played Zeus, father of Hercules, in several of the films. Old friend and associate Josh Becker directed *Maze of the Minotaur*, a clip show that starred Quinn.

Below:
Renee O'Connor and Ted Raimi in Xena: Warrior Princess.

Kevin Sorbo made an ideal Hercules, and the five TV movies were popular enough to generate a series, *Hercules: The Legendary Journeys*. Somewhat to everyone's surprise, it became not just a hit but a phenomenon, often the most popular off-network series on the air (other than game shows, of course — even Hercules can't defeat those). Production finally ceased in 1999. A New Zealand actress, Lucy Lawless, played the villainous Xena in a couple of episodes, and was so popular that she was revived as a heroine and given her own series, *Xena: Warrior Princess*. And that, too, became a major hit around the world. The success of the two series prompted other off-network adventure shows in the same vein, including one about Conan, but none of them had the flair, wit and style of the Renaissance series.

Xena was successful in another way, too. Rob Tapert was going to New Zealand often for the two series in production there, and spent lots of time with Lucy Lawless. Lots of time. Finally, in 1998, they were married. (Ironically, Lucy Lawless recalled seeing *The Evil Dead* at the cinema, and thinking that it must have been made by the sickest, most demented people she could imagine!). Of course, 1998 was also the same year that *Young Hercules* went on the air as Renaissance's latest series, and promptly disappeared, so it wasn't all beer, skittles and women warriors.

In 1993, Bruce Campbell starred as the title character in the television series *The Adventures of Brisco County, Jr.* The Fox network show never did well in the ratings, but it had a deeply loyal, almost fanatical, following, some of whom were long-time *Evil Dead* fans, but most of whom had never heard of Campbell before. For those who had followed Campbell's career closely, it was fascinating, even moving, to watch his ability as an actor and his ease in front of the camera visibly grow from episode to episode of the extremely entertaining series. And it accomplished his main goal in doing the series, making him a more visible, more bankable actor.

Bruce ranges from busy to phenomenally busy, from supporting roles in bigger-budgeted films (like *Congo*, *Escape from L.A.* and *McHale's Navy*) to starring roles in smaller films and television movies. Initially, he appeared in low-budget genre movies such as *Maniac Cop*, *Sundown: the Vampire in Retreat*, *Moontrap* and *Mindwarp*, while continuing to work for Renaissance Pictures in films like *Darkman* (he *is* Darkman — for one shot) and Becker's *Lunatics: a Love Story*. He appeared in both *Hercules* and *Xena* in a recurring role as Autolycus, King of Thieves, a part tailor-made for Bruce's jaunty rascal persona. He also directed several episodes.

The Coen brothers cast Campbell in a substantial role in *The Hudsucker Proxy*, co-written by Sam, and he began turning up as the star of some television movies — not necessarily genre outings, either, appearing in films like *Tornado*, *The Love Bug* remake and *Gold Rush*. He also gave an exceptionally good performance (as a *nice*

Left:

Bruce stars as Jack of All Trades.

demon) in a sixth season episode of *The X Files*, and has guest-starred in several TV series, from *Lois & Clark: The New Adventures of Superman* to *Weird Science*, *Ellen* to *Homicide: Life on the Streets*. Campbell maintains an active presence at conventions and, particularly, online, where he runs his own website, www.bruce-campbell.com. He's also putting the finishing touches to his autobiography, to be published in 2001 and tentatively titled *Confessions of a B-Movie Actor*, and producing and directing

Fanalysis, a documentary about horror movie fandom from his perspective.

In January 2000, Bruce's Renaissance Pictures television series *Jack of All Trades* began airing around the world. Campbell is a co-producer of the broad, even silly, series, which is very much in the tradition of the daffy movies they made back in Detroit. Like Sam and Rob, Bruce has now become a solid, continuing presence in Hollywood.

While Raimi, Tapert and Campbell established themselves professionally, the *Evil Dead* movies themselves moved into legend. As Rob Tapert points out, the films never did that well theatrically, but they developed a life on video and then on the Internet. Furthermore, the dazzling, unique visual style and ghastly, over-the-top horror of the *Evil Dead* trilogy became highly influential. Some movie-makers drew on both resources, combining exuberant gore with vivid style, while others were liberated by applying Sam's style to their own projects. Naturally, one would expect that Josh Becker's *Thou Shalt Not Kill... Except* and Scott Spiegel's *Intruder* would show some kind of debt to Raimi, if only because he's an actor in both of them and they've worked together on and off for so long, but there are countless others...

Below:

Dan Hedaya

is buried alive

in the Coens'

Blood Simple,

influenced by

Raimi's Evil

Dead *style.*

Film-makers Joel and Ethan Coen transposed elements of long-time associate Sam Raimi's style to their movies *Blood Simple* and *Raising Arizona*, while at the same time creating something entirely new. In Italy, where the *Evil Dead* pictures always did well, Lamberto Bava (son of the great horror director Mario Bava) was struck by Sam's work; he happily acknowledges that his films, including *Blastfighter*, *Demons* and its sequels, are strongly influenced by Raimi. Bava's *Demons* movies led to numerous American imitations, beginning with *Night of the Demons* in 1989, that were also influenced directly by the *Evil Dead* pictures.

In New Zealand, director Peter Jackson was influenced not only by Raimi's style, but by the way *The Evil Dead* was made. In 1987, Jackson shot his first movie, *Bad Taste*, on weekends with money he raised himself. His next film, *Brain Dead* (aka *Dead Alive*), is an exuberant, outrageous horror comedy, very much from the Raimi school — and is more gruesome than Sam ever thought of being.

In 1987, the movie world marvelled at *A Chinese Ghost Story*, while few realised that the dizzying camera moves, particularly the exhilarating rush through the forest, were largely inspired by *The Evil Dead*. Michele Soavi's very entertaining *Cemetery Man* (*Dellamorte Dellamore*) from the same year is an almost breezy horror comedy-drama with many Raimi-esque touches, including an ending that prefigures the original *Army of Darkness* climax.

Lesser films, including *Spookies*, *Il Bosco* (*The Evil Clutch*), *Kamillions* and many more, took inspiration from Sam's work. *Evil Ed* is so strongly influenced by Raimi that almost everything about the film, and certainly the title, can be seen as a tribute to Sam's style. *The Quest for _____* even features a character called Mr Fake Shemp.

In the movie *Idle Hands*, young actor Devon Sawa battled with his own murderous right hand, much in the manner that Bruce Campbell did in *Evil Dead II* — but this was a genuine homage, not a rip-off as some thought. Sawa recalls seeing *Evil Dead II*, "at a young age, and I watch it a lot; it's in my trailer right now. I loved Bruce Campbell's work, that was basically how I started building the character." When Sawa first auditioned for *Idle Hands*, he says, "they were looking for more of a serious hand, they weren't into the comedy. When I went in, I played it like Bruce had in *Evil Dead II*, sort of the Elmer Fudd-Bugs Bunny relationship, where the hand is Bugs and I'm Elmer." Sawa claims that, like Campbell, he too can grab himself by the scruff of the neck and throw himself onto his back. "Maybe Bruce and I will have a hand war someday," Sawa laughs, "although my hand is in retirement."

One of the most public endorsements of *Evil Dead II* came in *High Fidelity*, Stephen Frears' entertaining comedy about commitment. At one point, hero and record store owner Rob (John Cusack) is disturbed because his girlfriend, who's just moved out of their apartment and in with someone else, tells him that she hasn't made love with the new guy "yet." That "yet" bothers him, so the next day he asks his abrasive clerk Barry (Jack Black), a walking encyclopedia of pop culture history, how he would feel "if I told you 'I haven't seen *Evil Dead II* yet.'" Barry, stunned and almost embarrassed, responds, "I'd think you are a cinematic idiot and I'd feel sorry for you." He later adds that *Evil Dead II* is "so funny and violent and the soundtrack kicks fuckin' ass." Based on Nick Hornby's novel, *High Fidelity* was written by D.V. De-Vincentis, Steve Pink, John Cusack and Scott Rosenberg. Is one of these guys a closet Sam Raimi fan?

In terms of the ratio of cost to profit, the most successful movie to date is *The Blair Witch Project*, and while it's a very different movie to *The Evil Dead* and its sequels, it has a roughly comparable plot, and was financed in a similar manner — proof indeed that Sam's low-budget, kids-in-the-woods formula still works today.

Josh Becker feels that there are Raimi influences in films as diverse as Stephen Sommers' *The Mummy*, Coppola's *Bram Stoker's Dracula* and Scorsese's remake of *Cape Fear*, while customers of the hugely popular site the Internet Movie Database (IMDb) insist that they see references to the *Evil Dead* trio in any number of movies — some more plausible than others. For example, under *The Evil Dead* itself, the IMDb cites *A Nightmare on Elm Street*, *Splash*, *Tetsuo the Iron Man*, *The Wizard of Speed and Time*, *There's Nothing Out There*, *Jason Goes to Hell: The Final Friday*, *Scream* and *Barbacoa Sangrienta* as among the films that refer to *The Evil Dead* in some way. *Evil Dead II* references, the IMDb claims, can be found in, among others, *The Brave Little Toaster*, *Evil Ed* and Dario Argento's *Opera*. *Army of Darkness*, says the IMDb, was referred to in *Necronomicon*, Sam's own *The Quick and the Dead*, *Starship Troopers* and *Death: The Franchise*. Of course, some of these so-called 'references' are probably due to the classic *post hoc ergo propter hoc* logical fallacy — just because something came before something else doesn't necessarily mean it was an influence.

Then there are those films that, while not influenced by the *Evil Dead* movies, actually include the words "evil dead" in their titles — in every case the work of an opportunistic distributor, not necessarily the film-makers themselves. 1973's *El Ataque de los Muertos sin Ojos* is one of several Spanish/Portuguese horror movies about blind monks returning from the dead. On video in the United States, it was called *Return of the Evil Dead*. 1982's *Manhattan Baby* was sometimes shown as *Eye of the Evil Dead*, while *Mo Chun Jie* became *Holy Virgin vs The Evil Dead* in some markets. American movie *The Resurrected* was called *Evil Dead — Die Saat des Bosen* in Germany. *Siryo no Wana* was retitled *Evil Dead Trap*, and was popular enough that other Japanese horror films came out called *Evil Dead Trap 2* and *Evil Dead Trap 3*.

As movie and television writer Buzz Dixon points out, "The influence the *Evil Dead* movies have had on films extends far, far beyond just horror movies. While one can't say *The Evil Dead* inspired David Lynch or Quentin Tarantino, the success of Raimi's films certainly made it easier for their films to be made (yeah, I know Lynch was making movies before *The Evil Dead*, but *Twin Peaks* and his other TV series were helped by the success of the *Evil Dead* moves; at least it could be argued there was a market for that type of film-making). Sam Raimi's *Evil Dead* movies are, stylistically, a continuation of the hyper-reality first introduced to American films via Russ Meyer. Their sledge-hammer editing effects are what really sells them, not the genre. Raimi's greatest contribution to American and world cinema may be in establishing hyper-reality as a viable style."

Dixon correctly points out that another area where the *Evil Dead* movies made an impact was on music videos. For instance, the band Foo Fighters produced a video for their song 'Everlong' which, as Dixon says, has "typical Sam Raimi touches all through the video, but the last portion, set in a cabin in a swamp, is the most clearly *Evil Dead*-influenced."

Film students today report that Raimi's style has energised countless short films made in schools all across the United States. "I can confirm that the movies are certainly ones that every self-respecting film student has seen," agrees graduate Mike Bradford, "and many of us are in great awe of them. While I don't know first-hand of any direct *Evil Dead* rip-offs or homages made in film classes, Raimi's camera movements are often on our minds when planning shots. I've certainly tried to do 'Sam Raimi' shots in some of the student films I've made and worked on, even if the movies have had nothing to do with cabins or Deadites. The best little nugget I can give you is that at one North-Western film class, we analysed the scene in *Evil Dead II* where the unseen evil chases Ash from the broken bridge and ultimately through the windshield of the Olds, from a technical standpoint."

Mike Watt, once a film student and now a film-maker himself, says, "As a recent graduate (and hopeful 'professor') at Pittsburgh Film-makers, I got to witness firsthand a lot of *Evil Dead*-lite movies (including a few of my own). Plus, let's not forget that *The Evil Dead* has been seen and imitated all over the world." Indeed.

Over the years, there have been several video games — home and arcade — that imitate or allude to the *Evil Dead* films, and a lavish new game, tentatively called 'Evil Dead: Hail to the King' and based directly on the movies themselves is currently in development from THQ. Narrated by Bruce Campbell, it features Ash's first new adventure since *Army of Darkness* and continues the ongoing saga of Ash and the Necronomicon. It's an extensive horror survival game, in the vein of 'Resident Evil' and 'Doom' — the classic Deadites are back, along with various new ones, and Ash packs a variety of weapons as he travels around locations very familiar to *Evil Dead* fans.

With *Army of Darkness*, the *Evil Dead* series has probably come to a close. Rob Tapert says, "I don't know if there'll ever be a fourth *Evil Dead*, because they haven't made money. This is the truth. They've made money, but they haven't made *real* money, and it just doesn't pay for us to do it. That said, I think for Sam, Bruce and I, our best film experiences have been working together on those projects, and I think we'll all work together again some time."

Bruce Campbell goes to more conventions than ever since his success in *The Adventures of Brisco County, Jr*, and when his schedule permits, Raimi turns up at them too, often taking pratfalls, tumbling over backward and blowing his nose on his tie. Sam doesn't necessarily scorn the idea of another *Evil Dead* outing. "Another one? Yeah, if the audience wants it," he says, but adds, "they may have worn out their welcome

Evil Dead The Game - Ash Concept

with the audience, so it might be time to make a new type of movie with Bruce, and I think that's what I'd like to do." In fact, Sam and Ivan did finally write a script for *Evil Dead IV* — they've actually have written two and a half drafts, all of which are different, including one starring just Bruce and plenty of the Evil Dead. Rumour has it that the story takes place at a gas station. For now, though, the movie remains in the realm of unwrought things, and is likely to stay there.

The movies did achieve something remarkable, though — they took a group of high school friends (read the credits for *Army of Darkness*) on a journey from box-filled alleys in suburban Detroit all the way to Hollywood, creating careers when there had only been ambitions. As interviews for this book wound down, something quite surprising kept turning up in comments by Rob, Sam and Bruce. Independently, without prompting, each of them expressed a strong desire to work with the other two again, as soon as possible.

Hollywood is a town of impermanence. Life-long partnerships last a year; studio heads shuttle in and out of the top offices as if on greased tracks; actor-director partnerships burn out after two movies. But Bruce Campbell and Sam Raimi are still *friends*, as they were in high school. Rob Tapert came aboard a couple of years later, but the bonds are still as strong. All three talk about each other in glowing terms, with enormous humour, respect and affection. This is not just unusual in Hollywood, it's a one-off. All three *Evil Dead* movies are unique and remarkable, and so are the people who made them.

During the progression from Super-8 movies shot on weekends, to short films shot between classes at college, to a 16mm horror movie shot in the chilly woods of Tennessee, something great was forged, and it wasn't just their careers. These guys from Detroit are among the most decent, likeable people this writer has ever met, and it has been an enormous pleasure, one of the greatest of my professional life, to have been associated with them.

The making of the *Evil Dead* movies is not a prescription on how to break into films, but these guys did do it, starting from a standing stop. If your dream is to make movies, don't ever let anyone tell you otherwise: *you can do it too.*

CHAPTER 13

THE EVIL DEAD

IN ALL THREE FILMS, BUT MOSTLY THE FIRST TWO, THERE ARE MANY SCENES SHOT FROM THE POINT OF VIEW OF THE EVIL FORCE THAT DWELLS IN THE FOREST. IN THESE SHOTS, THE CAMERA SEEMS TO *BE* THIS FORCE, MOVING SWIFTLY THROUGH THE WOODS, KNOCKING DOWN, EVEN SPLITTING, TREES AS IT ROARS ALONG. IN THE SYNOPSES, WE WILL SIMPLY USE THE TERM "THE FORCE POV" FOR THESE SCENES.

THE COMMENTS IN ITALICS THROUGHOUT THE SYNOPSES ARE PRIMARILY FROM BRUCE CAMPBELL; AS HE WATCHED THE FILMS ON VIDEO, HE ADDED BACKGROUND NOTES SPECIFICAL-LY FOR THIS BOOK. CONSIDER THIS A LOW-BUDGET VERSION OF A LASERDISC OR DVD WITH A RUNNING COMMENTARY TRACK.

The movie opens and closes with the buzz of a fly on the soundtrack.

(The idea, Bruce Campbell says, was that this is the fly on the wall that observes the entire movie. The titles come up silently, with no music, and nothing on the audio track.)

RENAISSANCE PICTURES Presents
THE EVIL DEAD

A loose, almost floating camera prowls over the foggy surface of a lake, zoom-ing over branches, past bubbling fog, heading towards the far shore; we see a wrecked car off to the side.

(This is the 'Sam-o-Cam' shot. Sam Raimi fastened a small Arriflex camera to his hand with gaffer tape, and got onto a raft. The crew, wearing waders, pushed the raft through the swamp as Sam's camera-hand swooped low over the surface of the water, dodging the branches as you see in the film. This shot was done several times, with a fresh chunk of dry ice tossed into the water to make the fog for each take. It was at least the fourth version of the opening, too; most of the others were similar to the Force POV that accompanies the scenes of the car.)

A 1973 Delta 88 Oldsmobile drives along a mountain road. Shelly, the girl in the

front passenger seat, is singing; Scotty is driving, though we learn later that the car belongs to Ash, who's sitting behind Scott in the back seat with his girlfriend Linda and sister Cheryl. The camera picks out Ash.

Above:
A promotional
shot of Bridget
Hoffman.

(*Why call him Ash? Sam Raimi jokes that he chose it "because that's all that was going to be left of him in the end," but that's not likely, since Ash was scheduled to survive his little outing in the woods. Bruce says he thinks that it was initially short for 'Ash Holt', indicating Sam's opinion of Ash's character, and Cheryl calls him 'Ashley' in the film. For Army of Darkness, Sam toyed with calling him 'Ashley J. Williams'. Maybe the name just drifted in through the window.*)

The Force POV prowls through the woods, over the scattered leaves. On the road below, the car's wheels squeal as it rounds a corner, and there's ominous music on the track. "Hey Ash, where are we?" Scott asks.

"Well," says Ash, consulting a map, "we just crossed the Tennessee border..."

(*Campbell points out that in these scenes in the car, the first shot for the movie, you can see that he is growing sideburns, but that they aren't in yet. By the end of the film, the sideburns are fully formed. It was, after all, a hair-raising experience...*)

Elsewhere on the mountain road, a truck is approaching. There's intercutting between the Force POV, the oncoming truck, and Ash and his map. "Which would put us..." Ash says a couple of times, then exclaims, "Right here!" His finger stabs at the map as the Force POV arrives at a bluff above the car, the steering wheel twists in Scott's hands, and they almost meet the truck head on.

(*"This was actually the first 'stunt' we'd ever done," says Bruce. "Some local shmoe was driving the truck; in those days there was no stunt co-ordinator, there was no stuntman, it was, 'Okay, whenever you feel like turning, turn.' All these scenes were shot on back roads near the cabin."*)

One of the girls screams, but Scott manages to dodge the truck, exclaiming, "Hey, don't blame me, it's your steering wheel — the damn thing jerked right out of my hand!"

(*Shots in which the camera is actually below the seat and looking up at the driver were filmed in a driveway, not out on the road. Watch the view out of the window during these scenes — the car is up in the mountains one minute, then among trees or passing through pasture land the next, without any rhyme or reason.*)

A little shaken, Scott honks the horn a couple of times, and two guys by the side of the road wave at them.

(*They're fishermen, played by Sam Raimi and Rob Tapert*)

Scott scoffs at them. All of a sudden he's holding a jar of moonshine, without any explanation for it.

(*The jar of moonshine is left over from a deleted scene. If you watch closely, you can see Bruce Campbell still reacting to a swig. It was stunt moonshine, of course.*)

They all discuss the cabin they're heading for, which Scott got really cheaply, but none of them have seen yet. The idea that no one has checked it out disturbs Cheryl.

Ash points out where they should turn off, and the road takes them to a rickety bridge, past a sign reading "Dangerous Bridge. Travel at Own Risk". As they drive over it, a couple of timbers fall away, tumbling into the river beneath.

(*If you look to the right of the bridge just as the car starts across it, you can catch a glimpse of Rob Tapert, standing in camera view.*)

"This thing is solid as a rock," Scott says, just as one of the wheels plunges through the planks of the bridge roadway. Ash leans out to see the timbers hit the river below, but the car makes it across safely.

(*This was the abandoned bridge they were allowed to destroy later on; the hole was already there. "Generally speaking," a wiser Campbell now admits, "it wasn't a good idea to put that car out on that bridge.")*

To ominous music, the car drives along a narrow dirt road towards the cabin.

(That's not Teresa Seyferth you glimpse through the car window here; it's Sam Raimi, Fake Shemping like mad.)

Branches brush by the camera POV following the car from behind and above. A rhythmic, repetitive booming sound echoes down the road as they near the cabin; we see that it's caused by an old swing slamming into the cabin wall. The car stops some distance away, and they all get out. Low angles are used here to intensify the ominous mood. Scott approaches the cabin alone, with the camera following him.

(Steve Frankel made the swing on location, partly out of planks taken from another cabin seen only once in the film, at the beginning of the very last shot.)

He steps up onto the front porch, and as he reaches for the key over the door, the swing stops dead. With a couple of nervous glances at the swing, he unlocks and opens the door. In a shot from inside the cabin, we see him silhouetted in the doorway, with a mounted deer head on the wall in the foreground.

(The room is distinctly dusty — in movies made in Hollywood, this slight fogginess is generally created by either cigarette smoke or mineral oil fog. For this movie, Sam Raimi tossed a handful of dust into the air just before the camera rolled. Originally, the first shot of the inside of the cabin ran on uninterrupted until Scott finished checking out the interior.)

Outside, the others happily unload the car.

(Watch how fast it gets dark.)

Inside, Scott moves around the cabin, exploring a room in the back festooned with dangling bones, including a cow skull. He turns on a light, examines the unusual decorations and turns it out again. He seems to be in some kind of workshed.

(The hanging bones, and the gourds we see later, were inspired by similar set dressing in The Texas Chain Saw Massacre.)

The sun sets.

Later, the lights are on in the cabin, and we can hear the crickets crick. We see Cheryl from behind the clock's pendulum. The clock stops at eight minutes to six, with a lot of chiming. The window curtains beside her blow slightly, and we can hear ghostly voices crying, "Join us... Join us..."

(That's Sam Raimi's voice, altered by sound-editing magic.)

She looks down at her sketch of the clock — with a grimace, and apparently against her will, she clutches the pencil in her fist and draws a rectangle with a crudely-sketched face, tearing the paper as she does. There are strange dark lines on the back of her hand. Across the room, the trapdoor to the cellar noisily flaps a little.

The next scene is merely a dinner, although it starts with a jump when we cut abruptly to a blender whirring away loudly. All five people seem perfectly content as Ash rises to make a toast. In the other room, the trapdoor springs open completely.

(The eerie music here recalls Bernard Herrmann's title theme for Mysterious Island.)

In the cellar, the camera looks up at the five young people peering apprehensively into the cellar.

(The crew only dug out enough dirt from beneath the floor of the real cabin for five steps downward into darkness.)

They discuss what could have made the trapdoor move, and they're all nervous about going into the cellar to investigate. Scotty volunteers to go, and descends the staircase. The others wait, tensely, and all we can hear is the sound of crickets. After a moment or two, Ash calls after him, "Hey Scotty, you find anything?" No response.

Ash decides to go down into the basement himself, taking a lantern in the absence of a flashlight. The three girls watch from above. At the bottom of the stairs, Ash pauses, looking around. There's a noise like a motor running in the distance, some jingly sounds on the music track and dripping water. The camera pivots 360 degrees as Ash examines the dark, shadowy cellar. He calls out for Scotty. Water slowly drips from pipes above.

(This was actually Karo syrup, so the drips would fall slowly enough. These scenes were shot months later, in the cellar of the Tapert farmhouse.)

A sudden noise from behind a closed door catches Ash's attention. In close-up, he advances towards it.

(This is double-printed — each negative frame is printed twice, because Raimi felt that Campbell moved too quickly.)

Ash reaches out for the doorknob, turns it with a loud clunk, and the door creaks open. As he enters, we can see gourds hanging from the ceiling beams behind him. He enters the second room slowly, passing some pipes.

(If you watch carefully, you can spot a hidden cut. Once Bruce has passed the pipes, he's in the Raimi family cellar. This extended the scene a little, and added the small scare that follows, back in the Tapert cellar.)

BOO! Scott pops up. As Ash recovers, Scott says, "Look at all this stuff!" There's a tape recorder, a torn poster for *The Hills Have Eyes* and a shotgun — "I bet this still shoots," observes Scott. And there's also a strange book, with what seems to be a face carved into the leather cover. Ash opens it and sees depictions of demons, skeletal faces, eyeballs and a pile of skulls.

(There's a reason for the poster. "In The Hills Have Eyes,*" Campbell explains, "there's a poster for* Jaws *ripped in half. Sam took it to mean that however scary* Jaws *was, that was nothing compared to what's going on here. So Sam took* The Hills Have Eyes *poster and tore that — as scary as that film is, it's nothing. Then Wes Craven, who directed* The Hills Have

Eyes, *had a scene from* The Evil Dead *playing on TV in* A Nightmare on Elm Street. *In Evil Dead II, Sam included a poster for that movie, torn — or burned — in half.")*

Scott finds a long knife with a small, distorted skull on its hilt, then picks up the tape recorder and starts upstairs. Ash finds, rather mysteriously, an illustration within the Book *of* the Book, only here the face looks alive and somewhat resembles Cheryl's crude drawing.

Lightning forks across the sky, striking a tree. The full moon rises over the cabin.

(This is actually an effects shot, one of the few mattes in the film. It's pretty crude and obvious, so much so that Stephen King pointed it out in his rave review as evidence of the movie's low-budget origins.)

Later, they sit on the floor near the fireplace and play the tape.

(The tape recorder really belonged to Bruce's dad.)

"It has been a number of years," says the voice on the tape, "since I began excavating the ruins of Kandar with a group of my colleagues. Now, my wife and I have retreated to a small cabin in the solitude of these mountains. Here, I continued my research undisturbed by the myriad distractions of modern civilisation, and far from the groves of academe. I believe I have made a significant find in the Kandarian ruins. A volume of ancient Sumerian burial practices and funerary incantations. It is entitled *Noturan Demonto,* roughly translated, 'Book of the Dead.' The Book is bound in human flesh and inked in human blood. It deals with demons, demon resurrection and those forces which roam the forests and dark bowers of man's domain."

(Sam wrote the narration with Ethan Coen, and the voice is that of Bob Dorian, more recently the host of American Movie Classics. He was a friend of Joe Masefield, the sound editor on the movie.)

As the voice continues, we see close-ups of the friends listening, and at least one shot of the storm outside.

"The first few pages," the voice on the tape continues, "warn that these enduring creatures may lie dormant, but are never truly dead. They may be recalled to active life with the incantations presented in this Book. It is through recitation of these passages that the demons are given license to possess the living..."

Cheryl turns off the tape recorder, but Scott joshes them into turning it back on; however, he fast-forwards it before pressing 'play'. When the recording starts again, we hear the Sumerian chants. The words are hard to discern, but some sound like "Katra amistrobin azonda..."

The scene cuts to an exterior; as the voice continues. We see the cabin in the background, and in the foreground, earth begins to stir. Smoke rises in front of red light breaking through the fissures of the cracking earth.

In the cabin, the voice goes on: "Samand Robeesa dar ees heiker dan zee roadza.

Opposite:
Bruce Campbell
poses as Ash for
a publicity still.

Kandar! Kandar! Kandar!" Cheryl suddenly shouts, "Shut it off! Shut it OFF!" She clutches her head as a branch crashes through the window.

(It's real glass breaking, not the candy glass used in mainstream movies. The Renaissance partners simply couldn't afford stunt glass.)

Cheryl flees the room, then Ash and Scott quarrel, and Scott leaves. While Ash is alone, he takes a small box out of his pocket. When Linda joins him, he's resting on the couch, eyes closed, box on his knee.

(The intercutting that follows is the only scene in any of Sam's films in which he applies this bravura technique to romance.)

Ash watches Linda as she reaches for her present, with a lot of quick cutting between their eyes. Finally, he shyly gives her the box. Inside is a necklace, a small silver-framed magnifying glass on a chain. He puts it around her neck.

(The reason it is a magnifying glass, a rather unlikely lover's gift, is that, at the climax, Ash was supposed to use it to focus the morning sun's rays on the Book of the Dead. They scrapped that idea by the time they filmed the ending, but they were still stuck with the magnifying glass prop. Which, incidentally, was gold, not silver; if you watch closely, you can see flecks of silver paint on 'Linda's' fingers.)

She's knocked out by the gift. "Oh, Ash, it's beautiful; I really love it — I'll never take it off."

("Sam's a total romantic at heart," Campbell points out, "but he'd just never admit it.")

But now we're seeing them from the outside, from the POV of the Force. It looks in the window at them kissing, then goes around to the side and looks in another window as they finish their clinch and approach the fireplace. In another room, Shelly takes off her blouse, and we get a brief glimpse of her breasts.

(Scenes of a sexual nature are very rare in Raimi's movies).

Looking through another window, growling "Join us," the Force sees Cheryl, who peers out into the night, draws her bathrobe more tightly around her and leaves the room. She comes out of the back door of the cabin.

(This was one of the most involved shots in the film; lighting was very difficult, and so was the timing of all the actors.)

Cheryl looks around, calling, "Is anybody out there?" A wolf-like howl in the distance is the only answer.

(There's a subtle, interesting use of no sound here. A faint "wubba wubba" sound can be heard, a by-product of the sound mixing board that Raimi liked. It's almost literally the sound of silence.)

Cheryl walks along the side of the house, with the shadows of branches passing over her face.

(Made by Sam, off-camera, waving a branch.)

"I know someone's out there — I heard you," she insists. A cloud covers the moon. Cheryl unwisely enters the woods, the camera alternately following and preceding her.

(The sounds in this sequence are a combination of Raimi, Tapert, Campbell and their sound mixer Joe Masefield moaning "Join us," blended with the sounds of flies and bees.)

As Cheryl walks through the woods, a strangled growl is heard. There are some shots of swirling clouds. The Force POV moves in the woods, knocking down small trees, intercut with fog and Cheryl reacting in fear.

(This entire sequence is a combination of footage shot on location in Tennessee, later on in the Michigan woods and the Raimi back yard.)

Vines crawl along the forest floor, rising in the air, and looping themselves around Cheryl's wrist, then her neck, then her other wrist.

(Most of this involved simple reverse printing — the vines were really being pulled away from Ellen Sandweiss. If you watch carefully, you can see where her robe was pre-torn so the vines would follow a certain path; at other times, gaffer tape, holding the cloth together for later takes, can also be seen.)

Cheryl screams as the creepers tear away her bathrobe and drag it off into the woods. The vines strap her to the ground and spread her legs, and with sudden violence, one stabs into her vagina. Cheryl writhes in pain. More vines swarm over her, but one breaks as she struggles to free herself.

(For those interested in such things, you can glimpse her bare breast in this sequence.)

The Force POV is still moving through the woods, and now it sees her, freeing herself from the last of the creepers.

(Apparently, the Force and the vines are buddies, but not guided by the same mind.)

Half-naked, Cheryl runs headlong through the woods, looking back to see a tree toppling behind her. She makes it to the house with the Force POV still following her, knocking down trees. She grabs at the bunch of keys on top of the doorjamb, but they're stuck. Freeing them, Cheryl struggles to unlock the door as the Force POV advances on her from the woods. The suspense builds as she drops the keys, and Ash's hand grabs her wrist at the last possible moment. The Force POV, thwarted, withdraws into the woods with a frustrated growl.

"Did something in the woods do this to you?" Ash asks. "No," she sobs, "it was the woods themselves — they're alive, Ashley, they're alive!... I want to get out of here, I want to leave this place right now." Cheryl demands that Ash drive her into town immediately. He tries to talk her out of it, but then agrees.

(Campbell points out how Ash struggles to get his arm into the sleeve of his jacket. "I couldn't get it on to save my life," he says. When they're outside, the jacket's already on.)

They go out into the misty night, and once again the only sound is the innocent chirping of the crickets. Their friends, silhouetted against the light from the open door, watch as Ash and Cheryl get into the car. At first it won't start, but just as Cheryl says, "I know it's not going to start. It's not going to let us leave," the engine roars into life. They drive away, and the others go back inside.

Ash drives on until he sees something ahead, and stops. When he gets out, he walks past the front of the car at a strange angle. Fog drifts by as Cheryl leans out of the car, worried, then she too walks past the camera, also tilted to one side.

(This, one of the eeriest effects in the movie, was done quite simply on location. Sam found a slope next to the road and mounted the camera on it so the bottom frame line was parallel with the slope, ie, the camera tilted as much as the slope did. When the car drives up, it seems, therefore, to be level — and when Campbell and Sandweiss walk by, they seem to be tilting, as if gravity isn't working quite right.)

There are loud woodsy creaking sounds from the forest. The noises get louder as she approaches the bridge, only to find its girders bent upwards like the clutching fingers of a skeletal hand. There's lots of fog here.

(The bridge is real, and was really cut into the shape of a hand, but the way it's shot, it could have been a backyard miniature.)

Cheryl runs back toward the car, and Ash jumps out of nowhere and scares her. She's hysterical and he can't calm her down. If they can't cross the bridge, they have to return to the cabin.

Back at the cabin, Ash listens to more of the tape through an earphone.

(It is with this scene that Ash essentially becomes the hero, since he is taking the menace seriously. By not playing the tape aloud, he avoids upsetting the others.)

"I know now that my wife has become host to a Kandarian demon," says the voice on the tape. "I fear that the only way to stop those possessed by the spirits of the Book is through the act of" — pause — "bodily dismemberment. I would leave now to avoid this horror, but for myself I have seen the dark shadows moving in the woods, and I have no doubt that whatever I have resurrected through this Book is sure to come calling for me."

Despite the ominous mood, Linda and Shelly are fooling around with playing cards, testing each other's extra-sensory perception, if any. After they've tried predicting cards for a while, Cheryl, who's been staring out of the window in the background, gets a sequence exactly right. This amazes the others, but Cheryl, her voice now weird and unearthly, goes on naming cards that haven't even been turned over yet. She suddenly whirls on the others, her face distorted and demonic, her eyes blank.

Abruptly, Cheryl levitates, rising from the floor and hanging in the air in front of the window, her head jerking about. "Why have you disturbed our sleep?" she groans. "Awakened us from our ancient slumber? You will die like the others before you. One by one we will take you!" Cheryl collapses onto the floor.

(*To levitate Sandweiss, she was strapped to an X-shaped frame with a pole going straight out the back of the X and the window behind her. They called this the 'Ellievator'.*)

Everyone is virtually in shock. There's a close-up of Ash tentatively reaching out toward his sister.

(*Bruce has injuries on his face he actually received from Ted Raimi later in the shoot, due to filming out of sequence.*)

Cheryl's now monstrous hand finds a pencil on the floor. Holding it like a dagger, she abruptly sits up, her eyes blank, with a horrifying fixed grin, and plunges the point of the pencil into Linda's ankle, twisting it around.

(*That's the sound of an apple being stabbed.*)

Cheryl raises it to strike again, but Ash grabs her wrist. She knocks Linda flying across the room, then slams Ash into a bookcase, which tips over on top of him.

(*In these pre-stuntman days, Bruce simply flung himself backward into the\ bookcase.*)

Grinning demonically, the possessed Cheryl lurches across the floor. Scott tries to stop her, but she throws him aside. Ash is trying to get out from under the bookcase as Scott knocks Cheryl backward so that she falls through the trapdoor. He clouts her

Below:
Cheryl (Ellen Sandweiss) rises up, possessed.

head a couple of times, then laces the chain through the fasteners, and padlocks it.

(*There's a brutal shot of her hand being smashed here; actually a leftover fake hand from* It's Murder. *It's later seen being squashed in a door.*)

After all the upheaval, there's a very quiet scene. In a bedroom, Ash pulls the covers tenderly over Linda, who seems to be asleep. He kisses her softly, then leaves.

(*Bruce Campbell makes an interesting point: "One thing I really commend Sam for that isn't done much in movies any more is that he allows things to get very quiet for several minutes after major scare scenes. Otherwise, there is no release, there's no stop. It's interesting to try to make a movie that never stops, but in this case a quiet moment is more effective, because you mellow down, then you can get bashed again, whereas if you keep getting bashed, there's nowhere to go. It becomes a version of pornography, where it's no longer teasing and tantalising, it's just something that never stops. I think this wound up being very effective, and I only realised it when I went back in and did the remastering of the sound for the laserdisc release."*)

Outside, the Force POV advances on the house again. Inside, Shelly is hysterical as Cheryl growls away to herself in the cellar: "Why does she keep making those horrible noises? For God's sake, what happened to her eyes?" Scotty tells her that everything is going to be all right — famous last words if we've ever heard them... "Scotty," she says, "I think there's something out there," in an understatement matching his misplaced optimism.

The Force POV peers into the cabin, following Shelly along the house as she goes into her room. Turning toward the window, Shelly sees something outside in the dark, and backs away in horror, screaming as the Force POV smashes through the window.

(*This, says Rob Tapert, was a Ram-o-Cam shot. The guy behind the camera used a big rake-like device made out of nailed-together boards to punch out the window just as the camera reaches it. If you watch carefully, you'll see that the glass shatters before the lens hits it.*)

Scott enters the room with the smashed window, but there's no sign of Shelly. He looks out of the window, first one way, then the other. Nothing. And nothing happens to Scott, either, though audiences expected him to be decapitated. A noise from the closet catches his attention. He pulls the curtained door open as the music builds, but there's nothing in there.

(*There's a Camp Tamakwa T-shirt on the inside of the closet door, though*).

Cautiously entering the bathroom, Scott walks gingerly toward the shower curtain and pulls it aside. Nothing. As he turns to leave, a hand suddenly grabs his throat while another, with large red fingernails, rakes grooves down the right side of his face. He staggers into the front room with Monster Shelly clutching him. Scott manages to push her away and she falls into the fireplace, her head starting to smoulder. He grabs her legs and pulls her to safety, but she's still a monster. "Thank you. I don't know what

I would have done if I had remained on those hot coals," she says, sarcastically.

(Watch closely: in the rest of the scenes involving Scott, you can tell the reshoots from the original Tennessee footage by the length of Rich Demanincor's hair, which changes abruptly from fairly long and shaggy to shorter and neatly combed, then back again.)

Monster Cheryl bangs away at the trapdoor. Ash tries to help Scott, but he's flung back into yet another bookcase, while Monster Shelly grabs the skull dagger and tries to stab Scott, but he pulls his own hunting knife and slashes at her wrist.

Ash grabs the axe and raises it, but stops in horror as Monster Shelly bites her own hand off at the wrist. Scott stabs her in the back with the skull knife, which still has her dismembered hand clutching the hilt; she screams hollowly — for quite a while — and blood dribbles from the mouth of the skull on the knife's hilt, along with some smoke. Monster Shelly leans so far back that we can see where the make-up ends on her neck. With multiple groans and moans she falls backward onto the knife. White fluid spurts out of her wrist stump and her mouth, leaving her face not only monstrous but covered in red, black and white goo.

(This sequence was a mixture of locations; the Shelly monster is played by Sarah York [Teresa Seyferth], Rob Tapert and Rob's sister Dorothy. They filmed some of these shots much later in Michigan, in Bart Pierce's cellar. The white fluid is simply milk.)

Scott walks toward Shelly's recumbent form, unwisely, as she grabs him again.

(The legs you see here are those of stand-in Ted Raimi.)

He pulls away, but Shelly rises up and walks towards him, oozing blood and other unpleasant matter. Scott grabs the axe from Ash and whacks her in the head. After she collapses, he dismembers her in a series of violent blows. In one shot, blood covers the camera lens, which is aiming upward at Scott.

(Hiding out of camera range, people tossed Karo syrup blood upward for the splattering effect. Shots for this scene were done in Tennessee, in the Raimi garage and in Marshall, Michigan. Campbell says, "Rob and Sam made a conscious decision to make this cutting up scene very graphic, but did a lot of the extra shots back in Michigan. There's a fake floorboard here; a real hand was fastened to a prosthetic arm, with the person underneath, so the axe could seem to cut off the hand. It's an old magician's trick. The leg you see chopped is a chunk of bologna. If you watch closely, you can see a green garden hose pumping out fake blood.")

Finally, Scott stops swinging, and we see Shelly's various dismembered body parts scattered about the floor — legs here, torso there, head over here — twitching and squirming, making gloppy, gooey sounds.

(This was done just the way it looks — people were hiding under the floorboards sticking arms, legs or a head up through holes cut for this purpose. At this point, they had been shooting for something like sixteen hours. Rob Tapert, lying on his back with his leg sticking through a hole, got a terrible cramp, and he darkly suspects that Sam took his time lighting

the shot because he knew Rob was one of the body parts. "This is where the cabin became unmanageable," Bruce says. "Because we were using Karo and just dumping the stuff on the floor; the syrup got on everything. It got on the fog machines, it got on the cameras, it got inside the cameras, everywhere. Your hands would stick together, and your fingers.")

Ash and Scott are overwhelmed. "What are we going to do?" Ash asks. "We're gonna bury her," says Scott tersely. Ash responds, in a daze, "We can't bury Shelly. She's a friend of ours."

(This line generally gets laughs at screenings, but that wasn't intended.)

Dragging the body through the woods in a bloody sheet, Ash and Scott dig a hole and bury their bundle in it. Scott plants a cross.

(Just before filming this scene, Campbell wrenched his ankle. "Now, Rob and Sam will never admit to this, but they cornered me in a room with sharp sticks, and started poking at my ankle. These are my good friends.")

Later, the Force POV advances on the house again, amid plenty of fog.

Inside, Scott insists that he's leaving, but Ash says they can't take Linda out with her wounded foot.

(The scratches on Scott's face are now on his left cheek.)

"I don't care what happens to her," Scott says selfishly, thereby sealing his doom.

(The film does follow certain moral codes, like all good horror movies.)

"She's *your* girlfriend — you take care of her. I'm getting the hell out of here, right now." And with that, he heads off into the woods.

(It was around now that Campbell started doing something he regrets "to this day. At this point, my hair was starting to get messed up, so I would just put Karo syrup on it, because it would stay shiny and gooey; in all of Evil Dead II, I put Karo syrup on my hair. There are certain habits you pick up that you don't realise until years later how stupid it was. On Evil Dead II, I slept on the set with a fly swatter in my hand because of all the flies buzzing around. I didn't put anything on my hair for Brisco County, Jr." Sam says that's why the show was cancelled — insufficient Karo.)

Ash checks on Linda, who is sleeping and seems okay. He pulls the cover back to look at her foot where Cheryl stabbed it with the pencil — and the wound immediately turns black, with a spider web of black lines spreading out from it.

(The leg is actually that of Cheryl Guttridge, an old friend from the Super-8 days.)

Linda sits up abruptly, her eyes blank, with a doll-like grin on her face; she doesn't look like the other monsters. She's giggling and moving in a jerky, marionette-like fashion.

Horrified, Ash runs to the front door, and is startled when Scott falls in on him, begging for help. He's all banged up, with a big cut on his leg. The possessed Linda sits cross-legged on the floor in the doorway to the hall, giggling at their predicament.

To sneers from the monster women, Ash tries to reassure Scotty, claiming that they'll survive, and asks him if there's another way out besides the bridge. Scott says, "There's a trail, but the trees, Ash, they know, don't you see, Ash, they're alive!" Apparently, it was the trees that tore him up.

The two monster women both laugh fiendishly as blood runs from Scott's mouth. "Shut up!" yells Ash, rushing over to Linda and slugging her in the face. "Kill her," says Scotty. Ash picks up the shotgun and aims it at the cackling monstrosity before him, murmuring "God forgive me," but can't bring himself to shoot. "Kill her if you can, loverboy," cackles Cheryl, goading him. Without warning, Linda looks normal again, and whispers, "Oh, Ash, help me, please. Ash, help me, please. Oh, Ash, please don't let them take me away again."

(Did she really regain her own mind for a moment, or was it a trick on the part of the demons? We never know for sure.)

They embrace.

"Ashley, help me, let me out of here." Ash hears Cheryl's voice, sounding like herself again. He looks at the closed trapdoor. "I'm alright now. Unlock this chain and let me out," she says. The soundtrack is otherwise quiet.

(You'll notice the floor isn't especially bloody in these scenes. They knew they would chop up the possessed Shelly when they shot these sequences in Tennessee, but it wasn't until

Right:

Ash comforts Scott (Rich Demanincor) after his ordeal in the woods.

Left:
Cheryl peers out
through the
trapdoor.

they filmed the cutaways back in Michigan that the blood really flowed. So there are only some patches of gore here.)

"Cheryl?" Ash says, uneasily. He kneels by the trapdoor and pulls the keys out of his pocket. Peering into the crack, he's punched by her monstrous hands.

(The hands actually belonged to Ted Raimi, and Ted really punched Bruce in this shot, making those marks mentioned earlier).

Ash pulls back in terror, and Linda, now possessed again, chants, "We're gonna get you, we're gonna get you," in a taunting, sing-song voice. "Not another peep, time to go to sleep." "You bastards!" rails Ash. "Why are you tormenting me like this? Why?"

Grabbing her by the ankles, Ash drags Linda through the cabin door and outside. He hauls her over the leaf-covered ground as she writhes and screams. "We'll come for you!" she shrieks.

(When this scene was shot, Linda's make-up was monstrous in the same way as the others; the doll-like look came later.)

The tension is broken by another shot of the moon, to signify time passing.

Ash goes over to Scott, offering him some water. "The sun will be up in an hour or so," the numbed Ash says, more to himself than to Scotty, "and we can all get out of here together. You, me, Linda, Shelly... no, not Shelly, she... We'll all be going home

Above:

Ash and Linda

(Betsy Baker)

fight to the

death.

together... I bet you'd like that, wouldn't you?"

(*Some of the shots of Campbell in this sequence were taken well after all the other actors had left. "I had these horrible Moe bags [named for Moe of the Three Stooges, of course] under my eyes," he says. In other shots in this same sequence, "I'm all clean, I'm all pretty, no bags under my eyes."*)

But Scott is dead, and Ash lets the glass tumble to the carpet. He goes to the window and looks out. Nothing. He turns round just as Linda stabs him in the left arm with the skull knife. She licks the blood off the blade.

(*At the start of this shot, Bruce points out, "My left arm is tucked a little unnaturally into my side, because we tried to do this all in one — which of course didn't work — so my arm is pre-bloody. We had to go back later to pick up an insert of the actual stab." As for how Linda got back into the house, "Don't ask questions."*)

They struggle, and Ash falls on the couch, knocking Scott's body to the floor. He manages to turn the knife around to Linda's back, very much as Scott had done earlier with Shelly, stabs her and she falls backward onto the knife. Blood runs out of her mouth, but she finally lies still. Ash grabs Linda by the legs and drags her slowly across the carpet.

(Here's where they used what they called the Vas-o-Cam. They fastened the camera to a wooden block wrapped in gaffer tape; a two-by-four on the floor was also covered in tape, then both layers of tape were greased with Vaseline, enabling the camera to slide along smoothly only inches from the floor. However, it was so cold in the cabin that the petroleum jelly was thicker than usual, and you can see a few little hitches in the Vas-o-Cam's gitalong. The Vas-o-Cam was Philo's idea. The can here is Stroh's beer, because they were from Michigan. "These are important things, you know," Bruce asserts without much conviction.)

In the woodshed, a rat scampers away as Ash turns on the light. In quick cuts, with a distinctive sound emphasising each one, he chains Linda's body to the table.

(There's a sequence like this in all three films, and several in Army of Darkness.*)*

Ash pulls aside a curtain and finds a chainsaw. He starts it, standing over Linda's body, but loses his nerve when he sees the necklace he gave her still around her throat. He leans over her body, crying.

(Joe Lo Duca's music here performs what Bruce refers to as an "NBC dip. That's when the music goes way down and you hear a line of dialogue, then it comes back up again.")

Cut to outside. Ash passes the camera carrying Linda's body — he didn't hack her up after all. There's the shovel where they left it after burying the dismembered pieces of Shelly's corpse. He gently puts her body down, and starts to dig.

(The wind currents were very favourable to the fog they lay down, giving some of the exterior sequences the Hammer horror look they were aiming for.)

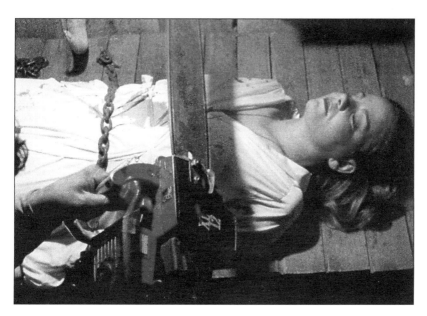

Left:
Linda lies
chained to
the workbench,
ready to be
dismembered.

Inside the cabin, Cheryl pounds away again at the trapdoor, as the metal hoop fastening the chain to the floor, and the hinges, begins to give way. This is intercut with close shots of Ash's and Linda's blank but open eyes. In an echo of the sequence earlier when he gave her the magnifying glass-charm, whenever Ash glances at Linda, she closes her eyes again. He picks up her body and lies it in the grave.

Now there's a POV shot from inside the grave as Ash tosses a shovelful of dirt in; by sheer chance, his face is still visible through an area the dirt doesn't cover. He finishes the grave and pats down the earth, then reaches for the necklace, which is on the ground beside the grave.

(*Watch here also for some good Shaky-Cam shots as the camera moves right over the open grave and back again. A local Tennessee woman named Barbara Carey played the body in this insert.*)

As Ash picks up the necklace, Linda's hand shoots out of the earth and grabs his wrist. He pulls away, but she still gets hold of his ankle, lacerating it with one hand while holding on with the other. Ash screams in pain.

(*The woman rising from the grave is actually Cheryl Guttridge, in scenes shot in Sam's cellar. She's rising "out of fertiliser," Campbell says, "which is essentially cow manure." In other scenes, the undead Linda is Barbara Carey again. "These are our actors-gone scenes," Campbell explains. Carey was determined to do a good job, and didn't tell anyone until after the take that she had torn her own fingernails badly when she clawed at Bruce's leg. "She's this nice, neat Tennessee girl, and she didn't want to say anything while she was obviously in horrible pain — she just wanted to do it right," Bruce says with admiration and regret.*)

Ash falls to the ground, but finds a charred timber, which he repeatedly pounds Linda with until she picks him up by the other end of the timber. Ash, surprised, is lifted right off the ground and falls hard.

(*Bruce and Sam both clouted Betsy Baker with the* It's Murder *beams, with Sam really nailing her. "She'd get all pissed and throw a hairy fit," Bruce says, "and Sam would apologise, and we'd start again — and he'd do the same thing all over again." She got her revenge, though; Betsy had milk in her mouth she was supposed to spew out, which she did — all over the camera, infuriating Tim Philo. An angry day all around. And you think you want to be in a Sam Raimi movie...*)

Linda leaps into the air and Ash swings the spade and lops her head off. It lands, plunk, right in front of the camera. In the background, Ash grapples with the headless body; the stump of the neck pumps black fluid onto his screaming face. On the ground, Linda's head laughs as the legs of the body straddle Ash's in an obscene parody of sex.

(*On the soundtrack, you can momentarily hear a few female groans lifted from the track of a real hardcore movie.*)

The head cackles. Finally, Ash staggers away.

(*This overhead shot is one in which the cherry-picker crane was actually used.*)

Breathing hard, he comes into the cabin — to find the trapdoor standing open, and Cheryl gone.

(*Compare the amount of blood on Bruce in this shot with how much was on him when he walked back to the cabin.*)

Ash hears a creaking sound as the door across the room opens slowly. He picks up the gun and enters Shelly's room, looking around. The closet is making strange noises, and as he moves around to get a better shot at it, Cheryl pops up outside the broken window, and grabs the barrel of the shotgun. He blasts her, but she stands up again, pumping blood.

(*The effect of shooting something with a shotgun was achieved by shooting something with a shotgun. Also, you can see a green garden hose pumping blood out of Cheryl's shoulder. "That's so lame," Bruce sighs; "it's always bothered me."*)

Running toward the front door, Ash leaps over the camera.

(*Sam was lying in a space where the floorboards had been torn up, as Bruce recalls. He gets a good shot of Ash's "stupid elf shoes."*)

Cheryl, heads for the front door, getting a hand in before he can close it altogether, and he smashes it bloody, until she withdraws.

(*This is one of the nastiest shots in the movie; it was done using a fake hand with balloons filled with Karo blood inside, and some broken glass to pop the balloons when the door slammed. In these scenes, Cheryl is played by Rob Tapert in drag.*)

Ash frantically runs to the back door, slams it shut and searches desperately for the shotgun ammunition. "Shells. Where'd I see that box of shells?" he sputters, grabbing them. He comes slowly down the cellar stairs, stumbling on a beer can. Overhead, there's a pipe wrapped in sheets, dripping blood. He looks up at it, and it breaks open, spewing gallons of blood over him.

(*There's an interesting shot of Bruce from above the pipe; a mirror was placed on the ceiling of the Tapert cellar over it, and Bruce's reflection was filmed in that.*)

An electrical outlet on the wall oozes blood, blood pours out from between the stones of the wall and a lightbulb fills up with blood.

(*An homage to the Three Stooges short* A Plumbing We Will Go, *in which the same things happen with mere water.*)

A wind-up record player pops open and starts playing 1920s-like jazz of its own accord. A movie projector bursts into life, catching Ash in its beam as blood drips onto the projector lens. The square of light on the wall and Ash turn red.

(*This was a tribute to long-time Detroit film distributor Andy Granger. Sam met with Granger in 1979 when they were raising money for the film, and asked his advice on making a horror movie. "Just keep the blood flowin' down the screen," said Granger. Sam follows his advice to the letter in this shot.)*

"We're gonna get you, we're gonna get you," Linda's voice chants. There are also layers of other sounds, including the voice from the tape repeating the "bodily dismemberment..." passage.

(These were added, as Bruce recalls, on the advice of sound editor Joe Masefield, who was worried that the audience would forget everything else that had happened by this point. As if that mattered.)

Ash grabs for the shotgun shells and loads the gun. The gramophone and projector continue to run. He rushes in, and sparks fly from the projector as it explodes. The blood-filled lightbulb bursts and the record player runs down.

(There's dust on the record so we can actually see that it's turning. Also, notice the Band-Aid box floating in the bloody slop on the floor. This is irony. Much of the floor is covered with wadded-up garbage bags too keep the liquid glop on them from soaking into the floor, but, as Bruce says, "You can kind of tell that they're just garbage bags." The shot of him wiping himself may seem out of place, since Ash isn't usually fastidious, but it was added to match the footage shot much earlier in Tennessee, when he wasn't as gore-besmeared.)

Ash goes back upstairs, fearfully. The clock hands whirl madly and we hear Big Ben-like chimes. From behind the pendulum, we see Ash in close-up at an extreme

Right:
Ash, pushed to the limits of his endurance.

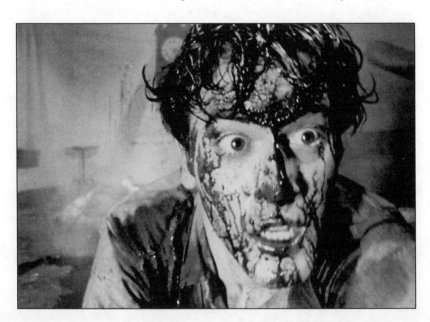

Dutch angle as it slams back and forth. We hear the sound of a heartbeat. The camera rights itself.

(These scenes were shot when there were only five people left on the crew. Rob tried to talk Sam out of using so many tricky shots in this sequence, but Sam wanted it all to look weird. Sam was right.)

We see Ash upside down from behind as he passes directly under the camera, which tilts to follow him right-side up.

("I can't figure out how Sam had his body," says Bruce, marvelling at his director's derring-do. "He was in some horrible, contorted position hanging down over the rafters. He had to bend over upside down, then do an inverted sit-up as I walked back. The camera was attached to his hand.")

From underneath Ash, we see his feet swivel.

("I'm on my heels on a box here," Bruce explains, "perched pretty precariously. I may have actually been held up from behind, so that all my weight is on my heels.")

There's an extreme Dutch angle from outside looking at Ash in the doorway. The Force POV moves closer and he slams the door closed. The shutters on the house bang wildly. There are many disorientating Dutch angles here, as well as straight down-shots from above the rafters as the camera moves along above them, following Ash. As the camera passes the rafters, there are distinct sounds counting off each one.

(The sounds were made by Sam himself. This is another Vas-o-Cam shot, with the camera elevated just enough to miss the beams, sliding along a board on the rafters. This one shot took a fourteen-hour day to complete.)

The heartbeat on the soundtrack increases in tempo as Ash stares into the oval mirror. He reaches out toward his own image, but his hand plunges into the mirror as if it were water.

(Which, of course, is exactly what it is. Raimi had read about a similar scene in Jacques Cocteau's classic Orpheus, in which an actor put his hand into a mirror, actually a vat of mercury, with the actor and camera at angles suggesting the reflecting surface was vertical. Raimi did the same thing here, but couldn't afford mercury, so he used a pool of water with black backing under it. Bruce is lying face-down on a board.)

Ash screams and pulls back, staring at his hand in horror. There's a bright light outside and he fires at the window, rather peculiarly knocking away the crossbeams of the frame but not the window itself.

("One of our few two-camera set-ups," Bruce says, "because to us it was a big stunt. I had to make sure I shot upward to miss the guys operating the cameras.")

Ash looks around the room, very frightened. There's a howling wind and mysterious creaking sounds. He remembers to reload the shotgun. Now he can hear footsteps on the roof.

(At last the dark secret can be told — the footsteps were made by Sam in high heels.)

More footsteps, but they don't sound human. Ash snaps his head back and forth, up and down, following the sounds. He remembers something, and fishes the necklace out of his trouser pocket.

"Linda," he says. He is looking around the now-silent cabin when monstrous hands crash through the door and clutch at him. "Join us!" a coarse voice bellows. It's Cheryl. Ash falls back onto the floor, and fires at her through the two holes she smashed through the door.

But — whoops! — Scott suddenly sits up, now a monster.

(There's a jump cut here, Bruce points out: "Watch my position at the door change when the monster pops up." They did this to speed up the action.)

They battle inside while Cheryl pounds on the door that Ash has barricaded. Scott lifts Ash off the floor by his throat, but Ash plunges his thumbs into Scott's eyes, gorily gouging them out. Scott drops him, screaming. Ash pulls a piece of wood out of Scott's belly and watery-looking blood pours forth.

(Despite what some have thought, Ash is not pulling Scott's penis off.)

Cheryl pounds on the door as Scott collapses. Ash sees the Book of the Dead near the fireplace as Cheryl smashes open the door. On his knees, Ash starts for the Book, but Scott, smouldering away, grabs him, while Cheryl picks up a poker. Ash, being dragged along by Scott, clutches at Linda's necklace. Drooling, smoking, Cheryl comes across the room toward him as he uses the necklace to try to snag the Book, still lying next to the fireplace. Cheryl slams him in the kidneys with the poker.

Below:

Ash gouges out

Scott's eyes.

(The logic here is a little muddled. If Cheryl can go clear across the room to get the poker, why doesn't she just pick up the Book of the Dead? On the other hand, just what the Evil Dead are actually after in this film isn't clear.)

Ash tries again to snare the Book, and she hits him again. Scott starts chewing on Ash's leg. He's still having no luck getting the Book, and he's being pulled backwards away from it, when — what ho — the chain catches on the cover of the Book, which is burning around the edges. He throws the Book into the fireplace.

Cheryl freezes, holding the poker above her head. Smoke drifts from her body, and chunks are missing from her face. She drops the poker, which stabs into the floor by Ash's face. Her head lurches to one side with a crunching sound.

(*There's something bright blue on her lip, and now the blown-away part of her face is her lower left cheek, when in the previous shot, it had been her right cheek.*)

She blinks, twitching strangely as her hair falls out. Scott's also crumbling away, the flesh literally crawling off his bones, and the same thing is happening to Cheryl. Bubbling, butterscotch-like matter oozes from Scott's head as something green tumbles slowly down his flayed cheek. Cheryl's tongue stabs out, and so does that on the Book of the Dead itself, which is having its own problems.

Above:
Cheryl advances,
armed with a
poker.

(*The face of the Book, and its tongue, are rendered in stop-motion animation. At one point during this sequence, the matte shifts, so a sound effect was added to cover the error. It's not likely anyone would notice, though. Furthermore, Bart Pierce had an ingenious idea — there's a sheet of transparent plastic between the camera and the action in some of the scenes, slowly moving, so that when flecks of decomposed Deadite stuff spatter, they're smoothly pulled away from the lens.*)

All is silent.

Scott's body moves slightly. Something like porridge squirts out of his sleeve. Cheryl's head turns a bit, and a giant hand erupts from her chest, as two of them stab upward out of Scott's back. There's an amazing shot of Cheryl's body, upright, with her own hands flailing, and the hands from inside her reaching out in opposite directions. Her throat erupts, she topples over and her head crumbles a little as she's falling, bursting apart on the floor.

(*One of Sam's favourite shots in the film, using dog food to stand in for the head's innards. Also, notice that when the head bursts, stuff falls up. This shot is actually inverted.*)

Bugs crawl out of one of the ruined bodies, which continue to flatten, change colour and rot. "Join us, join us," Ash hears again, but the voice is now fading away.

At last, it seems to be over. Slowly, painfully, Ash rises to his feet. He's covered in blood, his friends and his sister are dead, but he's alive. Outside, the sun is rising. Ash opens the cabin door and looks at the dawn sky. Limping, he starts towards the car.

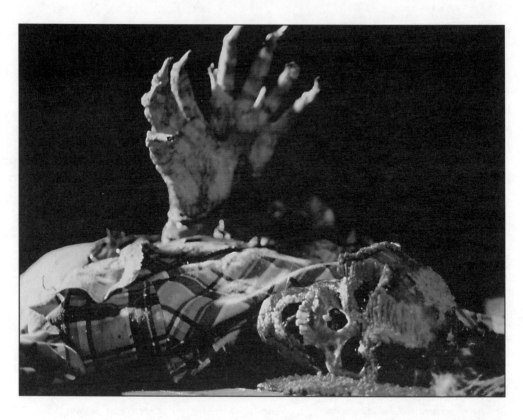

Above:
Giant hands
erupt from
Scott's corpse.

But the camera cuts to a shot of a leaf, very close; we hear a rumbling sound and we are again seeing via the POV of the Force. Close to the ground, dodging trees, the Force roars toward the cabin.

(And it's now a cabin we haven't seen before — we can also see the workshed near the main building.)

The Force rushes at the back door of the cabin, which bursts open; it zooms through the house, knocking open an interior door, then smashes through the front door. Ash limps towards the car. He turns and screams as the Force rushes up to his screaming mouth.

(THE END)

It is interesting to compare the final product with the original outline included in the prospectus lawyer Phil Gillis prepared for potential investors in *Book of the Dead:*

Book of the Dead (brief synopsis)

Something evil is lurking about the wooded mountains of Tennessee. It watches a carload of five youngsters drive across a narrow bridge over a deep mountain chasm, and arrive at an old wood cabin which they are renting for the weekend. That night they explore the cellar and find the ancient "Book of the Dead" which had been left there by a professor of Egyptian mythology who mysteriously disappeared from the cabin six months ago. Once they read passages from the "Book of the Dead" terrifying nightmares, evil sounds in the woods, and glimpses of shadows moving about at the forest's edge plague them.

Attempting to drive back to town because of the weird events, they are brought to a standstill when they see that the bridge over the chasm has been completely destroyed, isolating them totally in this mountain cabin.

As the evil force grows stronger, one by one the vacationers become possessed by it. Their eyes turn bone white and their bodies are jerked about like marionettes as they are driven to kill their own friends and lovers. The few remaining humans soon realise that the only way to stop this dark force which inhabits their possessed friends, is to dismember them so they can never walk the earth again. Struggle after struggle, battle after battle, the dwindling number of humans continue to destroy the white eyed possessed until only one man remains.

This man, now more than ever, has a driving will to survive and also has finally learned the secret behind the 'Book of the Dead'. In a final, bloody battle, he manages to destroy this demonic book, sending back to some dark and brooding place the evil which had possessed and murdered his friends, and almost cost him his own life.

Having used his courage and raw strength to survive the terrifying night, this last man leaves the cabin and walks off into the mists of the early morning hours to safety.

by Samuel M. Raimi

The final film is very close to this synopsis, of course, but you'll notice that there is a "secret" of the Book that enables the lone survivor to destroy it, though the synopsis doesn't reveal what that is — and the survivor gets away safely at the end.

EVIL DEAD II

NOTE: THE ACTUAL ON-SCREEN TITLE IS *EVIL DEAD II*. *EVIL DEAD 2: DEAD BY DAWN* WAS ONLY USED FOR PUBLICITY, AND SOME REFERENCE BOOKS THAT MISTAKENLY ASSUME THAT THE TITLE ON THE POSTER IS THE TITLE ON SCREEN. AT THE END, THE MOVIE DESCRIBES ITSELF AS "THE SEQUEL TO THE ULTIMATE EXPERIENCE IN GRUELLING TERROR."

Through a sea of clouds, the Book of the Dead rushes toward us with a creaking sound; the rough face on the front of the book changes, becomes more monstrous. It swallows the camera, and we see a swirling fog. Ghostly, skeletal shapes rush by us, the two most striking being a spider with a human skull for a body, and a bat-winged skull. The narrator speaks: "Legend has it that it was written by the Dark Ones — *Necronomicon Ex Mortis*, roughly translated, Book of the Dead. The Book served as a passageway to the evil worlds beyond. It was written long ago, when the seas ran red with blood." We see a red sea, the waves crashing. "It was this blood that was used to ink the Book." Animated drawings fill the pages, then lines of printing in an ancient, indecipherable text. More drawings and more lettering appear, faster and faster. "In the year 1300 AD, the Book disappeared." The Book slams shut and flies away.

RENAISSANCE PICTURES Presents
EVIL DEAD II

Suddenly, we're inside a tunnel, zooming out into the daylight, behind a yellow car; inside we find a young man, Ash, and his girlfriend, Linda. "So what's this place like?" she asks.

(This scene was filmed in a tunnel on the Blue Ridge Highway.)

"Well, it's a little rundown," he replies, assuring her that it's deserted. In a miniature shot, the car crosses a very high, precarious-looking bridge with three spans. Then we see the cabin, at this point also a model shot, the windows and door of which suggest a face. Inside, Ash plays a piano while Linda dances in her panties and a letterman's shirt from Michigan state.

("Typical Rob Tapert influence," Bruce grins. "The costumer said, 'Okay, she can wear a regular T-shirt, or she can wear this, like, vacuum-packed T-shirt.' Rob says, 'Well, there's no question about it.' So it's this ridiculously tapered, sexy T-shirt.")

They start to kiss by a window, but a necklace Linda's wearing — like the one in the first film, a small magnifying glass set in silver — digs into her. It's obviously a very recent gift, and she tells Ash she loves it.

(They shot some of the scenes with Denise Bixler on the duplicate set built in a warehouse in Dearborn, Michigan. They had always hoped to be able to use footage from The Evil Dead *at the beginning; when that proved impossible, new footage was necessary.)*

"I feel funny about being here," says Linda, still concerned. "What if the people who own this place come back?" Ash reassures her and goes to open some champagne.

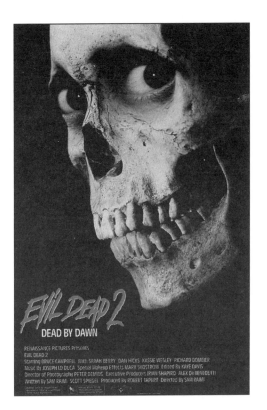

Singing, he wanders into the next room, where he finds a tape recorder. In the front room, she takes off her shirt and suggests Ash plays the tape recorder, which he does.

(It's actually the tape recorder used in the first film.)

We hear the voice of Dr Raymond Knowby, of the Department of Ancient History: "Log Entry Number Two. I believe I have made a significant find in the castle of Kandar, having journeyed there with my wife Henrietta, my daughter Annie and associate Professor Ed Getley. It was in the rear chamber of the castle that we stumbled upon something remarkable... the Book of the Dead." As the narration continues, we see a Jeep-like wagon approach some bleak spires of rock, then the four people identified on the tape inside an underground chamber.

(The castle here is not a matte painting; it's a very large miniature. They filmed 'the actual exteriors at a kaolin mine. "When we scouted," Bruce says, "they had a display in their offices of what kaolin is used for. It's used in paper so ink adheres to it, it's used in tyres, pencil erasers — and Kaopectate.")

"My wife and I brought the Book to this cabin where I could study it undisturbed. It was here that I began the translations." We see Dr Knowby at his table examining the book, talking into the tape recorder — his wife, Henrietta, is in the background in a rocking chair, knitting. "The Book speaks of a spiritual presence, a thing of Evil that roams the forests and the dark bowers of man's domain. It is through the recitation of the Book's passages that this dark spirit is given license to possess the living." Ash examines the Book; on one page is a distorted, monstrous face, like those of the later demon possessions we witness. Included here, the tape recorder says, are the phonetic readings of those passages, which play over our first Shaky-cam shot of the Force POV rushing through the woods.

The Force sees Linda through the window, then smashes it and rushes at her. Ash, in the other room, dashes in, dropping the bottle of wine in shock. He runs outside as wisps of fog drift by him. He's looking around, bewildered, when Linda pops up, screaming and cackling maniacally. Her face is distorted, her teeth long and reddish and her eyes blank. She holds her hands out, moving like a marionette.

Terrified, Ash falls backward, catching sight of a shovel lying nearby. As Linda leaps into the air, passing over the camera; he swings at her with the spade and neatly chops her head off.

(Why? All she's done has been to scare him and act weird. He couldn't have known at this point that she was a real menace. Ash is impulsive sometimes.)

The lopped-off head flies toward the camera, then rolls along the ground.

A few minutes later, Ash begins to dig a grave for Linda. He places her headless body in the grave. "Linda," he cries, clutching the magnifying glass charm. He fashions a big wooden cross and plunges it into the ground.

The next morning, the Force POV barrels through the woods, very much like the end shot of *The Evil Dead*. It charges headlong into the cabin, through the building and out the front, smashing the doors. It flies right up to Ash's screaming face, picking up where the first movie left off.

As he screams, Ash is lifted up bodily by the Force and carried through the woods ahead of it. He's moving extremely fast.

(In the first two films, people are clearly seeing something when the Force POV rushes at them, but what? At the end of Evil Dead II, the Force manifests itself as a giant, skinned head, but that's not likely to have been what people were seeing earlier. So just what was it?)

The Force carries Ash screaming through the air, occasionally revolving as if tied to a slow-moving propeller, whisking through overhanging leaves.

("This was an all-day shoot, the only sequence shot in South Carolina. We needed a long, straight road with trees on either side, and we found it [there]," Bruce recalls. "I'm on the arm of a crane that's going very slowly down a road, going up and down. I'm mounted on a big X on the end of the crane, spinning around; Sam could turn me either way. Sam had people down below running along with branches that they would slap into me.")

He slams into a tree and collapses, falling face-forward into a big mud puddle. He lies there quietly for a moment, blowing bubbles as if he's drowning, while mist drifts over him. This goes on so long that you suspect he's drowned.

(The effects crew created the bubbles, not an iron-lunged Bruce.)

Suddenly, he rears up with a horrendous gasp, his face distorted as if the bones are growing through it, his eyes blank, one of the Evil Dead.

("Of course," Bruce points out, "the tricky thing was having the white contact lenses underwater; we had to have clean mud, clean water, but I couldn't always tell whether my eyes were open.")

But the sun is rising, and he groans and screams under the power of its rays. Elsewhere, the fog pulls back quickly through the forest, past the cross on Linda's grave, into a tree and into the ground. Deadite Ash is still screaming and groaning. There's a close-up of his blank eye as Ash's normal eye, iris, pupil and all, reappears.

(Bruce explains, "We felt there was some need to see that he is saved by the morning sun, so that's why we show the eyes returning to normal." The effects team built an oversized replica of Bruce's eye; in reverse action, liquid was injected that blanked out the iris and pupil of the big eye.)

Back to normal, more or less, Ash's eyes cross, he goes "Aargh," and falls over. We see more fog being sucked into the ground. He lies there for a while in the woods, his position changing slightly, signifying the passage of time. The sound of a fly is faintly heard. Then his eyes pop open and the camera rushes upwards, away from him. Stunned, shocked, apprehensive, he looks around him at the woods, which seem harmless and quiet now. In a 360 degree shot, returning to Ash, there's the cabin, there's the car. "It's gone," he says aloud. "The sun's driven it away. For now."

("Sam loves these three-sixties," says Bruce. He points out that the trees weren't large enough, "So we built a couple of fake, foam-injected bases of trees." However, he can't explain why Linda's grave seems to have coal all around it.)

There are strange wailing sounds on the track, and Ash sees demonic eyes superimposed over the cabin's windows as a thick, garbled voice intones "Join us."

(Despite the Force's frequent, even plaintive attempts to get volunteers, no one ever joins up willingly. What would have happened if they had? That's Sam's voice calling him, incidentally.)

Ash gets up and walks toward the cabin, which now looks normal again. Then he glances at the car.

(This is the same car used in the first movie, and it's appeared in virtually every one of Sam's films since. They buy duplicates for destroying. Bruce thinks Sam is hanging on to it assuming it will eventually be a classic, but he's replaced every part of it over the years.)

There's a shock cut to the car roaring through the forest. Inside, Ash frantically wipes his face, then abruptly slams on the brakes.

The girders of the bridge are bent up like clutching fingers. Horrified, Ash tries to pull himself together. Then he hears something strange, and sees the setting sun plunging down, faster than it possibly could, disappearing into clouds beyond the car.

The Force POV rises up from the crevasse spanned by the bridge, rushing along the wooden road and right at the car, but Ash backs madly away from it, whirling the car around and taking off again.

(This scene is a combination of miniature and location shooting.)

Ash appears to be outrunning the Force, but it's hot on his heels. Raimi intercuts between the Force POV, close-ups of Ash and his point of view quickly and smoothly, despite the very fast pace.

(Again, people were stationed beside the road to whap the car with branches as it roared by; the branch that smacks Bruce in the face was held by Sam. Of course.)

The car slams into a stump, and Ash, groaning, is flung through the windshield and toward a tree, but he hits the ground first.

(Yes, that is a dummy, not Campbell, smashing through the window, although you can never be sure...)

The Force POV catches up with the car. Without a cut, it smashes in through the back window, then out the front.

Below:

Deadite Ash

(Bruce Campbell)

in the 'Sid Caesar'

make-up.

(This Ram-o-Cam shot was particularly difficult, Bruce says. "We tried to get this three times or so." They used "a forty-five foot metal arm with an attachment for this little Eyemo camera. We all had to run with it, and when we got to the back of the car, we had to feed the arm through the car window. The rod was attached to a cart, but we had to lift it up to feed it through the window. Once we hit the trunk, and another time ran into the rear-view mirror. Sam wanted it to lift up; he didn't want it to go straight in.")

Ash flees through the forest, pursued by the Force; there's more fast intercutting here. When we are seeing him from the Force's POV, we hear a rising, rushing drone of sound. He dashes into the cabin, and it follows.

("We never finished the interior of the location cabin," Bruce says. "[It] was all on sets over at the school, but for this shot we had to do a fake version of the front room because we had to start the evil entity

going into the house. We had to do a cut here; watch when the inner door shatters, there's a cut to the studio.")

Ash rushes into the hallway and slams the door. The Force keeps coming, crashing through the doors he slams behind him, following him when he smashes bodily through a door and on through the cabin in an S-shaped path, into the bathroom, then actually inside the *walls* of the cabin. Ash ducks to one side, and the Force doesn't see where he went. The Force POV looks around the front room of the cabin, then sort of shrugs and leaves, flying off into the forest.

(During the scene within the walls — surprisingly wide walls of an amazingly large cabin — watch for a moment where the camera jerks spasmodically; that's where Sam, who was operating the camera, ran into a wall. "The hard thing with using the wide-angle lens for the Force POVs," Bruce says, "is where to hide all the lights and all the crew, because this is a fish-eye lens and you can see the entire world.")

Back inside the cabin, two shutters bang. We hear the sounds of wind as the camera pans over the cabin, looking for Ash. The trapdoor we hadn't seen until now lifts a little.

(Many exterior shots of the cabin are of the miniature, so that the switch to all-miniature shooting during the attack by the trees wouldn't be too jarring.)

Unexpectedly, we cut to a shot of a small aeroplane landing. Annie, Dr Knowby's daughter, gets off the plane and is greeted by Ed Getley, both of whom we saw briefly in the flashback accompanying the tape recording.

(In the background, watch as airport workers try to open the doors of the plane; the guy on the right — Rob Tapert, as it happens — can't get the door open. "This," says an amused Bruce, "still torments Sam horribly." After a cut, both doors stand wide.)

Annie bears with her more pages of the Book of the Dead. Ed's impressed. They plan to begin the translations at the cabin; Ed says he hasn't heard from the doctor in a week, as there are no phones out there. They load her stuff into Ed's car. "Annie," Ed says, "you hinted in your telegram that your father was onto something with the first part of his translations. What has he found in the Book of the Dead?"

("Ed was supposed to be the young stud; the idea was that the audiences would assume he'd win the day," Bruce explains. The problem with that is that we've already become attached to poor bedevilled Ash, and Ed just isn't vivid enough. Looks like monster fodder to me.)

"Probably nothing," she replies, shutting the boot firmly, "but just possibly the doorway to another world."

(This line is a homage to Robert Wise's classic chiller The Haunting. *When asked what he expects to find in Hill House, Professor Markway answers, "Probably nothing, but maybe — just maybe — the key to another world.")*

In the cabin, Ash, troubled, dozes. Something makes him look up abruptly at the stuffed deer's head on the wall, hearing something we don't. He gets out of the chair painfully, and limps to a closed door, opening it with trepidation. He enters the room, still hobbling. It's dark in there. Did he hear something, or was it his imagination? He returns to the piano, which starts playing itself...

(We can now see that Ash has a scratch on his face. "This was some of the first stuff we shot," Bruce explains, "so there was a whole long list of what I had gone through, but we didn't know exactly how beat-up I should look.")

Ash takes out the necklace and stares at it, grief-stricken, as the camera moves around him. A sound from behind him makes Ash turn around as some of the boards nailed over the broken window of the room where the Force attacked Linda fall off. He rushes to the window and stares out.

(Notice that the windows are now boarded up. The screenplay included scenes showing Ash nailing boards everywhere, but they weren't shot.)

Cut to outside, as the cross on Linda's grave topples over and her hand thrusts up from the earth. Her shrivelled, headless body climbs out of the grave, and begins to dance.

(Good stop-motion animation by Doug Beswick.)

After a moment, it indicates with gestures that it misses its head. It bends over and the head tumbles along the ground and reattaches to the body.

(This is in reverse motion. "I am actually not interested in this movie," Bruce admits, "until from this point on; for me, it really gets going here, it really kicks in.")

Ash can't believe his eyes as the body dances, the head rolling down one arm and back again. The body pirouettes rapidly while the head stays in one spot, laughing at Ash. With a happy cry, the body runs off into the woods. Ash peers out after it and she suddenly appears in front of him, reaching through the window towards him with long bony fingers.

(Now played by the actress again.)

Linda bangs his face repeatedly against the boards of the window, then her head falls off again.

Screaming, writhing, Ash finds himself back in the chair. Was it all a dream?

(He jerks spasmodically here; it's not that he can't get out of the chair, it's that "I can't scream. Sam told me I was so scared I can't scream.")

Just as he decides it was all a dream, Linda's decapitated head falls into his lap. "Hello, lover," she hisses, chomping down on the web between his thumb and fingers.

(Originally, some of this was in reverse action — the head thrust a four-foot tongue down Ash's throat. But when he watched the dailies, an exasperated Sam exclaimed, "That's the worst reverse-motion acting I've ever seen!" Bruce says, "You'd only hear that from Sam; he's the only guy who shoots so much reverse action that he would create a class of acting.")

This scene, which looks simple, was "a total and utter nightmare rig," Bruce explains. "I'm in a ridiculously uncomfortable position; her real body is between my legs, propped up by eight sandbags. I had fake legs coming out around her head, and then we had two free-standing chair arms, all because we wanted her face to be alive, with a neck appliance.")

Ash leaps up, yelling, running around the cabin banging Linda's decapitated head against the mantel, against the bookcase, against the wall. He grabs a book from the shelf and pounds it against the head, which makes small noises of complaint and occasionally cackles. He flings himself around the room desperately as the head laughs. "Work shed!" he exclaims.

(Bruce reveals that Evil Dead II *fans often ask him to autograph a still with the word "workshed." They're amused because the sound and the movement of his lips in this shot don't match. "At conventions," Bruce sighs, "they love hassling me about that.")*

Ash rushes out of the door and trips over an oil barrel, slamming the head against a tree, then against the camera! He comes into the shed, puts the head in a vice and clamps it shut. The head releases its death-bite. "Even now," it shrieks, "we have your darling Linda's soul! She suffers in torment!" "You're going down!" Ash tells the gloating head. "Chainsaw!" he says to himself, pulling aside a curtain, but there's no chainsaw, just a chalk outline on the wall.

(We have to assume that Ash had been there before — otherwise, why would he expect

Left:
Linda's head
(Denise Bixler)
in Ash's lap.

to find a chainsaw, and how would he know where to look?)

The door bursts open and Linda's headless body, carrying the roaring chainsaw, stumbles in. Ash counters its move, and the chainsaw flips over, slicing down into the stump of the neck, spewing blood or black bile all over the place, and all over Ash.

(Sure, the walking, headless body is clumsy, but give it a break. Just be impressed it's walking around at all. It's a big marionette on a pole, with Howard Berger operating it on a mechanic's dolly below, and Greg Nicotero controlling the saw from above.)

The saw blade remains stuck in the neck, but after a struggle, Ash gets control of the chainsaw and jerks it into life. He starts for the head, but Linda has reverted to normal. "Please, Ash, please don't hurt me. You swore we would always be together. I love you." "Arrrggh," he cries. Without warning, she looks monstrous again: "Your love was a lie, and now she burns in hell!" In silhouette, Ash attacks the head with the chainsaw. Blood covers the lightbulb, and we see hanging bones in the red light. Fade to black.

It's later. Ash comes out of the work shed covered in goo, carrying the chainsaw. He staggers back into the cabin and closes the door behind him. He takes a shotgun off the wall, finds some cartridges, and begins to load it. Henrietta's rocking chair moves slowly with a rattling sound. Ash, frightened, cautiously reaches out, but just before he can touch the chair, it stops.

(That's actually Sam's voice making the sound of the chair. "We played around with the rocking chair squeaks," Bruce says, "and sort of blended them, so it's got a little more edge to it than a regular rocking chair.")

This is a strain on old Ash. He lurches around the cabin, over to the oval mirror we saw in the first film. "I'm fine, I'm fine," he tells himself. Then his reflection leans out of the mirror, grabs him by the shoulders, and says, "I don't think so. We just cut up our girlfriend with a chainsaw — does that sound fine?" The chuckling reflection clutches at Ash's neck, then after a cut the camera pulls back to find he's alone and choking himself. The mirror is back to normal, and he touches it to make sure. He makes a little jump at it, as if trying to catch it off guard.

(We first see the mirror in an over-the-shoulder shot from behind the real Bruce Campbell, looking at his reflection. Then there is a cut to a close-up of him, then to a double for Bruce in the foreground, seen over the shoulder, looking at the real Bruce in the hole in the wall that's masquerading as the mirror. This cuts very quickly, and the lunge forward by the reflection takes most audiences by surprise. The other guy in the scene, doubling for Ash, was a local college student. "Sam kept threatening me that if I wasn't any good he'd get the other guy. 'Shut up and get him. Leave me alone.'")

The mirror is okay, but his right hand suddenly develops black veins, and makes a high pitched gibbering noise. The hand flops back and forth, as if trying out its new-

found independence, then clutches at Ash's face. After a moment, he pulls free painfully, but the hand continues to gibber and claw at him. "You dirty bastards," he cries. "Give me back my hand!"

Above:
Ash fixes Linda's
head in the vice.

(*Campbell's miming is excellent throughout this sequence; the illusion that the hand has a mind of its own is almost unshakeable.*)

Elsewhere, Jake, a guy from the road department, and his girlfriend Bobby Joe meet Annie and Ed, who are trying to get to the cabin. Jake tells them the road is out, and there are the clutching-hand girders of the destroyed bridge.

Annie insists that there must be another way up there. Jake suddenly remembers that there's a trail. "You could follow Bobby Joe and me," he says. "But it'll cost ya." He starts to demand forty-five dollars until Bobby Joe nudges him. "A hundred buck," he says, singularly.

"Tell you what," says Annie, "take my bags and you've got a deal." He looks into Ed's car and only sees a briefcase, so he agrees.

Meanwhile, back at the cabin, Ash is still having problems with his hand, which is all wrinkled, with long nails. He rushes into the kitchen and plunges it into the sink. We see this action from somewhere down in the drain, looking up at Ash through the water in the sink. At first, he appears to be getting some relief, but he doesn't notice the hand grabbing some nearby dirty dishes, breaking them over his head. It grabs him by the hair and pounds his head on the counter, then picks him up by the back of the neck and flips him clear over onto his back. After more flinging around and more broken crockery, it finally knocks him out, still making squeaking noises that sound almost like words.

The hand stays awake while Ash is unconscious. It drops a bowl it was about to brain him with, then catches sight (!) of a cleaver nearby, and begins painfully dragging Ash's unconscious body across the floor of the kitchen. It makes little self-affirmation noises as it gets nearer and nearer the cleaver — which we see from the point of view of the crawling hand.

Just as it gets to the cleaver, however, Ash stabs it with a knife. Even though this hurts him far more than it does the hand, he roars, "Who's laughing now?!" With his rebellious hand pinned to the floor, he grabs the nearby chainsaw and starts it by pulling the cord with his teeth. Again, he bellows, "Who's laughing now?!" — and saws his hand off.

(We're spared this sight, but his face is sprayed with spattering blood.)

Below:

Ash is attacked by his own reflection.

Dark clouds scud away from the moon as four people with flashlights approach the cabin. Bringing up the rear is Jake, angrily lugging Annie's big trunk. A deal is a deal, after all.

In the cabin, the disembodied hand struggles and twitches as Ash puts a bucket upside down on top of it, saying, "Here's your new home." This time we can make out the hand's words, "No, no, no!") He weighs it down with some books, with Hemingway's *A Farewell to Arms* on top.

(*Many reviewers mentioned this painfully obvious joke, possibly grateful for the opportunity to laugh at a gag they would have groaned at in an out-and-out comedy.*)

He wraps the stump of his hand in cloth and duct tape, to good sound effects. Behind him, the hand mutters and shrieks. Ash doesn't notice the bucket suddenly zip away, but he sees it overturned on the floor... no hand.

Grabbing the shotgun, Ash looks around the cabin and sees the hand scampering through a mouse hole. He tries to spot it by sound — it's still muttering and gibbering — and blows a hole in the wall to no effect. We see the hand framed in the mouse hole, drumming its fingers, kind of going "Na na na na na." It gets caught in a mousetrap and squeals, but flings it aside and flips Ash the finger before scuttling back. Boom! Boom! Ash blows a couple of holes in the wall. "Aarghh," he hears, as if the hand is dying, and a little blood trickles from one of the shotgun holes. "Got, you, didn't I, you little sucker!" he exults, but it's not over yet, of course.

There's a bit more blood than you'd expect from a hand, and more — and then a torrent of blood hits Ash square in the face, as if he were being hosed with the stuff.

(*This is the scene in which a garbage bag was more or less disembowelled above Bruce, who was lying on his back with the camera on its side. "The blood flood sequence wasn't bad to do," Bruce confesses," because it felt cool. That shoot was unmercifully hot, and those were the coolest two days I spent.*")

A longer shot of the room shows several fountains of blood gushing out from the wall. The blood changes to black bile and the flow reverses, sucking everything back in. Covered in blood, bile and other gunk, Ash sits down in the chair triumphantly, but it collapses under him. Take that, Mr Hero Man.

He hears a strange sound and looks up. The deer head mounted on the wall has developed blank Deadite eyes and swivels toward him, laughing maniacally. The gooseneck lamp laughs too, nodding up and down on its flexible neck. The books on the shelves and the doors of the cupboards all laugh giddily at him. Finally, Ash joins in, his eyes bugged out, his jaw stretched wide. It's all just too much. He lurches around the room, where he matches movements with the lamp, which amuses both of them. He stands in the middle of the room, howling with laughter, having a great time.

Suddenly, wham! Wham! Something pounds on the door. Everything stops laughing and he lets fly with both barrels, blowing holes in it.

(*"If you look closely," Bruce advises, "the door implodes instead of flying outward."*)

Ash opens the door cautiously. There's no one there. He backs away, not sure if some new horror has arrived. Suddenly, Jake leaps in at him and they grapple, Ash punching him with his good hand, but the hick slugs him again.

(*"The over-zealous actor actually hit me on the lip," Bruce recalls. "Of all the carnage and mayhem in the movie, what the British censors cut was the shot of someone hitting a man while he was being held. You can cut people's heads off, but you can't kick an unconscious man."*)

Seeing the carnage in the living room, the newcomers assume that Ash has killed Annie's parents, and throw him into the cellar.

(*Bruce's eager stunt double, John Casino, did the fall down the stairs.*)

They look down at him, and spit. As if he hadn't been through enough already.

(*Two lines here have particular resonance: Jake says, "The crazy buck's gone blood simple," a tribute to Joel and Ethan Coen's movie of that name. He also calls Ash "a flat-mouthed son of a bitch." That was a line an actress came up with in audition which Sam liked enough to include in the film.*)

A little later on, Jake is binding Bobby Joe's shotgun wound, while Ed tells Annie that there's no sign of her folks. She starts playing the tape, listening to her father's recording: "It's only been a few hours since I've translated and spoken aloud the first of the demon resurrection passages from the Book of the Dead — and now I fear that my wife has become host to a Kandarian demon. May God forgive me for what I have unleashed onto this Earth. Last night Henrietta tried to kill me." Dr Knowby says he buried Henrietta in the earthen floor of the fruit cellar.

Ash, down below, keeping company with a rat, is hearing all this too.

(*They shot more footage with the rat, called Señor Cojones by the crew, but didn't use it.*)

The moment Ash realises the implications, the floor of the cellar erupts and Henrietta's head, crawling with worms bursts through it. Ash screams.

(*At Sam's insistence, Bruce screams "like a woman." Ted Raimi plays Henrietta in elaborate make-up and costume, with the worms rendered in stop-motion animation. Lu Hancock plays the pre-Deadite Henrietta, "but Sam realised the amount of abuse that was going to happen to her when she comes back from the dead was far too great to inflict on an older woman, so he used his younger brother," explains Bruce.*)

"Someone's in my fruit cellar," the monster's cackling voice gloats. "Someone with a fresh soul!" Henrietta advances on the terrified Ash, who's pounding at the chained trapdoor. "I'll swallow your soul!" she screams, and her head mutates into something even worse.

The others let Ash out, but Henrietta's distorted head pops through the opening and bites down on Ash's foot. He pulls free and Henrietta grabs Jake's face. Ed slugs her, but she hits back and he sails across the room, smashing into a picture. He falls to the ground.

(*After shooting one of these scenes, Bruce washed the Karo syrup out of his hair, had the make-up scars removed, put on his clothes and went out to his car, only to be called back for one more shot. Not much he could do, since he was both star and one of the producers.*)

Ash comes around behind the open trapdoor and smashes it down onto Henrietta's head. One of her eyes pops out and whizzes across the room, landing in Bobby Joe's mouth. There's even a shot from the disembodied eye's point of view as it zips toward her screaming mouth. She spits it out.

(*This 'Eyeball Flyball' shot is the supreme gross-out moment in any of Raimi's films, amateur or professional, and audiences fall apart with eeewwws! and laughter every time. At one point, says Bruce, "Sam had the idea that they'd be later sitting around quietly trying to figure out what to do, and Bobby Joe would start making noises like a cat hawking up a fur-ball, and she'd cough up the eye, and it would be looking at her from the palm of her hand."*)

Jake kicks Henrietta in the head and Ash jumps on the door, forcing the monster back down. He and Jake kneel on the door, which is lifting up with the force of Henrietta's blows, but she quiets down after a while.

Outside, the Force POV heads for the cabin again.

It's later. Inside, Ash puts a log on the fire and tells the others that there is something out there in the woods, in the dark, and that the witch in the cellar is only part of it. Abruptly, Bobby Joe jumps up, screaming.

Then from the cellar trapdoor, they hear someone singing 'Hush Little Baby'. It's Henrietta, apparently normal. "Unlock the chains," Annie says, moved by the sight of her mother, but Ash stops her, shaking his head. Henrietta, seeing their indecisiveness, continues talking about the day that Annie was born. "It was snowing. So strange it would be snowing in September..."

Suddenly Ed, now a Deadite, leaps up from the floor, his face hideously distorted. He hangs in mid-air, twitching unnaturally.

(*He's animated by pixilation.*)

"We are the things that were and shall be again," he cries. Still hanging, still twisting, he says, "Dead by dawn," and is joined by Deadite Henrietta from the cellar, both chanting, "Dead by dawn, dead by dawn," over and over.

Dead Ed swoops across the room and tears out some of Bobby Joe's hair with his teeth, swallowing it. He goes the other way, and Jake grabs him from behind — but Ed's head swivels completely around on its shoulders to glare at Jake, followed by the body a moment later. He picks Jake up and thrusts him toward the ceiling, breaking the lightbulb with his head.

Ash runs out of the room, and Annie calls him a "filthy coward."

Right:
Henrietta (Ted Raimi) trapped in the cellar.

(Well, he's undeniably filthy by this point, and Sam did want us to momentarily believe Ash was a coward).

Of course, Ash returns in an instant with an axe. He chops Ed's head in two, and Ed bleeds green. He chops and chops, although we don't see the wounds, with green bile splattering everywhere, all over the walls, on the deer head, and finally over the camera lens. A voice, which could be Henrietta's, says, "We live, we live still."

("We tried very hard to cut around the fact that Ed was going to be sliced to shreds, because we knew the MPAA would be coming after us," Bruce says. "The beheading is in silhouette, although we may have actually shot it live action. The bile is bright green; there's no red anywhere." When the bile was flung from behind the camera, Sam Raimi made sure he was always one of the flingers. "Sam was being referred to as the King of Bile," Bruce says. His aim was too deadly and he kept hitting actors in the eyes, so he was fired as a bile-flinger.)

The four shocked survivors stand in the middle of the room, panting.

There's a shot of the cabin from outside, cutting to the interior again. Some time has passed, because Ash looks cleaner and neater. Gazing out of the window, Jake muses, "That's funny... that trail we came in on — it just ain't there no more, like the woods just swallowed 'er up."

The clock stops. It's so quiet.

(In fact, the soundtrack is artificially silent — there's no sound whatsoever.)

Annie and Ash, then Bobby Joe and Jake, react to swooshing sounds, jerking their heads around as if following something moving very fast that keeps coming to abrupt halts.

(Sam shot some cuts here with a 'scope, or anamorphic, lens turned ninety degrees to the plane of the film, drawing things out vertically. Also, as Bruce says, "Sam was doing stop-motion with live actors on a main unit, which in film-making terms is ridiculous. Sometimes a take would last two or three minutes just to get two or three seconds of running time; you'd have to stand there with your eyes open for minutes at a time while the camera's racing past. But that's how he gets those quick, funky moves all through here.")

They hear galloping hoofbeats. Snuffling sounds at the door, like a giant dog.

(This is another brief homage to The Haunting, *in which this memorably occurs.)*

Maybe it's something trying to force its way into our world... Giant booming sounds surround them as the door to other room opens part way, letting in more booming sounds and flashing lights.

(Sam called this the Zoom-Zoom Room. There's also the Boom-Boom Room, and the Zoom-Boom Room. We will leave it to the reader to determine which is which.)

Ash suggests they all go in together, but Jake exclaims, "Hell no, you're the curious one." So he and Bobby Joe stay behind as, carrying a lantern, Annie joins Ash and they enter the bedroom from which the flashes came. Another Camp Tamakwa T-shirt is on the closet door.

With a wailing sound, the ghost of Annie's father appears, writhing and semi-transparent, with only his face and hands visible. A dark spirit is the menace, he tells them, and their salvation lies in the pages of the Book of the Dead that Annie brought with her. "Recite the passages, dispel the evil. Save my soul, save your own lives," he screams as he vanishes.

(There are strange flashing lights on the wall all through this sequence, the result of using mirrors mounted on springs. "Sam has this moosh-moosh," Bruce explains cryptically. "He adopts a motif for a sequence, so every shot will be at a forty-five degree Dutch angle, or something will be zooming and booming. In this case, he had a board that had little pieces of mirror on wiggly springs. All he had to do was slightly mess with the board, and you'd get all kinds of bizarre reflections.")

Bobby Joe tells Jake he's holding her hand too tight, "But I ain't holding your hand," he replies. She looks down to see she's actually clutching Ash's lopped-off hand.

(Again, this remarkably effective scare was borrowed from The Haunting.*)*

Everyone screams. The lantern crashes to the floor and the lights go out. When they come back on a moment later, Jake asks, "Where's Bobby Joe?"

Unfortunately, she's outside running through the forest. A tree with a malignant face laughs at her, and she's grabbed by vines. One thrusts into her mouth and more and more grab her as she's hauled screaming through the woods.

Above:
Deadite Ed,
dismembered and
covered in green
bile.

(*The actress is "on an elevated board, with the camera above her, looking down," Bruce explains. "The vines are already in her face. It's shot in reverse motion, so the background had to be going up. The 'ground' was on a long, flat runner — she wasn't moving at all, but the ground and vines had to be pulled backward with the vines being withdrawn from her face, so when it all played forward, it would look like she was being dragged feet-first, and the vines would go into her face. This was an idea of Sam's." The shot looks straight down at Bobby Joe, so all we see is her, the 'ground' and the vines.*)

The hapless Bobby Joe is jerked through mud puddles with big splashes, pulled faster and faster, roaring, until she's rocketing toward a tree.

(*They originally intended to have a long shot of the forest at this point, with a sudden geyser of blood erupting above the treetops. It was too expensive to shoot, but it made an appearance in* Army of Darkness *instead.*)

Shock cut to Ash in the cabin dropping the glass-enclosed new pages of the Book. The frame shatters.

(*There's a shot of the Book of the Dead with strange, distorted music playing over it as the camera moves in. "We took a can of Dustoff," Bruce explains, "and sprayed it into an oil filler tube and got these wuhzzoooo sounds. Then the sound guy sampled that digitally and put it into his keyboard. It's not a Joe Lo Duca thing, it's a sound effects thing."*)

Outside, the trees distort as the fog closes in, and Jake worries about Bobby Joe. "If she went out in those woods," says Ash coldly, while studying the Book, "you can forget about her." The pages of the Book show a man in a blue shirt, and Ash reacts "like someone just walked over my grave."

(*This was to relate the illustration in the Book — which actually has white trousers, not brown — to Ash himself.*)

"In 1300 AD," Annie explains, "he was called the hero from the sky, prophesied [sic] to destroy the evil." They find the relevant passages in the loose pages. The first passage will cause "the dark spirit to manifest itself in the flesh," then the second will create a rift in time and space, and the physical manifestation will be forced into it.

But Jake has the gun and tries to force the other two to help him find Bobby Joe, out there in the woods alone. He grabs the pages and throws them into the cellar. "These pages don't mean squat," he says. "Now you ain't got no choice. Now move."

(Bruce points out that this was shot very early in the production, way out of sequence, and the splashes on his clothes don't match what we've just seen. He is also much heavier in these night exterior scenes — he always loses weight working on a Sam Raimi movie.)

They leave the cabin and walk cautiously into the woods.

(There's a miniature shot of the trees acting strangely, branches moving on their own.)

"No trail," says Ash. "Where to now?"

(Of course, Jake noticed earlier that the trail had been swallowed up by the woods.)

Jake has power, but doesn't know what to do with it. "Bobby Joe?" he screams.

The Force POV moves toward them as Jake slugs Ash with the shotgun butt. "Bobby Joe!" he screams. "Bobby —" sharp cut to the Force POV "— Joe! Bobby Joe, where are you, girl?"

(Scott Spiegel wanted the Force to be wandering nonchalantly through the woods, unconcerned with the cabin until it hears Jake shouting.)

Then Ash, a Deadite once again, leaps up, grabs Jake and flings him headfirst into a tree. Annie flees into the cabin and she slams the door as Deadite Ash, backlit by a red glow, screams at her; "You're next!"

Inside the cabin, she sees the knife across the room and grabs it. There's a noise from another room. She opens the door — it's the hallway. Annie walks down the hall, knife upraised. A door moves. She waits, knife at the ready. The door bursts open and she stabs... Jake, sinking the blade into his belly and staggering back in shock. Suddenly, Deadite Ash leaps up at the window, roaring, clutching at her. Annie tries to shut the door, but Jake's in the way. She moves him, but not far enough, slamming the door against him again as Deadite Ash pounds at it.

Annie pulls the knife out of Jake and drags him, still groaning, down the hallway, screaming "Shut up!" at him when he makes too much noise for her jangled nerves.

(This sequence gets a lot of nervous laughter in cinemas, and even more when Scott Spiegel and Bruce

Below:
Bobby Joe
(Kassie Wesley)
is attacked by
the forest.

Campbell watch the movie together.)

Entering the room, Annie spots an axe and drags Jake over to it. She picks up the axe and looks around anxiously. Henrietta, meanwhile, flings the trapdoor open and drags Jake headfirst into the basement. A gigantic wave of blood, far too much for one person, erupts from below Jake and over Annie as she tries to hold on to him. His legs disappear into the cellar.

(The scene immediately after this was shot earlier in production; Bruce points out that here Annie is absolutely drenched in blood, but in the next shot she only has a few splashes on her clothes.)

Annie staggers into the middle of the room, and Deadite Ash suddenly lurches into frame, clutching at her. He picks her up, raising her over his head with both arms, and slams her into a nearby wall, breaking the plaster.

Deadite Ash, looking worse than ever, roars like a lion, then laughs with horrifying glee, advancing on Annie's recumbent form. But there on the floor near her is the silver magnifying glass charm, the chain coiled in the shape of a face. He looks puzzled, confused, blank eyes and all, and picks it up, gazing at it with something like the dawning of understanding. He looks tormented, then as the camera backs away from his kneeling form, he sobs aloud in horror. When we see his face again, he's normal — and just barely manages to dodge Annie's axe blow.

"No, wait, I'm all right now!" Ash cries. Not surprisingly, Annie isn't convinced. They grapple and he slumps against the wall, relieved. Then, wham! The axe strikes the wall beside him, but this time he really calms her down. "I'm all right," he insists.

"Maybe you are," she replies, "but for how long?" She reminds him that to beat this thing, they need the missing pages that Jake threw into the basement. Ash looks grimly determined. "Then let's head down into the cellar and carve ourselves a witch," he growls.

Here's this movie's series of quick cuts, a sequence that got a lot of critical comment, and which audiences invariably respond to very strongly. Ash takes the chain off the work shed. From inside the shed, we see the door bang open — Ash and Annie stand in the doorway, Annie holding the chainsaw. Click: Ash turns on the hanging lightbulb. Señor Cojones crawls away. A space is cleared, two metal rings clank down and Annie holds the chainsaw while Ash drills into its housing. We see glimpses of work on the chainsaw rig, each accompanied by a specific sound heard only once; clanks, ratchetings, strapping sounds, the thoonk of Ash thrusting the stump of his arm into the slot they've made for it on the chainsaw.

They've fixed a prong to his chest to catch the wooden handle of the saw's starter cord. It works — the saw comes to life and he revs it up. Lopping two feet off the barrel of the shotgun in a flare of sparks, he twirls it like a pro and thrusts the gun into a holster mounted on his back. As the music rises, the camera comes in close on Ash, whose eyes light with a new fire as he murmurs, "Groovy."

("The sequence where Ash cuts the barrel off the shotgun and then twirls it and shoves it in his holster," Bruce says, "is one of those nightmare shots where you have to do about eight things, all right." There were squibs on the plastic barrels of the shotgun that had to be hidden; the chainsaw had to seem to slice into the barrel. The barrel had to be struck at the right point to break properly, it had to be twirled just right and then flipped into the holster. The version in the film is two shots. As the chainsaw "cuts" the barrel, there's a momentary flare of light hiding the cut between two separate takes of the sequence.)

Outside, the roots of a tree with a demonic face writhe like the tentacles of an octopus, and it begins to pull itself out of the ground.

Inside, Ash uses his saw arm to cut a slot down the middle of the trapdoor. He kicks it open. Those pages are down there somewhere. The saw purrs quietly as he walks across the cellar, reaching for the door to another room. He turns the handle — a shot we see past a lot of hanging gourds.

(The smoking chainsaw motor "very rapidly became the absolute bane of my existence," Bruce grouses. "Our budget was not such that we could have a real little motor sputtering away, and it would have been bad for sound, so it only smoked. We attached tubes down my leg and out the bottom of my pants for the scenes where we needed it sputtering. The only smoke that would run for the twenty or thirty feet necessary was tobacco smoke. At

Left:
Jake (Dan Hicks)
is confronted by
Deadite Ash.

the end of the day, they'd pull the tubes out through my outfit, and all the nicotine from the tube would come pouring out.")

Ash advances slowly, finding a couple of the pages stuck to the wall. The cellar seems vast, larger than the house above it. A curtain hangs in front of him, the light-bulb visible beyond it. He pulls the curtain aside to see pipes, hissing with steam. Abruptly, a bloody skeleton — Jake's, from the clothes — topples against him. Under the skeleton and a couple of rats hide more pages. Maybe this is all of them. Ash backs away, out into the basement proper.

(If you watch carefully, you'll see in one shot that Bruce's chainsaw hand is suddenly on the other arm. A shot had to be flopped in editing.)

He tosses the pages up to Annie. She immediately pulls up a chair and starts to sort them out. As Ash backs up the steps, Henrietta grabs his ankles from under the stairs and yanks. He topples forward. The camera stays on his face, falling with him. He's pulled back through the stairs in an undercranked reverse action shot.

Upstairs, Annie begins the chant, reacting to something, apparently the sounds of Ash being tossed around in the basement. Henrietta levitates out of the hole, laugh-ing fiendishly, and grabs Annie by the hair, rotating above her like a ceiling fan. Ash, meanwhile, with his left arm now bare, climbs out of the trapdoor and whistles at Henrietta. "Let's go," he says, challenging her.

(When Henrietta turns angrily toward him, note the sweat pouring out of her ear.)

She flies across the room at him as he revs up the chainsaw. They trade blows, with Ash getting the best of it till Henrietta elongates her neck and changes her face into the distorted horror we saw earlier. Her human screams turn into bird-like screeches as she chants "I'll swallow your soul!"

There's a reverse angle shot of a stop-motion Henrietta puppet threatening Ash. The head lunges at him, he bats it back, the camera staying with the head; they slug at each other again and again, Ash using his fist, Henrietta her head. Ash and Henrietta are staring at each other in close-up, when Annie starts singing "Hush little baby, don't say a word..."

This catches the monster's attention long enough for Ash to stab it in the back with the chainsaw. Whack! One arm flies across the room. Whap! There goes another. Swack! Lopped off, the head drops to the floor by Ash's feet. The torso stands upright for a moment, then topples over. "I'll swallow your soul! I'll swallow your soul!" the head cries.

"Swallow this!" says Ash, pointing the shotgun straight at the head, and at us, the POV camera. Kablooey! The blast shatters the head into bloody chunks. With sparks. Ash blows the barrel clean, twirls the shotgun, then slams it back into the hol-ster on his shoulders.

He tries to comfort the sobbing Annie. They hold each other, the only people in a world of horror.

And then, wham! A horrendous blow strikes the wall of the kitchen, knocking shelves down. Outside, we see that several trees have walked up to the cabin on their roots and are bludgeoning it with their limbs. More approach.

The mirror shatters as the limbs smash into the house, coming through the walls in some places. There are several exterior shots here as the trees attack the house. Annie and Ash lurch back and forth. The door is broken, and there's a demon-faced tree outside. "I only completed the first of the passages," Annie cries, "and that was to make the evil a thing of the flesh." Oops.

(When the Force rushes at the door, we can't actually see the big trees outside pounding on the house.)

Outside, we follow another POV shot of the Force charging toward the house. Annie tells Ash that someone has to read the second passage aloud, to open the rift and send the evil back.

The evil Force POV rushes toward the house and the door smashes open, and we see it — at least the way it looks now; like the skinless head of a demon the size of Kong. It has big teeth, big eyes, big everything, but how big can it be overall? It's not standing in a hole, after all.

Below:

Ash emerges from the cellar, armed with the chainsaw.

(The giant head, called the Rotten Apple Head on the set, never worked quite right. "One thing I give Sam a lot of credit for," Bruce says, "is that he is pretty good at making something out of nothing. You'll see what I call motifs, but what Sam calls moosh-moosh — as soon as the head makes its appearance in the cabin, a gale force wind starts, lights flash, papers waft around the room, he's using variable speed on the shutter, and you don't see the Rotten Apple Head normally. It always has an anamorphic lens stretching it this or that way. So he does a very good job of faking something pretty good that could have really looked sucky and cheesy." The head, left in a warehouse in North Carolina, turned up in a 'haunted house' later on.)

Somewhere in here, because of the mystical power of what he's seeing, the hair on Ash's temples turns white.

(This effect was created using pixilation. "It's composited with a background element of a time lapse

Above:
Henrietta's bird-
like incarnation
attacks Ash.

shot of a flower wilting," explains Bruce. "They had to keep swirling my hair to make it look like wind was blowing it. We added a separate smoke element going through the frame to blend everything together.")

Annie keeps reading the passages, but she's interrupted when Ash's dismembered hand stabs her in the back with that chicken bone knife. She falls to the floor as Ash screams "Nooo!" A huge hand, made of wood, limbs, bark and the like, plunges through the doorway and grabs him, pulling him toward the massive head, which has red eyes. Annie doggedly keeps reading. Outside, beyond the car, a white spiral opens in the sky, pulling the car slowly towards it. Faces appear in the demon head — Ash's own and those of the other victims of the Force: "We've won! Victory is ours!"

(What with the head, which required several operators, the hand, likewise, and the various wind and lighting effects, just about everyone in the production, including secretaries, had to do something to make it all work. This was also true of the 'laughing room' scene. "There were many occasions," Bruce says, "when the production office had tumbleweeds rolling through it because they were all doing something on the set.")

Ash fires up the chainsaw and stabs the big head in its right eye — bile gushes forth. Dying, Annie manages to sigh out the last few words of the spell. We see the car and a tree plunge into the spiralling rift in space.

The big head is sucked out of the house. The door slams shut. Ash and he crawls over to Annie. "You did it, kid," he says, but behind him, the cabin door rips away, plunging into the vortex. The stove hurtles past him and out the door, and other objects fly out of the house. Ash tries to hold on to something and is lifted clear off the floor. He hangs onto a shelf, but it breaks in the doorway. Screaming "For God's sake, how do you stop it?" Ash sails towards the vortex.

(*This sequence involved several different effects. When he sits up and says "You did it," the wall behind him is matted in, and the door is a separate matte. "You can see I'm walking a little oddly here," Bruce admits. "It's because my feet are chained together with a cable running to them, so as soon as I got to a certain point, I grabbed on, they yanked, and I was lifted horizontally. It's tough to pretend you're moving normally when you've got your feet shackled.*)

Ash falls into the spiral to flashes, lightning and coloured sparks. He plummets toward the camera as the vortex closes behind him in a burst of light and strikes the dusty ground at the same instant as the car... and opens his eyes to find himself surrounded by men in armour. "Slay the beast!" cries one of them.

(*He's a wizard type, played by Sam's Uncle Sid. Most of the knights were actually the North Carolina National Guard.*)

Several raise their swords and shout, "Slay the Deadite!"

(*This is the first time the term is actually used in the movies.*)

But they halt when they hear a shriek from the sky. A winged monster swoops down at them. Ash stands up, resolutely aims the shotgun, and blows the head off the winged Deadite, then seems surprised by what he's done.

(*Initially, they intended to have a Ray Harryhausen-type stop-motion battle between one of the knights and the winged Deadite, knocking the knight down the hillside. The stuntman didn't do the job to Sam's satisfaction, so he sent the man home, donned the armour and did the stunt himself, tumbling down a rocky hillside again and again. "It was horrible," Bruce says; "he really banged himself up." The sequence, you'll note, isn't actually in the movie.*)

The armoured men react with joy. One of the knights raises his visor. He leads the cheers: "Hail he who has come from the skies to deliver us from the terrors of the Deadites! Hail! Hail!"

(*He's none other than Sam Raimi. Also among the knights in armour are Josh Becker and Scott Spiegel, who reports that it was something like 110 degrees that day.*)

"No! No! No!" screams Ash, as more fall to their knees around him and hail him. The camera swiftly draws back, and we can see a castle in the distance that looks distinctly like the drawing we saw earlier. Ash is trapped in the past.

Sound of a fly...

(THE END)

CHAPTER 15

ARMY OF DARKNESS

DINO DE LAURENTIIS COMMUNICATIONS Presents
A RENAISSANCE PICTURES Production

We see the hooves of a horse, followed by men in chains and stocks. The camera pans up to a familiar face. "My name is Ash," we hear, "and I am a slave." Yep, it's Ash all right, with the gashes on his face we remember from *Evil Dead II*. "Close as I can figure it, the year is 1300 AD, and I am being dragged to my death. It wasn't always like this; I had a real life, once — a job."

There's a dissolve to a rotating blue light, as the camera pans right to a close-up of Ash, smiling blandly. "Shop smart," he says. "Shop S-Mart."

(*Bruce points out that this was part of the original script, so that when Universal requested a different ending, it was easy to return to S-Mart. However, "When we did it, we had to dig out all the old costumes again and shoot it in a different place, because the original location was no longer available to us."*)

His narration continues: "I had a wonderful girlfriend, Linda," and we see her smiling at him. "Together we drove to a small cabin in the mountains."

(*Linda is played by Bridget Fonda this time, in a dialogue-less cameo. You'll note she is wearing the requisite Michigan State University T-shirt, and that the car is the same one as in the other* Evil Dead *movies. Fonda is in the picture because she asked to be, as she's a fan of the first two, and she was later one of the leads in Sam's* A Simple Plan.)

We see all this as his narration continues, filling us in about the archaeologist and *Necronomicon Ex Mortis* — the Book of the Dead.

(*The Book has a different cover this time around, and it's larger, too. But the drawings inside are similar.*)

He sums up the narration about the Book from the first two *Evil Deads*, concluding: "It was never meant for the world of the living. The Book awoke something dark in the woods; it took Linda." We see her scream as the Force POV slams in through the window.

(This cabin is, needless to say, a third version; the first burned down and the second was just a set. "We built portions of it on a stage," Bruce says.)

Ash continues: "And then it came for me; it got into my hand..." cut to a close-up of Ash's hand developing black veins, "... and it went bad, so I lopped it off at the wrist, but that didn't stop it — it came back."

(We've been watching original footage up to this point, but now scenes from Evil Dead II *are spliced in.)*

We see Ash hanging on for grim death as the vortex sucks him out of the cabin, getting caught in door and then falling backwards.

(To appear to be plummeting through the vortex, Bruce dangled from a Peter Pan-like flying rig with pivots at his hips. He hung in front of an illuminated blue screen and was supposed to do a flip, but ended up twirling.)

In letters composed of smoke, the film's title gradually appears:

BRUCE CAMPBELL VS ARMY OF DARKNESS

Boom! Here come Ash and the car falling out of the sky. He gets to his feet as medieval soldiers on horseback surround him. "Where the hell....?" he says.

(The shot looking upwards at the Oldsmobile plummeting down to earth is a new one; the shot of it hitting the ground is the last scene they used from the second movie. Since they weren't sure they could actually use that footage again, they did shoot a new version of Bruce and the car hitting the ground, but "they loaded it with this Fuller's Earth stuff, and there was just too much of a cloud when it landed," Bruce recalls.)

Ash tries to placate the leader of the knights, whom we soon learn is called Arthur.

(Could he be that King Arthur? *There's no way to be sure.)*

Arthur summons his confidant the Wiseman, a wise man with a long white beard and flowing robes. Wiseman says he thinks Ash is the one prophesied to "fall from the heavens and deliver us from the terrors of the Deadites."

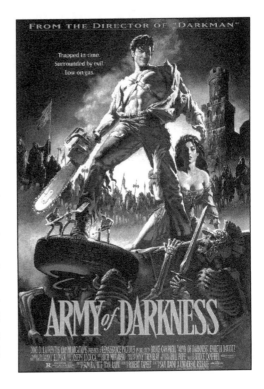

EIN FILM VON SAM RAIMI

Die ARMEE der FINSTERNIS

Above:

Ash (Bruce

Campbell), in

chains.

(Though he actually says "prophesised.")

Arthur expresses serious doubts about Ash's identity, and decides the newcomer must be one of Henry's men: "I say to the Pit with him!"

("Originally," says Bruce, "the king pulled out his sword, came racing by and sliced Ash across the chest. Later, you'll see a cut on my chest that I never had before." The fact that Ash bleeds makes Arthur doubt his validity as prophesied saviour, although everyone was happy to believe it at the end of Evil Dead II.*)*

Ash is taken prisoner, and loses his chainsaw. The Wiseman picks it up, curious. Sunlight glinting off the blade fills the screen in a matching dissolve to the blazing sun in the sky — and we're back to where the movie began.

A big castle lies ahead, and Ash and the other prisoners are marched toward it under the lash.

(Bruce says that the lower parts of the castle were still standing on that hill outside Acton until just before he shot an episode of The Adventures of Brisco County, Jr *on the same location. "When we I went back to the ranch, they had just torn the castle down. I had this big chase scene where I had to ride right across where that castle was, and it kind of gives*

you the chills, as if you're riding across your grave.")

They enter the castle courtyard, Ash still being jerked along in chains, a captive.

(You can't take Ash's word for things in this outing, though — he's clearly not the slave he claims to be in his opening narration.)

One young woman, Sheila, emerges from the crowd and asks Arthur where her brother is. Arthur says, "he fought valiantly, but fell in battle with Henry's men. I'm sorry, Sheila."

The children beat Ash and poke him with sticks, while other denizens of the castle pummel him with cabbages and rotten fruit.

("Sam would always be the guy who would aim at my head, just whale at me, because he knew the extras wouldn't. They never want to hit the star of the movie, or piss him off, for fear of being fired. Well, Sam's known me since high school, so he doesn't give a rat's ass.")

Sheila tugs at Ash, spits at him, and declares that her brother's death shall be avenged. It's still all a mystery to our hero, however.

(This sequence features a good example of a trademark Raimi shot. It begins with a close-up of Bruce's feet and ends as a high crane looking down as they halt near the pit, a hole in the courtyard floor surrounded by a metal ring and covered with a metal lid.)

Henry the Red, Duke of Shael, Lord of the Northlands, asks Ash whom he might be. Henry is another prisoner, the balding, redheaded bruiser who was just behind Ash all the way to the castle.

"Well, hello Mr Fancy Pants," sneers Ash insolently. "You ain't leading but two things right now, pal — Jack and shit, and Jack left town."

(It's worth pointing out at this point that in Army of Darkness, Ash's personality is somewhat different than in the other two movies; in the first, he was very quiet and romantic, just this side of a nerd; in the second, we didn't get to know him well, since he spent almost all his on-screen time being terrorised. Here he's rude, rather stupid, and not very likeable. This no doubt amused Sam and Ivan Raimi, who wrote the script, but apparently it didn't sit too well with audiences.)

Arthur advances and stands beside the metal-roofed pit. "There is an evil awakened in this land," he declares, "and well my people fight for their very souls against it." He gestures to Henry, who charges over to him and claims that Arthur started it — and that his people are suffering at the hands of the evil as well.

"Your people are no better than the foul corruption that lies in the bowels of that pit," Arthur sneers.

(This line came from a reading given by an actor auditioning for the role of Henry the Red, says Bruce: "We always encourage actors to bring a little speech with them, because when you're auditioning and the part being auditioned for has only a line here and there, it's hard to get a sense of whether the guy is right for the role, so you tell them to bring in

*Above:
Wiseman (Ian
Abercrombie)
with the
stranger's
device.*

a representational piece.")

The pit is cranked open, and we look up at Ash and Henry from inside it, as they're poised on the brink of a platform extending out over the mouth of the hole. One of Henry's men is shoved into the pit, screaming in protest. There's an ominous silence from within — everyone comes a little closer. In the crowd we can see a big bald blacksmith with a moustache.

(He's played by Tim Quill, a friend from the Super-8 days.)

We hear a scream, closely followed by a gigantic fountain of blood, and everyone backs away from the edge. In the confusion, one of the prisoners tries to flee. Arthur coolly takes a crossbow from a soldier, aims and lets fly. We follow the bolt from slightly ahead and to one side, then the camera seems to be mounted on the feathers of the arrow as it strikes the fleeing man squarely in the back.

The inhabitants of the castle turn one by one as the camera passes them, looking towards the pit — Ash turns too, and realises when someone nearby draws a sword that it's him they're looking at. "You gotta understand, man, I never even saw these assholes before," he declares passionately.

(According to Bruce, "Sam's very irreverent about how you handle the main character. Here, [Ash] is a coward and makes horrible mistakes. I think it's funny especially because of the fact that a studio released this movie in which the lead character is not even likeable. If this had been written for a studio, I can guarantee you a lot of this would have been reduced.")

Ash tries to get Henry to confirm that he isn't one of his men, but Henry says "I dinna think he'll listen, lad." Sheila flings a rock at Ash, catching him on the temple; he staggers right up the little ramp, teeters on the edge, and then someone pushes him in. Whooah...

Splash! Ash lands in water covered by a thin layer of fog. A manacled skeleton hangs from the wall in the background. Behind him, a pale hand with long nails rises from the water. A being, maybe a Deadite, rises from the water and advances on him, grabbing him by the back of the neck and pounding him in the face. The onlookers cheer from above. One calls out, "Isn't he wonderful?" but he's probably talking about Ash's opponent.

(And just what are these creatures in the Pit? Why is it there at all? What kind of bargain have Arthur and his followers made with its inhabitants?)

The thing in the pit pulls back and slugs the camera right in the lens, and we cut to Bruce recoiling from the blow. The wide angle lenses used here make the fist grow to enormous proportions as it strikes the camera.

(These bravura action shots are pure Sam.)

One blow sends Bruce flying back into the water as the thing tumbles toward him like an acrobat. "Why, you!" says Ash, grabbing it with his feet and flinging it to one side. Henry, above, cheers him.

Arthur mutters, "Spikes," and two of his men begin turning a wheel so that large spiked walls on either side of the pit start closing in. Ash slams his opponent against them, but it pulls free. Above, the Wiseman calls out, "Strange one!" and throws the chainsaw down to him. Ash leaps upward, plunging the stump of his hand into the housing he built for it on the chainsaw. *Thoonk!* He jerks the chainsaw into life and hacks at his opponent.

(Although Ash virtually dismembers it, we see very little blood on screen.)

Through the camera mounted on the wall we see four spikes around the lens, moving towards Ash. He's in real trouble, running this way and that, when an even worse-looking monster, the Pit Hag, erupts out of nowhere and runs at him. He swings the chainsaw and the thing's dismembered hand flies upward out of the pit, landing on the face of a bystander. The others laugh.

Below, Ash is still fighting the Pit Hag as he undoes his belt, wraps it around the ascending chain and is drawn upwards, but the Pit Hag grabs him. The walls get closer and closer and he almost loses the grip on his belt, but manages to lift his legs up and over onto solid ground as the walls slam together beneath him. Chainsaw first, he clambers out of the pit.

Ash walks up to Arthur. "You know, your shoelace is untied," he says. Puzzled, Arthur looks down, and he decks him. "All right," says Ash, furious. "Who wants some? Who's next? Who wants to have a little? You!" He points at a balding knight standing nearby. Ash walks up to him, pulls his sword away, slams the guy in the shoulder. The threatened knight shoves someone else aside.

Ash frees Henry: "Now get on those horses and get out of here." He orders Arthur's men to "Let 'em go," as Henry laughs, punches Ash in the arm companionably, and rides free. Arthur yells "Sword boy!", takes his sword from a flunky, and cries, "For that arrogance, I will see you dead!" He raises the sword, and bang! It shatters. Ash blows smoke from the barrel of his shotgun.

(And just when did Ash get his shotgun back? "There was an establishing shot earlier that got cut out," Bruce admits, "of the Wiseman with Ash's chainsaw and shotgun. Some of

that wonderful condensation where logic goes out of the window.")

"Alright, you primitive screwheads," he says, "listen up! See this?" He hoists the gun overhead, turning around so they can all see it. "This is my boom stick! It's a twelve-gauge double-barrelled Remington, S-Mart's top of the line. You can find this in the sporting goods department. That's right, this sweet baby was made in Grand Rapids, Michigan. It retails for about a hundred-nine ninety-five. It's got a walnut stock, cobalt blue steel, and a hair trigger. That's right. Shop smart, shop S-Mart."

The locals have no idea what he's saying, but he's speaking in authoritative tones, and he impresses the hell out of them. "Now, I swear, the next one of you primates even touches me — Yahhh!" he yells, and lowers the gun to blow away the Pit Hag, which has also climbed up via the chain.

(Of course, it doesn't seem likely that it would have survived the spikes.)

It takes two shots, but the Pit Hag is flipped over into the pit at last.

Below:
"Alright, you
primitive screw-
heads!"

Everyone is even more impressed. Ash twirls the gun in the light of the setting sun, holsters it on his back, and says, "Now, let's talk about how I get back home."

("One advantage of sequels," Bruce points out, "is you get to figure out how to do stuff. In Evil Dead II, we had a scene where I'm supposed to stick my sawn-off shotgun into my

EIN FILM VON *SAM RAIMI*

Die **ARMEE** der **FINSTERNIS**

holster. I tried it once with a real shotgun; didn't work at all. I jammed it into my arm and cut myself. We finally replaced the regular barrel with a plastic barrel, but the regular trigger caused problems. I tried to stuff it in the scabbard on my back in one shot, but it took some time to get it right.

Here we had an almost totally balsa-wood version of the gun with fishing weights at either end and a ring for the trigger guard; I could hold that thing out and twirl it for half an hour without stopping. After I walked into position, a prop person snuck up behind me, and I just made the motion of sticking it back there, while this guy pressed it to my back. We put in the sound effect later.")

Later, he's being fed grapes and a big chunk of roast meat by several beautiful young women. He belches a couple of times. Sheila approaches to beg his forgiveness, saying she thought he was one of Henry's men. "First you want to kill me," he says with curled lip, "now you want to kiss me. Blow."

Only the Necronomicon can help him, the Wiseman tells Ash, as it contains incantations that can return him to his time. Ash is demanding to go home when, suddenly, hot soup pours over his feet. The camera follows the soup back to an overturned pot, where woman with long hair has her back to the camera. As she whirls round, we see that she's a Deadite.

"You shall die!" the monster screams. It floats off the ground, levitating and jerking like a puppet. "We shall feast upon your soul!" It drops heavily to the floor.

Arthur approaches it cautiously, and we see the eyes pop open. He's about to touch the body but Ash stops him, warning him that it's a trick, and telling him to get an axe. With a scream, the Deadite sits up, knocks Ash and Arthur to one side and rushes at Sheila, but Ash slugs it with the butt of his gun.

The Deadite throws hot liquid into the eyes of a knight who charges at her. The blacksmith we saw earlier tackles her, and she's about to douse him with boiling water too when Ash shoots the pitcher out of the Deadite's upraised hands.

"Yo, she-bitch," he says. "Let's go."

(*As if there's any such thing as a he-bitch.*)

In a lot of fast action, with a very mobile camera and rapid intercutting, they battle; when he hits her, she twirls away, first spinning one direction, then the other. Finally, over his shoulder and facing in the opposite direction, he shoots the Deadite dead.

"If the Necronomicon falls into the hands of the Deadites, all mankind will be consumed by this evil," says the Wiseman. "Now wilt thou quest for the Book?" It looks like Ash has no choice.

(*This entire sequence was a reshoot, done six or seven months after principal photography wrapped, and was financed by Sam, Rob and Bruce.*)

Ash looks down at the stump of his hand and sighs. The doors to a cabinet full of armour slam open. "That one," he says, pointing. Ash and the blacksmith create a functioning artificial hand

(This scene utilises the swift intercutting between key moments of action accompanied by one loud distinctive sound, seen in the first two films. This time, a zoom in to the relevant image punctuates each shot. The whole thing only takes thirty-one seconds.)

We see the metal hand created, tested, mounted on Ash's arm and put into operation, easily crushing a metal goblet: "Groovy."

Later, Sheila enters, finding Ash tinkering with his new hand. "Raised in a barn? Shut the door," he sneers. "Probably was raised in a barn, with the other primitives."

"It's said thou wilt lead our people against the Evil," she says, but he replies that the only reason he's getting the Book is to go home. She picks up something from the table, but he snatches it away. "Don't touch that please," he snaps coldly. "Your primitive intellect wouldn't understand alloys and compositions and things with molecular structures..." He breaks off, apparently over-reaching his own expertise.

("How Ash treats the girl in this film is fairly chauvinistic and reprehensible," Bruce admits. *"We hoped the audience would stick with this guy because they realise they're stuck with him, not because he's necessarily nice — or they'll sympathise that he's completely out of his element.")*

Below:
Sheila (Embeth Davidtz) apologises to Ash.

Sheila persists: "All of my hopes and prayers go with you, and I made this for thee." She holds out a robe, smiling. "Good, he snarls, "I could use a horse blanket." She slaps him and heads for the door, but he catches up with her in the doorway. He pulls away her hair ribbon. "Gimme some sugar, baby," he says, and they embrace as flames lick up in the foreground.

(Bruce really was slapped in this scene, and since the slap happened in the master shot, it had to be done repeatedly for close-ups. Bruce darkly suspects that Sam, always prone to tormenting him, did it that way on purpose. Also, "As we're getting ready to shoot," Bruce admits, "I hear Sam giggling to himself over in the corner. He comes over, still sort of half giggling, and goes, 'Okay, I want you to say, "Give me some sugar, baby," just before you kiss her.' And it's one of those times where you go, 'Sam, are you out of your mind?' But it's one of the most-requested lines I get whenever women come up for autographs." This scene was originally followed by a fire-lit love-making scene, which still exists in cuts of the film released overseas.)

To heroic music, Ash and others charge out of the castle in the morning, as the rising sun sparkles on the dust their horses kick up.

(Bruce says that Sam has always wanted to do a scene where horses thunder across the countryside and everyone's yelling 'Heeyah!' One of the voices you hear yelling 'Heeyah!' in this scene is Sam's.)

They pause at a striking, familiar rock formation.

(Vasquez Rocks, used in many movies and television shows.)

This is clearly as far as everyone except Ash is going. The Wiseman says, "This path will lead you to an unholy place, a cemetery. There, the Necronomicon awaits."

(Bruce points out that in this scene, you can tell how long his hair is supposed to be in all of Army of Darkness.)

The Wiseman tells Ash that when he retrieves the Book from its cradle, he must recite the words "Klaatu birata niktoo."

(This is the famous phrase from The Day the Earth Stood Still *that Patricia Neal has to repeat to Gort, the giant robot. However, either accidentally or by design, no one in* Army of Darkness, *certainly not Ash, gets the phrase quite right.)*

Ash recites the words, actually saying "Klaatu varata nicto," but refuses to repeat it again. He insists that they send him back once he gets the Book, then rides off down the path between the rocks.

(This path was created for Army of Darkness.)

Soon, Ash is among pine trees, with fog blowing about him. He hears voices like distant singing, wails and weird sounds among the trees. Then the good old Force POV comes rocketing toward him through the sunny, misty woods. Faster and faster it comes, splitting trees as it gains on Ash, galloping along on his horse. A branch sweeps Ash off and he plunges headfirst into a muddy pool. He leaps out, starts running and tumbles down a hill, still followed by the Force.

(One of the ways Bruce landed the role in The Adventures of Brisco County, Jr *was to show the producers a reel of his horse and stunt action from* Army of Darkness. *In fact, he adds, "the nice thing about these movies I've done with Sam is that they're the hardest shoots I've ever worked on; other things pale in comparison, so that they seem much easier. It's been handy to get work because I can tell producers, 'Yes, I've done that. And I've done that, too.'")*

He runs up to a nearby windmill, dashes inside and shuts the door.

(The windmill is a hanging miniature mounted on an arm between the camera and the background. It's a Dutch windmill, not really appropriate for thirteenth century England, but who's counting?)

The Force slams against the door over and over as Ash leans against it from the inside, screaming with effort and fear. After a moment, he realises he's been screaming for a while without any further banging on the door. The windmill slowly stops turning.

It's night. Ash throws a log on the fire, then catches sight of someone — he runs forward and smashes into a mirror, shattering it. He picks up a piece and gazes at himself. Dropping it, he sees himself reflected many more times in the shiny fragments on the floor.

(Bruce says, "The scene inside the windmill is one of the most severely truncated in the film. I think it worked in its entirety, but it was a little slow, in that if Ash is on a journey to get this all-important Book, why would he stop and spend the night? It makes more sense that it be truncated.").

Ash walks away and doesn't notice that the reflections remain behind, then look at each other and climb out of the shards of glass.

(This is a very nice effect, and may be unique to this movie — hollows built into an oversize section of floor were lined with glass, so the illusion that they really are fragments of mirror reflecting Bruce Campbell is damned near perfect. We can even see the rafters overhead 'reflected' behind the tiny Ashes.)

The miniature Ashes are evil little bastards. Three of them grab a normal-sized fork, the one in the lead yells "Ramming speed!" and they charge at Ash's butt. There's a shot over the tines of the moving fork heading for his rear — "Yaahhhh!" he screams, jumping up and hitting his head. Other little doubles fire the shotgun at him, and bounce into the air from recoil.

The full-size Ash throws the fork at one of the miniatures, and we follow it until it impales this particular little Ash.

("I had to run in, stop at the wall, see that I was trapped, turn around, react as the giant fork came in, get skewered, and then die," says Bruce — and all of this had to be done

in reverse motion. "The reverse acting would have to be: dead, slowly coming to life, total agony, the fork is pulled away, turn, react to the wall, and run out in reverse.")

Ash bangs his head on a stovepipe, then falls onto the hob, landing on his left cheek. Stuck to the hot surface, he pries his face away with a spatula as you would a hamburger.

Catching sight of a little Ash on the floor, Ash stomps along after him, singing "London Bridge is falling down, falling down..." seen from the POV of Little Ash. This little Ash grabs a convenient nail and raises it just as big Ash's foot comes down. He reacts in pain and surprise as the nail stabs into his foot, screaming and bugging out his eyes. Four little Ashes — two riding piggyback on two others — conclude "My fair lady!" in falsetto.

("There was originally a sequence of him banging his head on the stovepipe until it finally smashed," Bruce recalls, "and all the soot comes out a la *the Three Stooges. When you cut a sequence, you've got to figure ways to condense it so there won't be big continuity shifts. It was all handled properly when we shot, but now there's a big jump, because my face is covered with soot without any explanation.")*

Ash slips, flying into the air and crashing to the floor on his back, knocking himself out as the little Ashes gibber. There's a blurry dissolve...

Ash comes to later (in a big close-up of his eyes); we hear him say "what a horrible nightmare..." and as he realises what's up, "Oh God! I can't move!" He's tied down *a la* Gulliver. Two little Ashes hold his mouth open as another is positioned over it. The little Ash plunges down into big Ash's mouth and is swallowed.

(Unfortunately, the Introvision shot here just doesn't work. You can't really tell what they're doing most of the time.)

Ash frees himself, but his belly roils in pain. He tries to make himself vomit, but can't, and looks around the room desperately. Spotting a kettle steaming on the stove, he grabs it. "Okay, little fella, how about some hot chocolate!" he laughs, and drinks the boiling water. He's momentarily satisfied, if scalded, as he hears a little scream from within.

Almost immediately, however, his right shoulder starts itching. He reacts in silent movie fashion, doing big takes, then pulls his shirt open to find an eye peering out of his shoulder. The eye blinks and protrudes a little.

(This scene is an homage to the peculiar movie The Manster, *which also featured a guy with an eyeball on his shoulder.)*

There's a high angle shot of Ash running out of the windmill screaming, "Oh dear God, it's growing bigger!" Ash runs up into close-up, howling at the moon, and he now has two heads (our Ash is the left head, Evil Ash is on the right). Our Ash pokes the other head in both eyes, Stooge fashion. "I'm blind, I'm blind," wails Evil

Right:

Ash splits

in two.

Ash, then snickers, opening undamaged eyes. The two-headed figure staggers back into a tree, then it's momentarily a creature with four legs, four arms and two heads, scuttling on its back through the forest. It pulls apart into two distinct entities — Good Ash and Evil Ash.

(An elaborate stop-motion effect was filmed for this sequence, with a little puppet double Ash running through the forest, but it was cut — more for reasons of timing than because the animation didn't work. Part of the sequence appears in foreign versions of the film.)

"I'm Bad Ash," says Evil Ash, "and you're Good Ash," with weird facial expressions and finger flips. "You're goody little two shoes, you're goody little two shoes," Evil Ash warbles, dancing on the spot. During the dance, he punches and kicks Good Ash — but then Good Ash he pokes the shotgun in his face and pulls the trigger. Kablooey! Evil Ash flips through the air, hits a tree. "Good, Bad," says Ash, "I'm the guy with the gun." Evil Ash's face is now, not surprisingly, in ruins. Ash drags the body back into the mill; there's a low angle looking up at the blades as they whoosh by the lens. The sound of the swooping blades is used to break up the shots of Good Ash strapping Evil Ash down for dismemberment.

(This is very similar to the equivalent scene in The Evil Dead.*)*

He raises the chainsaw, with lots of emphasis on the blade, but not a drop of blood is seen.

Later, under the full moon, Ash digs a grave and throws the remains of Evil Ash in a gunny sack into it; the head pops out and tells Ash that he'll die in the graveyard before he gets the Necronomicon. "Hey," asks Ash, "what's that you've got on your face?" "Huh?" grunts Evil Ash, as a shovelful of dirt hits him. Ash stabs another grave marker into the ground and gallops off into the night.

("We had a wireless mike on me during a lot of this stuff to get reference tracks," Bruce says, "and on the production track, in this scene you hear me going, 'Whoa, boy, whoa, easy boy,' begging the horse not to take off on a blind run. During looping, I could be brave again.")

At last, he arrives at the graveyard, which is on a hill. Weird monuments abound.

(This set is extravagant and theatrical, not in the realistic mode of the rest of the movie, but it works very well.)

The soundtrack music features church bells and a choir. Ash sees a skull on the ground, and its jaw slowly opens as he passes. The camera tilts back and forth as he approaches the altar holding the Necronomicon — but there are *three* of them. He's surprised: "Wait a minute. Hold it. Nobody said anything about three Books!" He doesn't know which or how many he should take. Oh well, he shrugs, and opens the nearest Book. Uh-oh — there's a whistling, sucking vortex in there that pulls his hand in, stretching it. We look out at Ash from inside the Book, seeing a hole with red sparks spinning around it, and Ash in the centre trying to escape.

Smoke is sucked into the hole as Ash tries to pull free, his arms getting longer and longer, in a reverse motion shot. Finally, he's pulled right into the Book, and it slams shut. There's silence for a beat or two, then the Book's cover flips open and Ash climbs out — but his face is very long, ending at the middle of his chest. He shakes his head until he's back to normal. Wrong Book.

Now Ash isn't sure what to do. He reaches for one, pauses, and reaches for the other, muttering to himself all the while. Ha, he thinks, almost fooled me... The Book he picks up opens the mouth on its cover and bites him, and he tries to throw it away but it flaps its pages like wings and flies at him. "Well," he concludes, "seems fairly obvious." Then he tries to recall the words.

Ash gets the first two right, but he can't remember the all-important third. "Necktie! Nectar! Nickel!" he tries desperately. "I think it was an 'n' word... definitely an 'n' word." Unwisely, he tries to outsmart the evil forces. "Klaatu Barada," he says firmly, then coughs loudly, making a vague 'n' sound. He looks around. Nothing's happened, nothing's changed. "Okay then, that's it," he announces. Ash picks up the Book to leave but all at once there's thunder and lighting, and tombstones start to explode.

Meanwhile, back at the castle, the thunder and lightning continues. "Something's amiss!" the Wiseman declares ominously. Sheila looks worried.

In the graveyard, tombstones continue to launch like little rockets. As Ash flees,

Above:

Ash chooses the

wrong book.

skeletal hands erupt from the ground and trip him. Others hold him to the ground while yet more wreak Stooges-like havoc on his face, stretching his mouth, poking into his nostrils, slapping him, pinching his nose, and so on. "Keep your damn filthy bones out of my mouth!" he cries, grabbing the Book, and riding away, declaring that he's through being their garbage boy.

Lightning smashes into Evil Ash's grave, and he bursts out of the ground and reassembles, announcing through his ruined face, "I live again."

Ash returns to the castle and gives the Necronomicon to the Wiseman, but has to admit that he didn't say the words exactly right. The Wiseman is furious, because failing to speak the words correctly has awakened the Army of the Dead. "Now, whoa right there, spinach chin," Ash exclaims. What about getting home? The Book can still send Ash home, Wiseman admits reluctantly, but right now it is useless to the people because the Evil has a terrible hunger for the Necronomicon, and will come looking for it.

(*This idea is new to* Army of Darkness; *in the first two films, the Evil Dead were awakened by the Book, which had a lot of power, but they didn't seem to want it themselves.*)

Ash insists on holding Wiseman to his deal, refusing to stay and help them — Arthur agrees because he is a man of honour. Everyone looks disappointed in Ash and walks away, leaving him embarrassed. "Wretched excuse for a man!" says Wiseman, and walks off. Everyone except Sheila mutters that Ash can't be trusted.

Ash and Sheila are alone in the courtyard. "I didn't have what it took. So long," he says, and starts to walk away. "But what of all the sweet words that you spoke in private?" she asks. "Well, that's just what we call pillow talk, baby, that's all," he responds, looking miserable.

"I still have faith in thee," Sheila says. But he looks helplessly untrustworthy, and can't say anything to gain her confidence. "Coward!" she sneers, and walks off.

A flying monster appears above the castle and swoops down toward Sheila. "Ash! Help me!" she screams, but it grabs her and flies off. Ash runs up the stairs to the castle wall with a sword, but he's too late: "Damn you!"

(*This winged Deadite resembles the one we saw at the end of* Evil Dead II.)

Elsewhere, the camera zooms in on gargoyle statues, then an optically-distorted shot of Evil Ash, complete with skull helmet. He's commanding the skeletal army to resurrect others. "I shall command every worm-infested son of a bitch that ever died in battle!" he declares. Skeletons help each other out of graves, and they all sound like Robert Newton as Long John Silver. One coughs dustily as he sits up.

(*There's a mixture of stop-motion and live action here, and it's pretty effective, the best optical work in the film so far, other than the Introvision scenes in the castle. Bizarrely, this sequence was singled out as one that bothered the ratings administration of the MPAA. "I just have to laugh every time I see the sequence of talking skeletons," Bruce says. "How seriously can you take that?"*)

The flying Deadite dumps Sheila, struggling, before Evil Ash, who snarls "Gimme some sugar, baby." He embraces her at the Necronomicon's shrine, as a field of skeletal warriors stir behind them.

Meanwhile, back at the castle, scouts warn that the Army of the Dead gathers in the woods. Should they abandon the castle? The men argue until — kaboom! Ash fires his rifle in the air. "Run home and cry to mama," he yells, having found his courage. "Me? I'm through runnin'. I say we stay here and fight it out."

"Are all men from the future loudmouthed braggarts?" Arthur sneers. "Nope,

Below:

The winged

Deadite captures

Sheila.

Above: Stop-motion skeletons emerge in the graveyard.

just me baby, just me," replies Ash. Arthur points out that he only has sixty men left, as the others have fled. Ash says they can get Henry and his men to join them. "Who's with me?" The blacksmith is the first to declare himself. "You can count on my steel" exclaims a bewigged and bearded Ted Raimi.

The Army of the Dead gathers. "Say hello to the boys," says Evil Ash. Sheila, corrupted by evil, unveils herself. "There's a sight for sore bones," says an offscreen warrior. "I may be bad," she sneers, "but I feel goooood." To the castle!

At the castle, Ash's Oldsmobile is dragged into the courtyard. He finds a coil of rope, a chemistry textbook, a lamp, shotgun shells, an issue of *Fangoria* and a bottle of *Coca Cola* in the boot. With the help of the blacksmith, he repairs and customises his car, and mixes gunpowder, handing it out in small leather bags and cautioning Wiseman for holding one to close to a candle flame. Outside, he trains the men to use pikes in battle.

(This does raise the question of how he knows about pikes, but never mind.)

The full moon rises over the castle as the Army approaches two days later —

there are a lot of horsemen out there. The defenders lock up The Necronomicon. "Maybe, just maybe, my boys can stop them from getting the Book," Arthur says hopefully. "Yeah, and maybe I'm a Chinese jet pilot," Ash retorts. He rallies the others, and they raise the drawbridge.

The evil Army are on the move, to Danny Elfman's 'March of the Dead'. They halt outside the castle, waiting... The camera pans across the skeletal ranks to where Evil Ash and transformed Sheila wait atop a hill. "Bring forth the Scout!" Evil Ash orders. A skeletal warrior and a fleshier one ride up; the skeletal warrior says the Book is most likely being kept beyond the wall in "the parapet."

(He points at the castle keep, however, not the parapets.)

"Bring me forth into that castle!" Evil Ash cries. "Death to the mortals!" cry the warriors, and begin their charge.

On the parapets, Ash's warriors ready explosive arrows. "Steady," says Ash. "Fire!" says Arthur. Bang: the explosive arrows blow up skeletons and their shields, one by one and in groups. More skeletal warriors, wheeling a battering ram. "Ready the catapults!" cries Ash. The catapults fling blazing balls over the walls, including one fastened to the camera for a unique POV shot.

Furious with his own men, Evil Ash cries, "Oh, you miserable bags of bones! Pick yourselves up and sally for — awk, sally for — awk." In the excitement, his jaw keeps threatening to drop off.

Inside the castle, the defending army brace the drawbridge, dropping rocks onto

Left:
Evil Ash takes
a bride.

Right:

Evil Ash goes

into battle.

the skeletons, some of which shatter. Live action and stop-motion skeletons charge across the temporary bridge into the castle. In the various battle scenes that follow within the castle walls, things are clearly not going well for the good guys.

Suddenly, Ash roars up in his customised car: "Say hello to the twenty-first century!" The steam-powered car has whirling blades mounted on the hood, and Ash chops, shoots and slugs his way through the Army of Darkness. Some of these shots are in slow motion, and one takes us to Sheila, standing in front of him, her gown blowing in the breeze, her arms outspread. Ash can't stop — he tries to turn aside and leaps from car, which crashes directly in front of her.

Sheila attacks Ash with a spear, and we follow Ram-o-Cam shots of her spear almost impaling him. He kicks her back into the pit and fights off several skeletal warriors, breaking one over his knee. Arthur, wounded, is still fighting too, but things look very dark for them.

(*The actor playing Arthur had a hard time of it here, Bruce reveals: "It's inside, it's hot, he had armour on, it was the end of the day. And he couldn't see what he's supposed to be reacting to, because it's all front screen work. He had to match all his actions to previously-shot footage while standing in front of what was to him a blank silver screen. All the blows were numbered; there's a guy going "Thirty-five! Thirty-six! Thirty-seven!" And you know at thirty-seven you have to do this, at forty-two you have to do that. They had to do this I don't know how many times.*

When they finally got it, the assistant director pushed a button, and over the walkie-talkie you could hear the whole crew cheering.")

Over the hill, here come Duke Henry and his men to save the day, Henry himself leading the charge, swinging a mace. Smashing their way through the warriors of evil, they ride into the castle.

Meanwhile, Evil Ash himself brings down Arthur, but doesn't kill him. "The Book is mine," he says to Ash, chortling. The two Ashes face each other, but Sheila leaps on our hero — he impales her on a pike and flings her over the wall. Evil Ash almost gets the Book, but Ash throws a spear at him. Evil Ash breaks it off, fore and aft, and they fight.

(At one point, Ash is fighting several opponents with spears, a scene that goes on for a while without any cuts — in the finished film, that is. "Doug Lefler's theory was that anyone could do it with enough cuts in the film," Bruce says. Sam agreed, and shot this long, unbroken scene of a fight. "Whenever you show a kung fu scene, there are thousands of cuts," says Bruce, "so he wanted to have some of these sequences in the battle where you just see it happen. He does undercrank a little, rolling at probably twenty-one frames per second.")

They keep fighting, up the stairs, and Ash flips over Evil Ash, stabbing him under the arm before setting fire to him. Ash calls out "Tally Ho!" and kicks the blazing Evil Ash over the battlements.

("In the sequence where Ash is fighting Evil Ash on the steps of the castle, I had to flip a stuntman, but a piece of armour got jammed into my face and gashed it," Bruce says. "It was deep enough it had to be stitched, so we stopped shooting for a bit, and I went rushing to the nearest emergency room. I came walking in with scars all over my face, mostly make-up, and we grabbed a plastic surgeon. He looked at me, and goes, "which — which one?" As soon as he was stitched shut, Bruce went back to the sent and kept filming; they realised no one would notice one more scar.)

Now a skeleton himself, Evil Ash jumps back over the wall. Ash fights his nemesis to the death yet again.

("When Evil Ash climbs back over the parapet, we switched over to Sam's voice," Bruce explains, "because we wanted it to sound raspier than the regular Evil Ash voice, which was mine. So now we switched over to Sam the Ham.")

Below, Ash sees a burning fuse on a catapult bomb. He slugs Evil Ash, whose head spins around; when it stops, the eyes keep rolling.

(Sometimes rendered in stop-motion and sometimes a puppet, the new incarnation of Evil Ash has living eyes in his skull, like the poster for Evil Dead II*).*

Evil Ash keeps fighting, knocking Ash off the wall next to the catapult bomb.

(At times, Bruce is battling an elaborate, life-size puppet of Evil Ash. "It was affectionately called Skeletor on the set," he says, "but sometimes these very expensive rigs don't

always work out right, so we also called it Drunkator and Strokator. It was one of these rigs that rolled around, using a series of cables and pulleys, and I was supposed to have a sword fight with it. The articulated head was good — the eyes move and the jaws move well enough so you could dub in lines later, but I never knew where that sword was going to go, because the cables weren't working right. It was worse than fighting a stuntman. Not much of that footage wound up in the finished film.")

Evil Ash has the Book, and lands atop the catapult, gloating. "Buckle up, bonehead," says Ash, picking up a sword, "because you're going for a ride." He chops off Evil Ash's right hand — the hand and Book go flying.

(Of course, Evil Ash's right hand shouldn't have been there at all.)

Ash slashes through the rope of the catapult, and Evil Ash sails into the air with the catapult bomb, exploding. The skeletal army retreats. Victory!

Meanwhile, Sheila has returned to normal.

(This shot was originally intended to have an effect over it.)

Arthur's men and Henry's men square off in the courtyard, and draw their swords with a lot of 'schwings'. Arthur and Henry advance towards one another... and embrace mightily. Everyone cheers.

The Wiseman gives Ash a phial and tells him to drink the liquid, uttering the words "Klaatu farata nikto," and he will awaken in his own time. Ash takes the bottle. "Remember, you must recite the words exactly," the Wiseman says.

Ash bids farewell to Sheila on the drawbridge, riding off into the morning light.

(Originally, he rode into the mountains, to a cave, filmed on location in Bronson Caverns. He was supposed to take six drops of the fluid to enable him to sleep until his own time. But, Ash being Ash, he took one extra drop and overslept, waking up in the future, still in England, to find it virtually destroyed: "No! I slept too long!" That's where the alternate version ends.)

We see the rotating blue light again, and we're back in S-Mart. Ash, with the cuts on his face almost healed, is saying that he thought about staying: "they offered me the chance to lead them, to teach them, to be king." Stock clerk Ted Raimi is listening, looking rather bored. "But my place is here," Ash concludes, "so I swallowed the juice, said the words, and here I am." "Did you say the words right this time?" asks his colleague. "Maybe I didn't say every tiny little syllable, no, but basically I said 'em, yeah. Basically."

Ash is working, pricing up toasters. A pretty girl says his story was kinda cute. He's starting to get interested when the lights flicker as the Force POV moves down an S-Mart aisle and up to a hapless shopper who whirls around, a Deadite.

Wham! She knocks Ash into a pile of boxes, picks up a cash register, and is about to brain the girl. Ash recovers near a display of guns, smashes it open with his

EIN FILM VON SAM RAIMI

Die **ARMEE** *der* **FINSTERNIS**

metal hand, leaps onto a counter and orders her to leave the store. "Who the hell are you?" growls the Deadite.

Above:

Ash bids farewell to Sheila.

"Ash," he says, twirling the gun. "Housewares."

Ash throws the rifle into the air, leaps onto a cart and catches the gun while rolling forwards. Pow! Pow! Pow! Rapidly cocking and firing, he blasts the Deadite. She does a huge backflip and lands on her feet, screaming, "I'll swallow your soul!" and charges at him. At last, he puts her down.

Ash sweeps the girl into his arms to the narrative that opened the movie: "Sure, I could have stayed in the past, could have even been king. But in my own way, I am king."

"Hail to the king, baby!" he says, aloud, and kisses her.

(THE END)

GLOSSARY

By Bill Thomas, with explanations courtesy of Bruce Campbell.

Chem wipes: using acetone or a similar fluid to primitively edit a sound track. "It's great to be able to get in there and mess around where you never could before. You were always dealing with the magnetic stripe, and I remember taking chemicals; we did what we called chem wipes. You get rid of stuff. You take a little acetone or a razor blade, and get in there."

Dutch angle: a drastically tilted camera angle, an example of moosh-moosh (qv).

Elf shoes: the uncomfortable soft shoes (Wallabies) Bruce wore in *The Evil Dead* on Sam's assumption that they'd never go out of style. He had to wear similar shoes in *Evil Dead II*, but not *Army of Darkness*.

Ellievator: the mechanical effects rig used to elevate Ellen Sandweiss in *The Evil Dead*. "She's hoisted up on an X with straps, with a pole going straight out the back. It's on a fulcrum, so she's being raised by a couple of guys in back. It's an old magic trick."

Eyeball flyball: the effects shot in *Evil Dead II* in which dead Henrietta's eye is violently popped out and shoots into Kassie Wesley's screaming mouth.

Fake Shemp: (a) someone doubling for an unavailable actor. "Fake Shemp is very simple. The [Three] Stooges used to make a bunch of shorts at the same time, because if Columbia had a giant castle set that they did an 'A' picture with, before they tore it down, the Stooges would say, 'No, let us come in and throw some pies.' Shemp was in his fair share of the shorts, and he died... They had to finish off about three or four, and Shemp had shot some scenes for each, but not all of them. So it would be Moe going, 'Shemp, guard the door!' And some Fake Shemp would go, 'Right! Mee-mee-mee-mee-mee!' And they'd dub in old lines, with some guy

with black stringy hair faking it. Even in high school we could tell how fake it was."
(b) In the credits for *Army of Darkness*, someone who helped by "doing weird things."
(c) A bit player in later Sam Raimi movies.

It's Murder beams: prop beams made from expanded plastic, used to simulate wooden beams in *The Evil Dead*. "*It's Murder* beams were tied with fishing line to the bottom of the bridge. They're the things you can get at Costco that are supposed to be ceiling beams, but are really U-shaped Styrofoam beams painted like wood. We thought they were the greatest props ever, so we brought tons of *It's Murder* beams to Tennessee, tied them to the bottom of the bridge, and released them as the car went over. They don't match anything else."

It's Murder hand: the rubber prop hand used in *The Evil Dead*. "There's a scene in *It's Murder* where a bad guy is reaching to get in a car; a pretty good sequence with a guy smashing a car with a sledge hammer. At one point he reaches in, and the guy inside slams the door on his hand. It was one of those rubber hands you can get at magic shops. So that was an *It's Murder* hand. Very useful. Because they were very resilient, too, you could beat on them all day long."

Kandarian plotzing: gruesome sound effects in *The Evil Dead*. The Book of the Dead was found in the ruins of Kandar, and plotz is from the Yiddish for crack, split or burst. "We got a turkey baster that gives you a SPLUSH SQUITCH SPLORK kind of sound; [sound editor] Joe Masefield referred to it as 'Kandarian plotzing.'"

Moe bags: prominent bags under the eyes, like Stooge Moe Howard's. "The effects of the shooting were starting to take their toll. I [had] these horrible Moe bags under my eyes at that point."

Moosh-moosh: effects calculated to distract the audience. "I think Sam is really good about making what I call moosh-moosh... He'll have the camera just sort of wiggling. It's not only hand-held, but it's the guys going for a little extra motion. They'll throw wind into it, or he'll have some kind of flashing lighting effects. He'll immediately kick into what we nicknamed moosh-moosh."

NBC dip: a music cue/accent, referring to the NBC TV network. "That's when the music goes way down and you hear a line of dialogue, then it comes back up. That's what Mel Zelniker, our sound mixer, called it."

Ram-o-Cam: originally a camera mounted on boards nailed together, used in *The Evil Dead* to get the effect of the Force smashing through a window. "A big rake kind of thing."

Recap of the Decap: recapitulation of the decapitation; that is, the establishing sequence at the beginning of *Evil Dead II*.

Rotten Apple Head: the giant special effects demon head that materialises in the doorway at the climax of *Evil Dead II*.

Sam-o-Cam: "For the opening shot of *The Evil Dead*, Sam taped an Arri camera to his hand. Sam was on a raft in a swamp, and I was behind him in these waders, pushing the raft. He would go up over a branch, down and swoop around it; it was all on his hand."

Señor Cojones: one of the rats that appears in *Evil Dead II*; named after the Spanish for Mr and slang Spanish for testicles.

Shaky-Cam: a camera rig used in *The Evil Dead* (and elsewhere) to get a Steadicam effect. A 16mm camera with a wide-angle lens is mounted on a length of two-by-four board, with "a guy on either end to stabilise it, a camera in the middle, and you could go over bushes." Despite its name, the Shaky-Cam gives smooth results. It is one of many customised camera rigs Sam has had built for his films.

Skeletor: a rolling skeleton puppet rig of Evil Ash used for a swordfight with Ash in *Army of Darkness*. Also known as Drunkator and Strokator because of its unpredictable movements. "The articulated head was good, the eyes moved, the jaws moved well enough so you could dub in lines later, but I never knew where that sword was going to go, because the cables weren't working right. It was worse than fighting a stuntman."

Vas-o-Cam: a camera rig used in *The Evil Dead* for a dolly effect in cramped or unusual circumstances. Two two-by-fours were nailed together, then, "you take gaffer tape, you put it across the whole thing, then you have a U-shaped thing that sits on top of it, and you bolt the camera to that. You put Vaseline all over the gaffer tape, so it would slide. This little thing was your dolly, you could go really smooth. The problem we had during the winter was really cold Vaseline, which didn't work as well."

THE SUPER-8 MOVIES

Thanks to Scott Spiegel, this is the first complete list of the Super-8 amateur and college movies Spiegel, Bruce Campbell, Sam Raimi and their friends made while teenagers (a few were shot in 16mm). This doesn't include the shorts Sam shot on video, as they are not currently viewable.

Inspector Klutz Saves the Day, 1969
Directed by Bill Ward, Matt DeWan and Scott Spiegel. Cast: Ward, DeWan and Spiegel.

Pies and Guys, 1971
Directed by Bill Ward and Scott Spiegel. Cast: Spiegel, Ward and Matt Taylor.
Corny Casanovas, 1971
Directed by Bill Ward and Scott Spiegel. Cast: Spiegel, Bill Ward, Matt Taylor, Lisa Reid.

Out West, 1972
Directed by **Sam Raimi**. Cast: **Raimi**, Chris Cornetta, Bill Ritter, Liz Larsen, and others. See Chapter One for description.
Oedipus Rex, 1972
Directed by Josh Becker. Cast: Becker, **Bruce Campbell**, Scott Spiegel.

Supa' Bad, 1973
Directed by **Bruce Campbell**. Cast: Don Campbell, Scott Tyler, **Bruce Campbell**, Roger Bick.
D-Day, 1973
Directed by **Bruce Campbell**. Cast: Don Campbell, Scott Tyler, **Bruce Campbell**, Roger Bick.
Day of Violence, 1973
Directed by **Bruce Campbell**. Cast: **Bruce Campbell**, Scott Tyler, Roger Bick, Don Campbell, Steve Davis.
Son of Hitler, 1973
Directed by **Bruce Campbell**. Cast: **Bruce Campbell**, Don Campbell, Scott Tyler, Roger Bick.
Hitler, goose-stepping around suburban Michigan, is too young to drive so his mother picks him up in a station wagon.
For Crimin' Out Loud, 1973
Directed by Bill Ward and Scott Spiegel. Cast: Ward, Spiegel, Arn Rosen, Greg Kosrin.

A Night in a Sanitarium, 1973
Directed by Bill Ward and Scott Spiegel. Cast: Ward, Spiegel, Mike Coatney, Carol Sahakian, Dave Souder, Chuck Baker.
Three Smart Saps, 1973
Directed by Bill Ward and Scott Spiegel. Cast: Ward, Spiegel, **Bruce Campbell**, Matt Taylor, Scott Taylor, Mike Coatney.
Loose Loot, 1973
Directed by Bill Ward and Scott Spiegel. Cast: Ward, Spiegel, Matt Taylor, Mike Lewis, Scott Taylor.
Piece of Mind, 1973
Directed by Bill Ward and Scott Spiegel. Cast: Ward, Spiegel, Matt Taylor, Scott Taylor, Mike Coatney, Jim Lossia.

Booby Bartenders, 1974
Directed by Bill Ward and Scott Spiegel. Cast: **Bruce Campbell**, Ward, Spiegel, Mike Coatney.
Three on a Couch, 1974
Directed by Scott Spiegel and **Bruce Campbell**. Cast: Tim Quill, Matt Taylor, Spiegel, **Campbell**.
Three Pests in a Mess, 1974
Directed by Bill Ward and Scott Spiegel. Cast: Ward, Spiegel, Matt Taylor, **Bruce Campbell**, Mike Coatney, Mike Ditz.
Half-Wits' Holiday, 1974
Directed by Scott Spiegel. Cast: Spiegel, Matt Taylor, Tim Quill, **Bruce Campbell**, Tom Williams, Sue Diezel, Dave Sedustrum.
Manhunt, 1974
Directed by **Bruce Campbell**. Cast: **Campbell**, Matt Taylor, Scott Spiegel.
Curse of the Werewolf, 1974
Directed by Scott Spiegel. Cast: Spiegel, **Bruce Campbell**, Matt Taylor.

All the World's a Stooge, 1974
Directed by Scott Spiegel. Cast: Matt Taylor, Tim Quill, Spiegel, **Bruce Campbell**, Mike Ditz.
No Dough Boys, 1974
Directed by Scott Spiegel. Cast: Spiegel, Matt Taylor, Tim Quill, **Bruce Campbell**, **Sam Raimi**, Tom Williams.
The Singing Nuts, 1974
Directed by Scott Spiegel. Cast: Spiegel, Matt Taylor, Tim Quill, **Bruce Campbell**, Amanda Cote.

I'll Never Heil Again, 1975
Directed by Scott Spiegel and **Bruce Campbell**. Cast: Spiegel, Matt Taylor, Tim Quill, **Campbell**, **Sam Raimi**, Doug Sills, Tom Williams.
The Great Bogus Monkey Pignuts Swindle, 1975
Directed by **Sam Raimi**. Cast: **Raimi**, Scott Spiegel, **Bruce Campbell**, Gary Parks, Jim Herrold, Peggy Jamison, Laura Locke, Diane Ricoz, Joady Broad.
A scarfaced gangster called Scarface, sporting a colossal cigar, orders a case of monkey pignuts. The pignuts turn out to be bogus. Bruce plays several roles, mostly gangsters, and does a pratfall over a wall into a creek. Sam Fake Shemps as a newsboy. Bruce Gangster and Scarface fight, but stop to adjust each other's collars. A very weird short even by their standards.
The James Hoffa Story, 1975
Directed by Scott Spiegel and **Bruce Campbell**. Cast: **Campbell**, Spiegel, **Sam Raimi**, Rudy Bublitz, Tim Quill, Peggy Jamison.

The James R. Hoffa Story, Part II (aka Home Sweet Homicide), 1976
Directed by Scott Spiegel and **Sam Raimi**. Cast: Spiegel, **Raimi**, **Bruce Campbell**, Rudy Bublitz, Matt Taylor, Tim Quill, Christie Gritton.
A gangster (Quill) left over from the first film has comic adventures on a beach, unaware he's now targeted because he knows who dumped Hoffa in the dumpster. Back at the Red Fox restaurant, he is killed and tossed into the same dumpster — but Hoffa is still alive (and still Bruce). He flees, encountering Sam as a pie salesman in pith helmet and sunglasses. Scott and Sam do a bunch of slapstick takes until Scott throws Sam over a table of pies. Everyone gets one in the face, sooner or later. Bruce, Fake Shemping, does another role as a guy with a goofy grin, among several others.
James Bombed in Here Today... Gun Tomorrow, 1976
Directed by Scott Spiegel. Cast: **Bruce Campbell**, **Sam Raimi**, Spiegel, Annette Laduke, Brett Sherran, Bill Aaron, Tim Quill, Rudy Bublitz.
Attack of the Pillsbury Doughboy, 1976
Directed by Scott Spiegel and **Sam Raimi**. Cast: **Raimi**. Sam eats breakfast, pouring curdled milk onto cereal. He set his finger on fire in a microwave oven, and falls headfirst over a turkey. He summons up the Pillsbury Doughboy, from the commercials, and immediately attacks it, flattening it out, with jelly pouring out like blood.
Uncivil War Birds, 1976
Directed by **Sam Raimi**. Cast: **Bruce Campbell**, Scott Spiegel, John Cameron, Bill Kirk, George Zania, Dan Nelson, Tom Williams, Matt Taylor, Ted Raimi and a cast of hundreds.
Mystery No Mystery, 1976
Directed by **Sam Raimi** and Scott Spiegel. Cast: **Raimi**, Spiegel, **Bruce Campbell**, Tom Williams, Matt Taylor, Peggy Jamison and Monty the Bulldog.
(a) Super-8 version: Bruce, as an old man, is seen writing; he's murdered. Sam, doing Jerry Lewis stuff, is a detective come to investigate, and Scott is the butler. There are some scenes in a graveyard, including a fight, lots of slapstick, some violence, Bruce Fake Shemping as a gardener, and Sam getting thrown off a balcony. Scenes at Pasquale's Family Restaurant.
(b) 16mm: this stars Scott as the old man and Bruce as the detective, but is only a short scene, not the entire plot, which is featured in the Super-8 version and the later *It's Murder* remake.
Topanga Pearl, 1976
Directed by Josh Becker. Cast: Becker, Ellen Sandweiss, Scott Spiegel, **Sam Raimi**.

Picnic, 1977
Directed by **Sam Raimi** and Scott Spiegel. Cast: **Bruce Campbell**, Annette Laduke, **Raimi**, Spiegel.
This won an award for best stunts from Joe Sasso at

Detroit's WXYZ radio. Bruce, in a Groucho moustache, baseball hat and goofy grin, is having a picnic with a girl. He waves at Scott and Sam, offering them some food. They run toward the two on the blanket, but Sam trips and falls headlong down the hill, landing on all the picnic goodies. More slapstick follows with the remaining food.

Charlie's Angels, 1977
Directed by Scott Spiegel and **Sam Raimi**. Cast: Annette Laduke, Pat Jamison, Linda Butler, Spiegel, **Raimi**.

The soundtrack seems to have been lost for this comic variation on the TV series, featuring lots of scenes of girls running down office building hallways carrying guns. Scott has the David Doyle role. There is no discernible plot because of the lack of a soundtrack. However, there are gags with a bicycle, and a man in a blanket falls down.

The Kids' Film, 1977
Directed by **Sam Raimi** and Scott Spiegel. Cast: a whole bunch of little kids from Walnut Lake School. Sam and Scott taught a class at Walnut Lake School one summer, and this is one of the most charming of their Super-8 movies. It features young children doing more or less the same stuff Sam, Scott and Bruce do in the other movies, including Three Stooges-like slapstick gags, and lots of gangsters (few of whom are twelve yet). There are even some stunts, which must have caused a few parental faces to blanch. Everyone looks like they are having a wonderful time.

Six Months to Live, 1977
Directed by **Sam Raimi** and Scott Spiegel. Cast: **Raimi**, Spiegel, **Bruce Campbell**, Jane Bultrud, Kathy Stepanian, Matt Taylor, Jon Page, Tim Quill, Rudy Bublitz, Bill Aaron, Ivan Raimi, Bill Kirk, Ted Raimi. Crew: Mike Ditz, Clay Warnock, Bruce Campbell. Includes much of *Attack of the Pillsbury Doughboy*. Bruce's airy doctor tells Sam that he has only six months to live. "I can't die!" Sam wails. "I'm too good looking. I'm not going to die, am I? There's no future in it." "Relax," sneers Bruce, "that's the last thing you're going to do." Sam tries to find a way to have fun in the six months remaining, seeking the help of Scott and

others. It's one of the funniest shorts, with Sam's best comedy performance and lots of good sight gags (and Bruce Fake Shemping like mad), but it loses sight of the basic idea, and concludes with Sam killing himself.

The Happy Valley Kid, 1977
Directed by **Sam Raimi**. Cast: **Rip Tapert**, Ivan Raimi, Scott Spiegel, **Bruce Campbell**, **Raimi**, Ruth Taubman, John Cameron, Pierre LaBlanc, Josh Becker, John Kata. See Chapter Two for description.

Lonely Are the Brave (aka *The Drama Movie*), 1977
Directed by **Sam Raimi**. Cast: Bill Kirk, Linda Quiroz, Jane Bultrud, Richard Smith, Don Shand, Dan Nelson, Doug Sills, **Raimi**, Mrs Labatt.

This was made for Groves High, and is really just an introduction to the drama department, with some gags, including some violence. We see parts of a rehearsal for *How to Succeed in Business Without Really Trying*.

Civil War Part II, 1977
Directed by **Sam Raimi**. Cast: **Raimi**, Doug Fierberg, Steve Chickeral, **Bruce Campbell**, Scott Spiegel, Ted Raimi, Dean Casparian.

Sam, in strange, racoon-like makeup, rushes in to interrupt a ponderous narrator who's been telling us there's no film footage of the Civil War. Sam shows us a lot of leftover footage from his first Civil War movie, only without sound. As in the first, we see people — mostly in 1977 clothing — marching along with modern guns and replicas. This includes some odd angles, smoke and gunfire, and tumbles down hills and into streams.

Final Round, 1977
Directed by Josh Becker. Cast: Becker, Stanley Schwartz, **Sam Raimi**, **Bruce Campbell**, Bill Aaron, Scott Spiegel, Matt Taylor.

Acting and Reacting, 1978
Directed by Josh Becker. Cast: **Bruce Campbell**, Ruth Taubman, Scott Spiegel, Matt Taylor, Charlie Campbell, Ted Raimi, John Cameron, Pam Becker, Debbie Raucher.

Holding It, 1978
Directed by Josh Becker. Cast: Bill Kirk, **Sam Raimi**, **Bruce Campbell**, Bill Aaron.

Shemp Eats the Moon, 1978
Directed by John Cameron. Cast: **Bruce Campbell**,

Jane Bultrud, Ellen Sandweiss, Matt Taylor, Bill Kirk, Bill Aaron, **Sam Raimi**, Scott Spiegel, Kelly Pino. Among the other incidents, a private eye named Shemp swallows a large pearl called the Moon. In case you were wondering.

It's Murder, 1978
Directed by **Sam Raimi**. Cast: Scott Spiegel, **Raimi**, Ted Raimi, Richard Smith, **Bruce Campbell**, Cheryl Guttridge, Bill Aaron, Matt Taylor, Tim Quill, John Cameron and Monty the Bulldog.

Note for completists: Cheryl Guttridge later turned to writing fiction under the name of Margery Allingham. She specialises in romantic suspense novels, and her books include *Promise Me, The Last Curve* and *Indiscretion*.

William Shakespeare — The Movie, 1979
Directed by **Sam Raimi**. Cast: **Bruce Campbell**.
A narrator tells us about Shakespeare, holding up pro-grammes and the like, then Bruce and a college actress play out a scene ("Some-times Kate the curs'd..." from *The Taming of the Shrew*) outdoors in a snowy wood. The camera moves a lot, but the sound isn't good. It's a handsome, energetic film with lively performances.

Attack of the Helping Hand, 1979
Directed by Scott Spiegel. Cast: Linda Quiroz, **Sam Raimi**.

Clockwork, 1979
Directed by **Sam Raimi**. Cast: Cheryl Guttridge, Scott Spiegel. See Chapter Two for description.

Night Crew, 1979
Directed by Scott Spiegel. Cast: Linda Quiroz, John Cameron, **Sam Raimi**, Tim Quill, Christie Gritton, Bill Aaron.

Spiegel later remade this as *Intruder*, a feature film.

Within the Woods, 1979
Directed by **Sam Raimi**. Cast: **Bruce Campbell**, Ellen Sandweiss, Scott Spiegel, Mary Valenti. See Chapter Two for description.

Spring Cleaning, 1979
Directed by **Bruce Campbell**. Cast: Scott Spiegel, Jane Bultrud, **Sam Raimi**, Ted Raimi, **Campbell**.

Fish Sticks, 1979
Directed by **Bruce Campbell**. Cast: **Sam Raimi**.

The Blind Waiter, 1980
Directed by Scott Spiegel and Josh Becker. Cast: **Bruce Campbell**, **Sam Raimi**, **Rob Tapert**, Spiegel, John Cameron, Jane Violassi, Liz Dennison, Tim Quill.

Stryker's War, 1980
Directed by Josh Becker. Cast: **Bruce Campbell**, Cheryl Guttridge, Charlie Campbell, **Sam Raimi**, Scott Spiegel, David Goodman, Don Campbell, Richard DeManincor, Tim Philo, Jane Bultrud, Bill Kirk, Ted Raimi, Nancy Karpowitz.

Becker later remade this as *Thou Shalt Not Kill... Except.*

Toro Toro Toro, 1981
Directed by Scott Spiegel and Josh Becker. Cast: Spiegel, **Bruce Campbell**, John Cameron, Bill Kirk, Matt Taylor, Bruce Jones, Pam Becker, **Rob Tapert**.

Cleveland Smith, Bounty Hunter, 1982
Directed by Josh Becker and Scott Spiegel. Cast: **Bruce Campbell**, Cheryl Guttridge, **Sam Raimi** and a lot of stock footage.

The Sappy Sap, 1985
Directed by **Sam Raimi**. Cast: Scott Spiegel, Cheryl Guttridge, **Rob Tapert**, Bruce Jones, and **Bruce Campbell** as the Goofy Goof.
Made well after *The Evil Dead*, this is the best of Sam's short films. It's broad slapstick with a very funny per-formance by Scott Spiegel in the title role, playing a guy who wants to cross a busy street to make time with a sexy girl in a polka-dot dress. The gags vary from the familiar to the fresh, it's well paced, with good use of music and sound, and it's utterly unafraid of going for the gross-out. Scott does an octuple take at one point.

Projects are listed chronologically by year, and alphabetically within each year.

The Magic Balloon
c1980.
Note: Vern Hyde directed this Detroit-made film. **Bruce Campbell** was billed as second assistant director, and says it had a few showings around 1980. Not to be confused with the 1990 film of the same title.

The Evil Dead
1982, Renaissance Pictures. 85 min.
Director/Screenplay: **Sam Raimi**; Producer: **Robert G. Tapert**; Executive Producers: **Robert G. Tapert, Bruce Campbell, Sam Raimi**; Assistant Producer: Gary Holt; Music: Joseph Lo Duca; Cinematography: Tim Philo; Editor: Edna Ruth Paul; Supervising Sound Editor: Joseph R. Masefield; Dialogue Editor: Lou Kleinman; Assistant Sound Editor: Dolores Elliott; Assistant Film Editor: Joel Coen; Creator of Special Make-up Effects: Tom Sullivan; Supervisor of Photographic Special Effects: Bart Pierce; Location Sound Recording: John Mason; Second Unit Sound: Josh Becker; Sound Mixer: Mel Zelniker; Production Assistant: Don Campbell; Music engineered at Audio Graphics by: Ed Wolfrum; Music Editor: Sheb Wooley; Construction Supervisor: Steve 'Dart' Frankel; Transportation Captain: David H. Goodman; Story Consultant: Sheila Roberts; Post Opticals: Dynamic Film Lab; Negative Matching: J.G. Films; Still Photography: Mike Ditz; Special thanks to: Simon Nuchtern, Carol Valenti, Sheila Roberts.
Cast: **Bruce Campbell** (Ash), Ellen Sandweiss (Cheryl), Richard Demanincor *aka* Hal Delrich (Scott), Betsy Baker (Linda), Teresa Seyfirth *aka* Sarah York (Shelly), Philip A. Gillis, Dorothy Tapert, Cheryl Guttridge, Barbara Carey, David Horton, Wendall Thomas, Don Long, Stu Smith, Kurt Rauf, Ted Raimi, Ivan Raimi, Bill Vincent, Mary Beth Tapert, Scott Spiegel, John Cameron, Joanne Kruse, Gwen Cochanski, Debie Jarczewski (Fake Shemps), Bob Dorian (Voice on tape recorder), **Sam Raimi, Robert G. Tapert** (Fishermen by the side of the road).

Generations
1982. TV series.
Note: **Bruce Campbell** had a regular role as Paul Carr. This was shot in Detroit, and should not be confused with any other series of a similar title. Scenes from the show can be glimpsed playing on a TV set in *Fargo*.

Going Back
1983.
Director/Screenplay: Ron Teachworth; Producers: Ron and Jill Teachworth.
Cast includes: **Bruce Campbell**, Christopher Howe, Perry Mallette, Vern Teachworth.
Note: **Campbell** plays Brice Chapman, and describes the film thus: "Boyhood chums spend an idyllic summer travelling in rural Michigan and attempt to repeat it again in their post-college days, only to find that time doesn't stand still. Sometimes you just can't go back..."

Crimewave
1985, Renaissance Pictures/Avco Embassy. 83 min.
Director: **Sam Raimi**; Screenplay: **Sam Raimi**, Ethan Coen, Joel Coen; Producer: **Robert G. Tapert**; Executive Producers: Edward R. Pressman, Irvin Shapiro; Co-producer: **Bruce Campbell**; Art Direction: Gary Papierski; Cinematography: Robert Primes; Editors: Michael Kelly, Kathie Weaver; Music: Joseph Lo Duca, Arlon Ober; Assistant Director: John Cameron.
Cast includes: Louise Lasser, Paul Smith, Brion James, Sheree J. Wilson, Edward R. Pressman, **Bruce Campbell**, Reed Birney, Richard Bright, Emil Sitka, Richard DeManincor, Julius Harris, Bridget Hoffman, Frances McDormand, Ted Raimi.

Evil Dead II
1985, Renaissance Pictures/Rosebud Releasing Corp. 85 min.
Director: **Sam Raimi**; Screenplay: **Sam Raimi**, Scott Spiegel; Producer: **Robert G. Tapert**; Executive

Producers: Irvin Shapiro, Alex de Benedetti; Co-producer: **Bruce Campbell**; Music: Joseph Lo Duca; Special Make-up Designed and Created by: Mark Shostrom; Director of Photography: Peter Deming; Director of Night Exterior Photography: Eugene Shlugleit; Edited by Kaye Davis; Production Manager: Joseph C. Stillman; 1st Assistant Director: Joseph Winogradoff; 2nd Assistant Director: K. Siobhan Phelan; Art Directors: Philip Duffin, Randy Bennett; 2nd Unit Director of Photography: Tim Philo; Sound Mixer: Tom Morrison; Transportation/Studio Manager: David Goodman; Animator: Tom Sullivan; Special Make-up Effects Unit Crew: Howard Berger, Robert Kurtzman, Gregory Nicotero, Mike Trcic, Shannon Shea, Aaron Sims, Bryant Tausek; Still Photographer: Mike Ditz; Assistant Editors: Michael Jonascu, Paul Harris; Supervising Sound Editor: David West.
Cast: **Bruce Campbell** (Ash), Sarah Berry (Annie), Dan Hicks (Jake), Kassie Wesley (Bobby Joe), Theodore Raimi (Possessed Henrietta), Denise Bixler (Linda), Richard Domeier (Ed), John Peaks (Professor Knowby), Lou Hancock (Henrietta), Featuring the Amazing Voice of William Preston Robertson.

Spies Like Us
1985, Warner Bros. 102 min.
Director: John Landis; Screenplay: Dan Aykroyd, Lowell Ganz, Babaloo Mandel; Producers: George Folsey Jr, Brian Grazer.
Cast includes: Chevy Chase, Dan Aykroyd, Mark Stewart, Sean Daniel, Bruce Davison, William Prince.
Note: **Sam Raimi** and Joel Coen are the guards at the drive-in.

Thou Shalt Not Kill... Except (aka *Stryker's War*)
1985, Renaissance Pictures. 84 min.
Director/Cinematographer: Josh Becker; Screenplay: Josh Becker, Scott Spiegel; Producer: Scott Spiegel; Music: Joseph Lo Duca.
Cast includes: Brian Schulz, Robert Rickman, John Manfredi, Timothy Patrick Quill, **Sam Raimi**, Cheryl Hausen, Ted Raimi, Scott Spiegel.
Note: In the world's worst wig, Sam Raimi plays the

vaguely Charles Manson-like villain who comes to a violent end. **Bruce Campbell** has an uncredited cameo as a video newscaster.

The Dead Next Door
1988, Amsco Studios/Surburban Tempe Co. 84 min.
Director/Screenplay: J.R. Bookwalter; Producers: J.R. Bookwalter, Jolie Jackunas.
Cast includes: Pete Ferry (as 'Raimi'), Bogdan Pecic, Michael Grossi, Robert Kokai, Roger Graham, J.R. Bookwalter.
Note: **Bruce Campbell** has an uncredited, voice-only role.

Intruder
1988, Phantom Productions. 85 min.
Director/Screenplay: Scott Spiegel; Story: Scott Spiegel, Lawrence Bender; Producers: Lawrence Bender, Douglas Hessler.
Cast includes: Elizabeth Cox, Renee Estevez, Dan Hicks, David Byrnes, **Sam Raimi**, Eugene R. Ted Raimi, Alvy Moore, Emil Sitka, **Bruce Campbell**, Howard Lawrence Bender, Scott Spiegel, Gregory Nicotero.
Note: Sam Raimi plays a worker in a supermarket who meets a violent end.

Maniac Cop
1988, Shapiro-Glickenhaus Entertainment. 85 min.
Director: William Lustig; Screenplay/Producer: Larry Cohen.
Cast includes: Tom Atkins, **Bruce Campbell**, Laurene Landon, Richard Roundtree, William Smith, Robert Z'Dar, Sheree North, **Sam Raimi**.
Note: Sam appears as a TV news reporter covering a Thanksgiving Day parade towards the end of the movie.

Easy Wheels
1989. 94 min.
Director: David O'Malley; Screenplay: David O'Malley, Ivan Raimi, Celia Abrams (**Sam Raimi**); Producers: **Bruce Campbell**, Dimitri Villard; Executive Producer: **Sam Raimi**.
Cast includes: Paul Le Mat, Eileen Davidson, Marjorie Bransfield, Jon Menick, Ted Raimi, Dan Hicks.

Moontrap
1989, Magic Films. 92 min.
Director: Robert Dyke; Screenplay: Tex Ragsdale;
Producers: John Cameron, Robert Dyke; Music: Joseph
Lo Duca.
Cast includes: Walter Koenig, John J. Saunders, Reavis
Graham, **Bruce Campbell**, Judy Levitt.

Sundown: The Vampire in Retreat
1989, Vestron Pictures. 104 min.
Director: Anthony Hickox; Screenplay: John Burgess
and Anthony Hickox; Producer: Jefferson Richard.
Cast includes: David Carradine, Morgan Brittany, **Bruce
Campbell**, Jim Metzler, Maxwell Caulfield, Deborah
Foreman.

Darkman
1990, Universal/Renaissance Pictures. 96 min.
Director: **Sam Raimi**; Screenplay: Chuck Pfarrer, **Sam
Raimi**, Ivan Raimi, Daniel Goldin, Joshua Goldin;
Producer: **Robert G. Tapert**; Cinematography: Bill
Pope; Production Design: Randy Ser; Editor: Bud S.
Smith, David Stiven; Music: Danny Elfman, Jonathan
Sheffer.
Cast includes: Liam Neeson, Frances McDormand,
Colin Friels, Larry Drake, Nelson Mashita, Danny
Hicks, Ted Raimi, Nicholas Worth, William Dear,
Bridget Hoffman, Philip A. Gillis, Sean Daniel, John
Landis, Carrie Hall, John Cameron, Craig Hosking,
Stuart Cornfeld, William Lustig, Scott Spiegel, **Bruce
Campbell**, Jenny Agutter (uncredited).
Note: **Sam Raimi** has two very tiny cameos — he's on
the tilt-a-whirl with Liam Neeson and Frances McDormand, and you can see him in the background on the
street after Pauly is tossed out the window.

Maniac Cop 2
1990, Medusa Pictures. 90 min.
Director: William Lustig; Screenplay/Producer: Larry
Cohen.
Cast includes: Robert Davi, Claudia Christian, Michael
Lerner, **Bruce Campbell**, Laurene Landon, Robert
Z'Dar, Clarence Williams III, Leo Rossi, **Sam Raimi**.

Note: The character **Sam Raimi** plays is presumably the
same guy as in the first film, promoted to anchorman.
His role only survives in the TV version.

Miller's Crossing
1990, Twentieth Century Fox/Circle Releasing. 115 min.
Director: Joel Coen. Screenplay: Ethan Coen, Joel Coen;
Producer: Ethan Coen.
Cast includes: Gabriel Byrne, Marcia Gay Harden, John
Turturro, Jon Polito, J.E. Freeman, Albert Finney.
Note: **Sam Raimi** plays the 'Snickering Gunman', and
meets a violent end.

Mindwarp
1990, Columbia Pictures/Fangoria Films. 91 min.
Director: Steve Barnett; Screenplay: John D. Brancato,
Henry Dominic, Michael Ferris; Producer: Christopher
Webster.
Cast includes: Marta Alicia, Angus Scrimm, **Bruce
Campbell**, Mary Becker, Brian Brill.

Lunatics: A Love Story
1991, Renaissance Pictures. 87 min.
Director/Screenplay: Josh Becker; Producer: **Bruce
Campbell**; Executive Producers: **Sam Raimi, Robert
G. Tapert**; Music: Joseph Lo Duca.
Cast includes: Ted Raimi, Deborah Foreman, **Bruce
Campbell**, George Aguilar, Brian McCree, Eddy
Roumaya, Philip A. Gillis, John Cameron.

Army of Darkness
1992, Universal Pictures/Dino De Laurentiis
Communications. 81 min.
Director: **Sam Raimi**; Screenplay: **Sam Raimi**, Ivan
Raimi; Producer: **Robert G. Tapert**; Co-producer:
Bruce Campbell; Music: Joseph Lo Duca; 'March of the
Dead' Theme: Danny Elfman; Cinematography: Bill
Pope; Edited by Bruce Campbell (as R.O.C. Sandstorm),
Bob Murawski; Production Design: Tony Tremblay; 1st
Assistant Director: John Cameron; 2nd Assistant
Director: Sarah Addington; 2nd Unit Director: Doug
Leffler; Sound Mixer: Al Rizzo; Optical Supervisor:
Robert Habros; Stop-Motion Supervisor: Pete Kleinow;

Special Make-up Effects: KNB EFX Group, Inc; Visual Effects: Introvision International; Make-up Effects: Alterian Studios; Still Photographer: Melissa Moseley. Cast: **Bruce Campbell** (Ash), Embeth Davidtz (Sheila), Marcus Gilbert (Arthur), Ian Abercrombie (Wiseman), Richard Grove (Duke Henry), Michael Earl Reid (Gold Tooth), Timothy Patrick Quill (Blacksmith), Bridget Fonda (Linda), Patricia Tallman (Possessed Witch), Theodore Raimi (Cowardly Warrior), Deke Anderson (Tiny Ash #1), Bruce Thomas (Tiny Ash #2), Sara Shearer (Old Woman), Shiva Gordon (Pit Deadite #1), Billy Bryan (Pit Deadite #2), Nadine Grycan (Winged Deadite), Bill Moseley (Deadite Captain), Micheal Kenny (Henry's Man), Andy Bale (Lieutenant.#1), Robert Brent Lappin (Lieutenant #2), Tower Guard (Rad Milo), Chief Archer (Brad Bradbury), Sol Abrams, Lorraine Axeman, Josh Becker, Sheri Burke, Don Campbell, Charlie Campbell, Harley Cokeliss, Ken Jepson, William Lustig, David O'Malley, David Pollison, Ivan Raimi, Bernard Rose, Bill Vincent, Chris Webster, Ron Zwang (Fake Shemps).

Innocent Blood
1992, Warner Bros. 112 min.
Director: John Landis; Screenplay: Michael Wolk; Producers: Leslie Belzberg, Lee Rich.
Cast includes: Anne Parillaud, David Proval, Rocco Sisto, Chazz Palminteri, Robert Loggia, Anthony LaPaglia.
Note: **Sam Raimi** plays a dopey worker at a meat-packing plant, confused by newly-minted vampire Robert Loggia.

The Nutt House
1992, Triboro Entertainment Group. 90 min.
Director: Adam Rifkin; Screenplay: Roc Sandstorm (**Bruce Campbell**), Alan Smithee Sr (Ivan Raimi), Alan Smithee Jr (**Sam Raimi**); Story: Peter Perkinson (Scott Spiegel).
Cast includes: Stephen Kearney, Amy Yasbeck, Robert Trebor, Robert Colbert, Sandra Gould, Barry Livingston.
Note: This was written under the title *The Nutty Nut*, with Scott Spiegel scheduled to direct. When he was unwillingly removed from the project, he and his friends used pseudonyms in the credits.

Waxwork II: Lost in Time
1992, Electric Pictures. 104 min.
Director/Screenplay: Anthony Hickox; Producer: Nancy Paloian.
Cast includes: Zach Galligan, Monika Schnarre, Martin Kemp, **Bruce Campbell**, Michael Des Barres, Jim Metzler.

The Adventures of Brisco County, Jr
1993. TV series.
Created by: Jeffrey Boat and Carlton Cuse.
Cast includes: Bruce Campbell, Julius Carry, Christian Clemenson, Kelly Rutherford, Billy Drago.
Note: **Bruce Campbell** played the title role in this series, which only ran for one season but is repeated regularly.

Hard Target
1993, Renaissance Pictures. 94 min.
Director: John Woo; Screenplay: Chuck Pfarrer; Producers: Sean Daniel, James Jacks; Executive Producers: **Sam Raimi, Robert G. Tapert**, Moshe Diamant.
Cast includes: Jean-Claude Van Damme, Lance Henriksen, Arnold Vosloo, Yancy Butler, Ted Raimi.

Indian Summer
1993, Outlaw Productions/Touchstone Pictures. 97 min.
Director/Screenplay: Mike Binder. Producers: Robert F. Newmyer, Jeffrey Silver.
Cast includes: Alan Arkin, Matt Craven, Diane Lane, Bill Paxton, **Sam Raimi**.
Note: Sam Raimi's most substantial (and best) acting role to date as Alan Arkin's dorky assistant.

Journey to the Center of the Earth
1993, High Productions. TV movie. 90 min.
Director: William Dear. Screenplay: David M. Evans, Robert Gunter; Producer: John Ashley.
Cast includes: David Dundara, Farrah Forke, Kim Miyori, John Neville, F. Murray Abraham.
Note: **Sam Raimi** plays Collins, a lab assistant who dies screaming and plunging into a pit of molten lava.

Body Bags
1994, 187 Corporation/Showtime Networks Inc. TV movie. 91 min.
Directors: John Carpenter, Tobe Hooper; Screenplay: Dan Angel, Billy Brown; Producers: Dan Angel, John Carpenter, Sandy King.
Cast includes: John Carpenter, Tom Arnold, Tobe Hooper, Robert Carradine, Alex Datcher, Wes Craven.
Note: Already dead, **Sam Raimi** falls out of a closet. He's also in a photo labelled 'Employee of the Month'.

Darkman II: The Return of Durant
1994, Renaissance Pictures/Universal Home Video. 93 min.
Director/Cinematography: Bradford May; Screenplay: Steve McKay; Based on Characters Created by: **Sam Raimi**; Producer: David Roessell; Executive Producers: **Sam Raimi, Robert G. Tapert**.
Cast includes: Larry Drake, Arnold Vosloo, Kim Delaney, Renee O'Connor, Lawrence Dane, Jesse Collins.

The Flintstones
1994, Universal Pictures/Hanna-Barbera Productions/Amblin Entertainment. 92 min.
Director: Brian Levant; Screenplay: Tom S. Parker, Jim Jennewein, Steven E. De Souza; Producer: Bruce Cohen.
Cast includes: John Goodman, Elizabeth Perkins, Rick Moranis, Rosie O'Donnell.
Note: **Sam Raimi** plays the stand-in for Kyle McLachlan in Jay Leno's 'reality show' about the Fred Flintstone scandal. He's very hard to spot.

Hercules and the Amazon Women
1994, Universal/Renaissance Pictures. TV movie. 91 min.
Director: Bill L. Norton; Screenplay: Andrew Dettman, Jule Selbo, Daniel Truly; Created by: Christian Williams; Executive Producers: **Sam Raimi, Robert G. Tapert**, Christian Williams; Music: Joseph Lo Duca.
Cast includes: Kevin Sorbo, Anthony Quinn, Roma Downey, Michael Hurst, Lloyd Scott, Lucy Lawless, Christopher Brougham, Tim Lee, Kim Michalis.

Hercules and the Circle of Fire
1994, Universal/Renaissance Pictures. TV movie. 91 min.
Director: Doug Lefler; Screenplay: Andrew Dettmann, Barry Pullman, Daniel Truly; Created by: Christian Williams; Executive Producers: **Sam Raimi, Robert G. Tapert**, Christian Williams; Music: Joseph Lo Duca.
Cast includes: Kevin Sorbo, Anthony Quinn, Tawny Kitaen, Kevin Atkinson, Stephanie Barrett, Christopher Brougham, Nell Weatherly, Mark Ferguson.

Hercules and the Lost Kingdom (aka *Hercules: the Journey Begins*)
1994, Universal/Renaissance Pictures. TV movie. 91 min.
Director: Harley Cokeliss; Screenplay: Christian Williams; Created by: Christian Williams; Executive Producers: **Sam Raimi, Robert G. Tapert**, Christian Williams; Music: Joseph Lo Duca.
Cast includes: Kevin Sorbo, Anthony Quinn, Renee O'Connor, Robert Trebor, Eric Close, Elizabeth Hawthorne, Nathaniel Lees, Onno Boelee.

Hercules in the Maze of the Minotaur
1994, Universal/Renaissance Pictures. TV movie. 91 min.
Director: Josh Becker; Screenplay: Andrew Dettman, Daniel Truly; Created by: Christian Williams; Executive Producers: **Sam Raimi, Robert G. Tapert**; Music: Joseph Lo Duca.
Cast includes: Kevin Sorbo, Anthony Quinn, Tawny Kitaen, Michael Hurst, Ray Anthony Parker, Nic Fay, Andrew Thurtell, Paul McIver, Simon Lewthwaite, Rose McIver, Katrina Hobbs.

Hercules in the Underworld
1994, Universal/Renaissance Pictures. TV movie. 91 min.
Director: Bill L. Norton; Screenplay: Andrew Dettmann, Daniel Truly; Created by: Christian Williams; Executive Producers: **Sam Raimi, Robert G. Tapert**, Christian Williams; Music: Joseph Lo Duca.
Cast includes: Kevin Sorbo, Anthony Quinn, Tawny

Kitaen, Marlee Shelton, Cliff Curtis, Jorge Gonzales, Timothy Balme, Michael Hurst, Michael Mizrahi.

Hercules: The Legendary Journeys
1994-99, Universal/Renaissance Pictures. TV series.
Producer: Bernadette Joyce; Created by: Christian Williams; Executive Producers: **Sam Raimi, Robert G. Tapert**.
Cast includes: Kevin Sorbo, Michael Hurst.
Note: **Bruce Campbell** had a recurring role as Autolycus, the King of Thieves. He also directed several episodes.

The Hudsucker Proxy
1994, Silver Pictures/Working Title Films. 113 min.
Director: Joel Coen; Screenplay: Ethan Coen, Joel Coen, **Sam Raimi**; Producer: Ethan Coen.
Cast includes: Tim Robbins, Jennifer Jason Leigh, Paul Newman, Charles Durning, John Mahoney, **Bruce Campbell**, Harry Bugin.
Note: **Sam Raimi** is a silhouette on a frosted window.

M.A.N.T.I.S.
1994, Renaissance Pictures. TV series.
Created by: Sam Hamm; Executive Producers: Sam Hamm, **Sam Raimi, Robert G. Tapert**.
Cast includes: Carl Lumbly, Bobby Hosea, Gina Torres, Steve James.

The Stand
1994, Greengrass Productions/Laurel Entertainment. TV miniseries.
Director: Mick Garris; Screenplay: Stephen King; Producer: Michell Galin.
Cast includes: Gary Sinise, Molly Ringwald, Jamey Sheridan, Laura San Giacomo, Rob Lowe.
Note: **Sam Raimi** plays Terry Bobby, one of demonic Randall Flagg's more stupid minions, and, yet again, comes to a violent end.

Timecop
1994, Universal/Renaissance Pictures. 98 min.
Director/Cinematographer: Peter Hyams; Screenplay:

Mark Verheiden; Producers: Moshe Diamant, **Sam Raimi, Robert Tapert**.
Cast includes: Jean-Claude Van Damme, Mia Sara, Ron Silver, Bruce McGill, Gloria Reuben, Scott Bellis.

American Gothic
1995, Renaissance Pictures. TV series.
Created by: Shaun Cassidy; Producers: Edward Ledding, Shaun Cassidy, David Eick; Executive Producers: **Sam Raimi, Robert G. Tapert**; Music: Joseph Lo Duca.
Cast includes: Gary Cole, Paige Turco, Jake Weber, Brenda Bakke, Sarah Paulson, Lucas Black, Nick Searcy, Sonny Shroyer.
Note: **Bruce Campbell** guest-starred in one episode, and met a thoroughly unpleasant end.

Congo
1995, Paramount Pictures. 108 min.
Director: Frank Marshall; Screenplay: John Patrick Shanley, Michael Crichton; Producers: Kathleen Kennedy, Sam Mercer.
Cast includes: Dylan Walsh, Laura Linney, Ernie Hudson, Tim Curry, Grant Heslov, Joe Don Baker, **Bruce Campbell**.

The Demolitionist
1995, A-pix Entertainment/Le Mont Entertainment/Planet Productions. 100 min.
Director: Robert Kurtzman; Screenplay: Brian DiMuccio; Producer: Donald P. Borchers.
Cast includes: Richard Grieco, Randy Vasquez, Jack Nance, Heather Langenkamp, Tom Savini, **Bruce Campbell**.

Lois and Clark: The New Adventures of Superman
1995-6, December 3rd Productions/Warner Bros. TV series.
Cast includes: Dean Cain, Teri Hatcher, Lane Smith, Eddie Jones, K. Callan, John Shea.
Note: **Bruce Campbell** appeared in several episodes of the third season of the series (which ran from 1993-97) as Bill Church Jr.

The Quick and the Dead
1995, TriStar Pictures. 105 min.
Director: **Sam Raimi**; Screenplay: Simon Moore;
Producers: Joshua Donen, Patrick Markey, Allen
Shapiro; Executive producer: **Robert G. Tapert**.
Cast includes: Sharon Stone, Gene Hackman, Russell
Crowe, Leonardo DiCaprio, Tobin Bell, Roberts
Blossom, Kevin Conway, Keith David, Lance Henriksen,
Pat Hingle, Gary Sinise, Woody Strode, Scott Spiegel,
Timothy Patrick, John Cameron, Mick Garris.
Note: **Bruce Campbell**'s scenes were cut.

Xena: Warrior Princess
1995-, Universal/Renaissance Pictures. TV series.
Created by: John Schulian, **Robert G. Tapert**;
Producers: Bernadette Joyce, Liz Friedman; Executive
Producers: **Sam Raimi, Robert Tapert**, R.J. Stewart;
Music: Joseph Lo Duca.
Cast includes: Lucy Lawless, Renee O'Connor.
Note: **Bruce Campbell** appeared in this *Hercules* spin-
off as Autolycus, and has directed several episodes.

Assault on Dome 4
1996, The Sci-Fi Channel/Avatar Filmworks. 91 min.
Director: Gilbert Po; Screenplay: Hesh Rephun;
Producers: Jimmy Lifton, Brian Shuster.
Cast includes: Joseph Culp, **Bruce Campbell**, Jocelyn
Seagrave, Brion James, Ray Baker, Jack Nance.

Darkman III: Die Darkman Die
1996, Renaissance Pictures/Universal Home Video.
87 min.
Director/Cinematographer: Bradford May; Screenplay:
Michael Colleary, Mike Werb; Based on Characters
Created by **Sam Raimi**; Producer: David Roessell;
Executive Producers: **Sam Raimi, Robert G. Tapert**.
Cast includes: Jeff Fahey, Arnold Vosloo, Darlanne
Fluegel, Roxann Biggs-Dawson, Nigel Bennett, Alicia
Panetta, Ronn Sarosiak, Peter Graham.

Ellen
1996-97, Black-Marlens Company/Touchstone
Television. TV series.

Cast includes: Ellen DeGeneres, Joely Fisher, David
Anthony Higgins, Clea Lewis.
Note: **Bruce Campbell** had a recurring role as Ed Billik
in the 1996-97 season of Ellen DeGeneres' TV series,
which ran from 1994-98.

Escape from L.A.
1996, Paramount Pictures/Rysher Entertainment.
101 min.
Director: John Carpenter; Screenplay: John Carpenter,
Debra Hill, Kurt Russell; Producers: Debra Hill, Kurt
Russell.
Cast includes: Kurt Russell, A.J. Langer, Steve Buscemi,
Stacy Keach, Michelle Forbes, **Bruce Campbell**.

Fargo
1996, PolyGram/Working Title Films. 98 min.
Director: Joel Coen; Screenplay: Joel Coen, Ethan Coen;
Producer: Ethan Coen.
Cast includes: Frances McDormand, William H. Macy,
Steve Buscemi, Peter Stormare.
Note: **Bruce Campbell** appears unbilled on TV in
Generations, the soap opera he made in Detroit.

Menno's Mind
1996, Regent Entertainment. 95 min.
Director: Jon Kroll; Screenplay: Mark Valenti; Producer:
Larry Estes.
Cast includes: Bill Campbell, Stephanie Romanov,
Corbin Bernsen, Michael Dorn, Robert Picardo, Marc
McClure, **Bruce Campbell**.

Tornado!
1996, Von Zerneck-Sertner Films/Hallmark
Entertainment. TV movie.
Director: Noel Nosseck; Screenplay: John Logan;
Producers: Artie Mandelberg, Stacy Mandelberg, Randy
Sutter.
Cast includes: **Bruce Campbell**, Shannon Sturges,
Ernie Hudson, L.Q. Jones, Bo Eason, Charles Hornet.

In the Line of Duty: Blaze of Glory
1997, Patchett Kaufman Entertainment. TV movie.

Director: Dick Lowry; Screenplay: Stephen Harrigan, Susan Rhinehart; Producer: Dick Lowry.
Cast includes: Lori Loughlin, **Bruce Campbell**, Brad Sullivan, Susanna Thompson, Mariangela Pino, Victor A. Morris.

The Love Bug
1997, Walt Disney Television/ZM Productions.
Director: Peyton Reid; Screenplay: Gordon Buford, Don DaGradi, Bill Walsh; Producers: Irwin Marcus, Joan Van Horn.
Cast includes: **Bruce Campbell**, John Hannah, Alexandra Wentworth, Kevin J. O'Connor, Mickey Dolenz, Dean Jones.

McHale's Navy
1997, Sheinberg Productions/The Bubble Factory.
109 min.
Director: Bryan Spicer; Screenplay: Peter Crabbe; Producers: Bill Sheinberg, Jonathan Sheinberg, Sid Sheinberg.
Cast includes: Tom Arnold, Dean Stockwell, Debra Messing, David Alan Grier, Tim Curry, Ernest Borgnine, **Bruce Campbell**.

Missing Links
1997. TV pilot.
Cast includes: **Bruce Campbell**.
Note: Campbell plays Ray, a golfer, in this one-off pilot based on the movie *Tin Cup*.

Running Time
1997, Panoramic Pictures. 70 min.
Director/Screenplay: Josh Becker; Producers: Josh Becker, Jane Goe; Music: Joseph Lo Duca.
Cast includes: **Bruce Campbell**, Jeremy Roberts, Anita Barone, Stan Davis, Gordon Jennison Noice, Art LaFleur.

Spy Game
1997, Renaissance Pictures. TV series.
Created by: **Sam Raimi**, Ivan Raimi, John McNamara.
Producer: Edward Ledding. Executive Producers: **Sam Raimi, Robert G. Tapert**, John McNamara.
Cast includes: Linden Ashby, Allison Smith, Bruce McCarty, Keith Szarabajka.

Timecop
1997, Universal/December 3rd Productions/Dark Horse Entertainment. TV series.
Cast includes: T.W. King, Cristi Conaway, Dan Stark, Kurt Fuller.
Note: **Bruce Campbell** appears in this ABC series, which only ran for half a season.

Amazon High
1998, Universal/Renaissance Pictures. TV movie (unaired).
Director: Michael Hurst; Producers: Liz Friedman, Eric Gruendemann; Executive Producers: **Sam Raimi, Robert G Tapert**; Screenplay: R.J. Stewart; Story: **Robert G. Tapert**, R.J. Stewart; Cinematography: Allen Guilford; Production Designer: Robert Gillies; Music: Joseph Lo Duca.
Cast includes: Selma Blair, Danielle Cormack, Karl Urban, Monica McSwain, Claudia Black, Peta Rutter, Chris Bailey, John Callen.

Gold Rush: A Real Life Alaskan Adventure
1998, Walt Disney Television/Gold Rush Productions/Hugget Productions. TV movie.
Director: John Power; Screenplay: Jacqueline Feather, David Seidler; Producer: Fitch Cady.
Cast includes: Alyssa Milano, William Morgan Sheppard, Stan Cahill, Peter Flemming, Tom Scholte, Frank C. Turner, **Bruce Campbell**.

Hercules and Xena —The Animated Movie: The Battle for Mount Olympus
1998, Universal Home Video/Renaissance Pictures. 80 min.
Director/Producer: Lynne Naylor; Screenplay: John Loy; Executive Producers: **Sam Raimi, Robert G. Tapert**; Score: Joseph Lo Duca.
Voices include: Kevin Sorbo, Lucy Lawless, Michael Hurst, Renee O'Connor, Kevin Smith, Ted Raimi.

A Simple Plan
1998, Paramount Pictures. 121 min.
Director: **Sam Raimi**; Screenplay: Scott B. Smith, from his novel; Producers: James Jacks, Adam Schroeder; Cinematography: Alar Kivilo; Production Designer: Patrizia von Brandenstein; Editors: Arthur Coburn, Eric L. Beason; Music: Danny Elfman.
Cast includes: Bill Paxton, Bridget Fonda, Billy Bob Thornton, Brent Briscoe, Chelcie Ross, Gary Cole, Becky Ann Baker, Jack Walsh, John Paxton.

Young Hercules
1998, Universal Home Video/Renaissance Pictures. TV pilot. 60 min.
Director: T.J. Scott; Screenplay: Andrew Dettmann, **Robert G. Tapert**, Daniel Truly; Producers: Liz Friedman, Eric Gruendemann; Executive Producers: **Sam Raimi, Robert G. Tapert**; Music: Joseph Lo Duca.
Cast includes: Ian Bohen, Dean O'Gorman, Chris Conrad, John Stewart-Bowden, Kevin Smith, Meighan Desmond, Nathaniel Lees, Rachel Blakely, Michael Hurst, Taungaroa Emile.
Note: A one-season series followed.

For Love of the Game
1999, Beacon Pictures/Universal. 137 min.
Director: **Sam Raimi**; Screenplay: Dana Stevens, Michael Shaara; Producers: Armyan Bernstein, Amy Robinson; Cinematography: John Bailey; Music: Basil Poledouris.
Cast includes: Kevin Costner, Kelly Preston, John C. Reilly, Jena Malone, Brian Cox, Vin Scully, Billy V. Costner, Sharon Rae Costner, Ted Raimi.

From Dusk Till Dawn 2: Texas Blood Money
1999, Dimension Films/A Band Apart/Los Hooligans Productions. 88 min.
Director: Scott Spiegel; Screenplay: Scott Spiegel, Duane Whitaker; Producers: Michael S. Murphey, Gianni Nunnari.

Cast includes: Robert Patrick, Bo Hopkins, Duane Whitaker, Muse Watson, Danny Trejo, Brett Harrelson, Tiffani-Amber Thiessen, **Bruce Campbell**.

Icebreaker
1999.
Director: David Giancola; Producer: Peter Beckwith.
Cast includes: Sean Astin, Alison Brooke, **Bruce Campbell**, Rusty De Wees, John James, Stacy Keach.

La Patinoire
1999, Canal Plus/Les Films des Tournelles. 77 min.
Director: Jean-Philippe Toussaint; Producers: Pascal Judelewicz, Anne-Dominique Toussaint.
Cast includes: **Bruce Campbell**, Pierre Belot, Aleksiejus Budrytis, Jean-Pierre Cassel, Dolores Chaplin, Ilya Claisse.

Cleopatra 2525
2000, Renaissance Pictures. TV series.
Created by: **Robert G. Tapert**, R.J. Stewart; Executive Producer: R.J. Stewart; Music: Joseph Lo Duca.
Cast includes: Gina Torres, Victoria Pratt, Jennifer Sky.

The Gift
2000, Lakeshore Entertainment.
Director: **Sam Raimi**; Screenplay: Tom Epperson, Billy Bob Thornton; Producers: James Jacks, Tom Rosenberg, **Robert G. Tapert**.
Cast includes: Cate Blanchett, Gary Cole, Katie Holmes, Greg Kinnear, Keanu Reeves, Giovanni Ribisi, Hilary Swank.

Jack of All Trades
2000, Renaissance Pictures. TV series.
Executive Producers: Sam Raimi and Robert G. Tapert, Alex Kurtzman and Roberto Orci; Co-executive Producers: Bruce Campbell, Eric Gruendemann; Music: Joseph Lo Duca.
Cast includes: Bruce Campbell, Angela Dotchin, Stuart Devenie, Stephen Papps.

THE FILMS SAM RAIMI *DIDN'T* MAKE

Like all directors, Sam has been linked with many properties he didn't finally direct, though in most cases, someone else eventually did. Some of these were announced in the movie trade magazines, others were offers that he turned down. This list is included to show the range of material he has been asked to work on over the years. The final film may, in some cases, be very different from the project Sam would have been considering.

The date shown is when the film in question was released (or, in some cases, merely announced), and the final director is also indicated.

Austin Powers: International Man of Mystery (1997, Jay Roach)

The Beast (1998 TV movie, Jeff Bleckner)

Crossroads (offered in 1997)

The Damocles Net (offered in 1995)

Day of the Triffids (based on the John Wyndham novel, as yet unmade)

The Devil's Advocate (1997, Taylor Hackford)

Dracula (from a script by Kevin Jarre, as yet unmade)

Dragon Tears (based on the Dean Koontz novel, as yet unmade)

Ender's Game (based on the Orson Scott Card novel, as yet unmade)

Face/Off (1997, John Woo)

The Fly II (1989, Chris Walas)

Friendly Voices (offered in 1996)

Frosty the Snowman (1998 as *Jack Frost*, Troy Miller)

Godzilla (1998, Roland Emmerich)

The Guardian (1990, William Friedkin — Sam developed this simultaneously with *Darkman,* then had to choose one or the other)

Hard Rain (1998, Mikael Salomon)

Hideaway (1995, Brett Leonard)

I Am Legend (based on the Richard Matheson novel, as yet unmade)

Interview with the Vampire (1994, Neil Jordan)

The Killer (an American remake of the John Woo movie)

Last Action Hero (1993, John McTiernan)

Last Boy Scout (1991, Tony Scott)

The Mummy (1999, Stephen Sommers — Sam was offered this in 1993 with a script by John Sayles that had initially been prepared for Joe Dante. Sommers film has nothing to do with that script.)

Musketeer (1993 as *The Three Musketeers*, Stephen Herek)

The Phantom (1996, Simon Wincer)

Planet of the Apes (the Oliver Stone version)

The Postman (1998, Kevin Costner)

The Shadow (1994, Russell Mulcahy)

The Shipping News (based on the novel by E. Annie Proulx)

Sleepy Hollow (a different project from the 1999 Tim Burton release)

Speed Racer (from the Japanese cartoon)

Tales from the Crypt (not the script that was eventually filmed)

V for Vendetta (from the graphic novel by Alan Moore and David Lloyd)

White House (offered in 1995)

I N D E X

Sam Raimi, Bruce Campbell and Rob Tapert appear on almost every page, so this index lists pages featuring their photographs only. If a title does not refer to the film version (eg A Farewell to Arms), this will be noted.

BIBLIOGRAPHY

Becker, Josh. *The Evil Dead Journal*
Boxoffice Magazine (Pasadena, CA)
Daily News (Los Angeles, CA)
The Detroit News (Detroit, MI)
Drama-Logue (Hollywood, CA)
Dutton, Mark, 'Within the Woods'
The Entertainment Litigation Reporter (Los Angeles, CA)
Fangoria (New York, NY)
The Hollywood Reporter (Los Angeles, CA)
Holverson, Cliff, 'Ash's Evil Dead Page'
L.A. Village View (Los Angeles, CA)

L.A. Weekly (Los Angeles, CA)
Los Angeles Herald-Examiner (Los Angeles, CA)
Los Angeles Reader (Los Angeles, CA)
Los Angeles Times (Los Angeles, CA)
The New York Times (New York, NY)
The New Yorker (New York, NY)
Rod Serling's 'The Twilight Zone' Magazine (New York, NY)
Screen International (London, England)
SPIN (New York, NY)
Variety (Los Angeles, CA)
The Village Voice (New York, NY)

INTERNET SITES

This list is representative, and definitely not exhaustive, but *Evil Dead* sites worth checking out include:

'Ash vs the World':
http://members.tripod.com/~asherald/
'Ash's Evil Dead Page':
www.geocities.com/Hollywood/Set/9683/
'Evil Dead Interactive':
http://members.aol.com/edinteract/index.html
'Evil Dead Online':
http://homes.arealcity.com/evildeadonline/
'Evil Dead Trilogy Unofficial Website':
http://ace.alleg.edu/%7Etruby/holy_triumvirate/stars poof/home.html
'House of Horrors Presents Evil Dead':
www.houseofhorrors.com/evildead.htm
'ISZ's Tribute to The Evil Dead':
http://the-isz.org/evildead/
'The Land of the Evil Living':
http://geocities.yahoo.com/toto?s=76000006
'Robert's Evil Dead Fan Page':
www.europa.com/%7Erew1977/dead/dead.htm
'Within the Woods':
www.dutton67.freeserve.co.uk/index.htm

There are several websites devoted primarily to *Army of Darkness*. These include:
'The Essential Army of Darkness Homepage':
http://hometown.aol.com/darkageprodu/index.html
'Justin's Army of Darkness Page':
http://geocities.yahoo.com/toto?s=76000006

There are several websites devoted to Bruce Campbell, but the best by far is the one that Bruce himself runs. Check it out at:
www.bruce-campbell.com

Josh Becker has his own jam-packed site, which includes the full text of his *Evil Dead* journal, called Becker films — Directing from the Edge at:
www.beckerfilms.com

Tom Sullivan's Dark Age Productions website can be viewed at:
http://hometown.aol.com/darkageprodu/index.html